SETTLE T

Here are all the facts you need to find out who did what in the amazing world of sports. Now you can test your knowledge and that of your friends in every major area of athletics.

Which professional football team was penalized the most yards in one game?
Who was the greatest money-winner in horse racing?
Where was the first world heavyweight title fight held?
What is the most expensive of all sports?
Here, in one volume, are all the answers plus thousands more! The one truly indispensable book for any sports enthusiast.

The Giant New 3rd Edition of
GUINNESS SPORTS RECORD BOOK

FASTEST MILER: Paola Cacchi (Italy) is the woman who has come closest to breaking the 4-minute mile—with a record run of 4 minutes 29½ seconds.

GUINNESS SPORTS RECORD BOOK

3rd Edition

by Norris McWhirter and Ross McWhirter

Enlarged from the sports section of the
Guinness Book of World Records

BANTAM BOOKS · TORONTO · NEW YORK · LONDON

GUINNESS SPORTS RECORD BOOK

*A Bantam Book / published by arrangement with
Sterling Publishing Company, Inc.*

PRINTING HISTORY

*Sterling edition published April 1972
Revised edition published December 1972
New revised edition published May 1974
Bantam edition published June 1972*

2nd printing	October 1972	4th printing	December 1972
3rd printing	October 1972	5th printing	January 1973

Revised Bantam edition published September 1973

2nd printing	September 1973	5th printing	December 1973
3rd printing	October 1973	6th printing	January 1974
4th printing	November 1973	7th printing	June 1974

New revised Bantam edition published September 1974

World rights reserved.
Copyright © 1974, 1972 by Sterling Publishing Co., Inc.
*This volume is taken in part
from the "Guinness Book of World Records"
Revised American Edition © 1973, 1972, 1971, 1970, 1969,
1968, 1966, 1965, 1964, 1963, 1962
by Sterling Publishing Co., Inc.*

CONTENTS

EVOLUTION OF SPORTS RECORDS IN THE 20TH CENTURY

	Start of the Century—January 1, 1901	*Middle of the Century—January* 1, 1951	*Present Day Record—August*, 1973
Greatest Weight Lift	4,133 lbs.—Louis Cyr (Canada), 1896	4,133 lbs.—Louis Cyr (Canada), 1896	6,270 lbs.—Paul Anderson (U.S.), 1957
Fastest 100 yards	9.8 secs.—John Owen (U.S.) and 12 others, 1890–1899	9.3 secs.—Mel Patton (U.S.), 1948	9.1 secs.—R. L. Hayes (U.S.), 1963; H. W. Jerome (Canada), 1966; J. R. Hines (U.S.), 1967; S. Williams (U.S.), 1973
Fastest One Mile	4m 12.8s—W. G. George (U.K.), 1886	4m 01.3s—Gunder Hägg (Sweden), 1945	3m 51,1s—J. R. Ryun (U.S.), 1967
One Hour Running	11 miles 932 yds.—W. G. George (U.K.), 1884	12 miles 29 yds.—Viljo Heino (Finland), 1945	12 miles 1,609 yds.—G. Roelants (Belgium), 1972
Highest High Jump	6′ 5⅝″—M. Sweeney (U.S.), 1895	6′ 11″—Lester Steers (U.S.), 1941	7′ 6½″—D. Stones (U.S.), 1973
Highest Pole Vault	11′ 10½″—R. Clapp (U.S.), 1898	15′ 7¾″—Cornelius Warmerdam (U.S.), 1942	18′ 5¾″—R. Seagren (U.S.), 1972
Long Jump	24′ 7¾″—P. O'Conner (U.K.), 1900	26′ 8¼″—Jesse Owens (U.S.), 1935	29′ 2½″—R. Beamon (U.S.), 1968
Longest Shot Put	48′ 2″—D. Horgan (U.K.), 1897	58′ 10¾″—Jim Fuchs (U.S.), 1950	71′ 7″—A. Feuerbach (U.S.), 1973
Longest Discus Throw	122′ 3½″—R. Sheldon (U.S.), 1899	186′ 11″—Fortune Gordien (U.S.), 1949	224′ 5″—L. J. Silvester (U.S.), 1968; R. Bruch (Sweden) 1972
Longest Hammer Throw	169′ 4″—J. J. Flanagan (U.S.), 1900	196′ 5″—Imre Németh (Hungary), 1950	250′ 8″—W. Schmidt (E. Germany), 1971
Longest Javelin Throw	161′ 9¾″—E. Lemming (Sweden), 1899	258′ 2″—Yrjo Nikkanen (Finland), 1938	308′ 8″—K. Wolfermann (W. Germany), 1973
One Hour Walking	8 miles 270 yds.—W. J. Sturgess (U.K.), (Amateur), 1895	8 miles 1,025 yds.—John Mikaelsson (Sweden), 1945	8 miles 1,294 yds.—G. Panichkin (U.S.S.R.), 1959
Longest Ski Jump	116½′—O. Tanberg (Norway), 1900	442¾′—Dan Netzell (Sweden), 1950	554′ 6″—H. Wosiwipo (E. Germany), 1973
Fastest 500 meters Ice Skating	45.2 sec.—P. Ostlund (Norway), 1900	41.8 sec.—Hans Engnestangen (Norway), 1938	38.0 sec.—L. Linkovesi (Finland), 1972; H. Borjes (Sweden), 1972; E. Keller (W. Germany), 1972
Fastest 100 meters Swim (long course)	1m 14.0s (no turn)—J. Nutall (U.K.), 1893	55.8 sec.—Alexandre Jany (France), 1947	51.2 sec.—Mark Spitz (U.S.), 1972
Cycling (m.p.h.) Paced	62.27—C. M. Murphy (U.S.), 1899	>80—L. Vanderstuyft (Belgium), 1928	140.5—Allan V. Abbott (U.S.), 1973
Fastest 1 mile Race Horse (excluding straightaways)	1m 35.5s—*Salvator*, in U.S., 1890	1m 33.4s—*Citation* in U.S., 1950	1m 32.2s.—*Dr. Fager* in U.S., 1968
Highest Mountain Climbed (feet)	22,834—Aconcagua, Argentina, 1897	26,492—Annapurna I, Nepal, 1950	29,028—Everest, Nepal-Tibet, 35 men, 1953–73

SPORTS, GAMES AND PASTIMES

Earliest. The origins of sport stem from the time when self-preservation ceased to be the all-consuming human preoccupation. Archery was a hunting skill in Mesolithic times (by *c.* 8000 B.C.), but did not become an organized sport until about 300 A.D., among the Genoese. The earliest dated evidence for sport is *c.* 2450 B.C. for fowling with throwing sticks and hunting. Ball games by girls, depicted on Middle Kingdom murals at Ben Hasan, Egypt, have been dated to *c.* 2050 B.C.

Fastest. The governing body for aviation, *La Fédération Aéronautique Internationale*, records maximum speeds in lunar flight of up to 24,791 m.p.h. However, these achievements, like all air speed records since 1923, have been para-military rather than sporting. In shooting, muzzle velocities of up to 7,100 feet per second (4,840 m.p.h.) are reached in the case of a U.S. Army Ordnance Department standard 0.30 caliber M1903 rifle. The highest speed reached in a non-mechanical sport is in sky-diving, in which a speed of 185 m.p.h. is attained in a head-down free falling position, even in the lower atmosphere. In delayed drops, a speed of 614 m.p.h. has been recorded at high rarefied altitudes. The highest projectile speed in any moving ball game is *c.* 160 m.p.h. in pelota (jai-alai). This compares with 170 m.p.h. (electronically-timed) for a golf ball driven off a tee.

Slowest. In amateur wrestling, before the rules were modified toward "brighter wrestling," contestants could be locked in holds for so long that single bouts could last for 11 hours 40 min. In the extreme case of the 2 hours 41 minutes pull in the regimental tug o'war in Jubbulpore, India, on August 12, 1889, the winning team moved a net distance of 12 feet at an average speed of 0.00084 m.p.h.

Longest. The most protracted sporting test was an automobile duration test of 222,618 miles by Appaurchaux and others in a Ford Taunus. This was contested over 142 days in 1963. The distance was equivalent to 8.93 times around the equator.

The most protracted non-mechanical sporting event is the *Tour de France* cycling race. In 1926, this was over 3,569 miles, lasting 29 days. The total damage to the French national economy of this annual event, now reduced to 23 days, is immense. If it is assumed that one-third of the total working population works for only two-thirds of the time during *Le Tour* this would account for a loss of more than three-quarters of one per cent of the nation's annual Gross National Product. In 1972 this was more than $125,000,000,000 so the loss would have been about $938,000,000.

Shortest. Of sports with timed events, the briefest recognized for official record purposes is the quick draw in shooting in which electronic times of 0.02 of a sec. have been returned in self-draw events.

Largest Field. The largest field for any ball game is that for polo with 12.4 acres, or a maximum length of 300 yards and a width, without side-boards, of 200 yards.

Most Participants. The annual Nijmegen Vierdaagse march in the Netherlands over distances up to 50 kilometers (31 miles 120 yards) attracted 16,667 participants in 1968. The greatest number of competitors in any competitive event is for the "Vasa Lopp" Nordic skiing race in Sweden. There were 8,755 starters in 1973, of whom 7,565 finished.

Worst Disasters. The worst disaster in recent history was when an estimated 604 were killed after some stands at the Hong Kong Jockey Club race course collapsed and caught fire on February 26, 1918. During the reign of Antoninus Pius (138–161 A.D.) the upper wooden tiers in the Circus Maximus, Rome, collapsed during a gladiatorial combat, killing some 1,100 spectators.

Youngest Sports Record Breaker. The youngest age at which any person has broken a world record is 12 years 328 days in the case of Karen Yvette Muir (born September 16, 1952), of Kimberley, South Africa, who broke the women's 110-yard backstroke world record with 1 minute 08.7 seconds at Blackpool, England, on August 10, 1965. (See photo.)

Youngest and Oldest Internationals. The youngest age at which any person has won international honors is 8 years in the case of Joy Foster, the Jamaican singles and mixed-doubles table tennis champion in 1958. It would appear that the greatest age at which anyone has actively competed for his country is 73 years in the case of Oscar G. Swahn (Sweden), who won a silver medal for shooting in the Olympic Games at Antwerp in 1920.

Youngest and Oldest Champions. The youngest person to have successfully participated in a world title event was a French boy, whose name is not recorded, who coxed the winning Netherlands pair at Paris on Aug. 26, 1900. He was not more than 10 and may have been as young as 7. The youngest individual Olympic winner was Marjorie Gestring (U.S.), who took the springboard diving title at the age of 13 years 9 months at the Olympic Games in Berlin in 1936. The greatest age at which anyone has held a world title is 60 years in the case of Pierre Etchbaster, who retired in 1955, after 27 years as undefeated world amateur tennis champion from May, 1928.

Longest Reign. The longest reign as a world champion is 27 years by the Basque tennis player, Pierre Etchbaster (see above).

Greatest Earnings. The greatest fortune amassed by an individual in sport is an estimated $47,500,000 by Sonja Henie (1912–69), of Norway, the triple Olympic figure skating champion (1928–32–36) as a professional ice skating promoter starring in her own ice shows and 11 films. The most earned in a single event is the reported $2,500,000 each by Joe Frazier and Muhammad Ali (*né* Cassius Clay) in their world heavyweight boxing title fight in Madison Square Garden, New York City on March 8, 1971. This is at a rate of $925.92½ per second of actual fighting. The highest contract announced for any sportswoman is $2,500,000 for 3 years to Janet Lynn, the 1972 Olympic bronze medal figure skater, on June 20, 1973.

Heaviest Sportsmen. The heaviest sportsman of all-time was the wrestler William J. Cobb of Macon, Georgia, who in 1962 was billed as the 802-lb. "Happy Humphrey." The heaviest player of a ball game was Bob Pointer, the 487-lb. tackle, formerly on the 1967 Santa Barbara High School team, and still playing in California in 1972 at 480 lbs.

Most Expensive. The most expensive of all sports is the racing of large yachts—"J" type boats and International 12-meter boats. The owning and racing of these is beyond the means of individual millionaires and is confined to multi-millionaires or syndicates.

Largest Crowd. The greatest number of live spectators for any sporting spectacle is the estimated 1,000,000 (more than 20 per cent of the population) who line the route of the annual San Sylvestre road race of 8,600 meters (5 miles 605 yards) through the streets of

YOUNGEST EVER TO SET WORLD RECORD IN SPORTS: Karen Muir of South Africa at the age of 12 years 328 days broke the women's 110-yard backstroke swimming mark.

São Paulo, Brazil, on New Year's night. However, spread over 23 days, it is estimated that more than 10,000,000 see the annual *Tour de France* along the route. (See also page 7.)

The largest crowd traveling to any sporting event is "more than 400,000" for the annual *Grand Prix d'Endurance* motor race on the Sarthe circuit near Le Mans, France. The total attendance at the 1969 Stampede at Calgary, Alberta, Canada, was 853,620 from July 9 through 18. The record stadium crowd was one of 199,854 for the Brazil *vs.* Uruguay match in the Maracanã Municipal Stadium, Rio de Janeiro, Brazil, on July 16, 1950.

Most Sports Participants

According to a report issued in April, 1971, some 28,400,000 men and 15,200,000 women are actively involved in 209,000 physical culture and sports groups in the U.S.S.R., where there are 6,100,000 track athletes, 5,600,000 volleyball players, 3,900,000 footballers and 891,000 weightlifters. The report lists 2,918 stadiums, 430 indoor and 475 outdoor swimming pools for 791,000 swimmers.

HOLDER OF THREE FLIGHT-SHOOTING RECORDS: Harry Drake is the master with the footbow (over 1 mile 101 yards), handbow and crossbow. Here he is trying to break his own unlimited footbow record.

Archery

Earliest References. Late Paleolithic drawings of archers indicate that bows and arrows are an invention of *c.* 1500 B.C. Archery developed as an organized sport at least as early as the 4th century A.D. The world governing body is the *Fédération Internationale de Tir à l'Arc* (FITA), founded in 1931.

Flight Shooting. The longest flight shooting records are achieved in the footbow class. In the unlimited footbow division, the professional Harry Drake of Lakeside, California, holds the record at 1 mile 101 yards 21 inches, shot at Ivanpah Dry Lake, California, on October 3, 1970. The unlimited handbow class (*i.e.* standing stance with bow of any weight) record is 856 yards 20 inches and the crossbow record is 1,359 yds. 29 inches, both held by Drake and set at same venue on October 14–15, 1967.

Highest Scores. The world records for a single FITA Round are: men 1,268 points (of a possible 1,440) by John C. Williams (U.S.) at Munich on September 10, 1972; and women 1,235 points (possible 1,440) by Emma Gapchenko (U.S.S.R.) at Noraya Kukhovka, U.S.S.R., in April, 1973.

The record for a FITA Double Round is 2,528 (possible 2,880) by Williams in securing his Olympic title (see above). The feminine record is 2,426 points by Anna Keunova (U.S.S.R.) at Tallin, U.S.S.R., on June 5, 1972.

Most Titles. The greatest number of world titles (instituted 1931) ever won by a man is four by H. Deutgen (Sweden) in 1947–48–49–50. The greatest number won by a woman is seven by Mrs. Janina Spychajowa-Kurkowska (Poland) in 1931–32–33–34, 1936, 1939 and 1947.

Marathon. The highest recorded score over 24 hours by a pair of archers is 30,709 during 31 Portsmouth Rounds (60 arrows at 20 yards with a 2-inch diameter 10 ring) shot by Barry Davison and Corporal Bob Pritchard at the Odeon Cinema, Colchester, Essex, England, on February 26–27, 1972.

Auto Racing

Earliest Races. The first automobile trial was one of 20 miles in France, from Paris to Versailles and back on April 20, 1887, won by Georges Bouton (1847–1938) of France in his steam quadricycle in 74 minutes, at an average of 16.22 m.p.h.

The first "real" race was from Paris to Bordeaux and back (732 miles) on June 11–13, 1895. The winner was Emile Lavassor (d. 1897) (France) driving a Panhard-Lavassor two-seater with a 1.2-liter Daimler engine developing $3\frac{1}{2}$ h.p. His time was 48 hours 47 min. (average speed 15.01 m.p.h.). The first closed circuit race was held at the Circuit du Sud-Ouest, Paris, in 1900.

The oldest auto race in the world, still being regularly run, is the R.A.C. Tourist Trophy (37th race held in 1973), first staged on the Isle of Man on September 14, 1905. The oldest continental races are the Targa Florio (57th in 1973) in Sicily, first held on May 9, 1906, and the French Grand Prix (51st in 1973) first held on June 26–27, 1906.

Fastest Circuits. The highest average lap speed attained on any closed circuit is 212.766 m.p.h. by Bobby Unser (b. Colorado Springs, Colorado, 1934) who lapped the 2-mile 22-degree banked oval at Texas World Speedway, College Station, Texas, in 33.84 seconds, driving a 2,611-c.c. 900-b.h.p. turbocharged Olsonite Eagle Model VI-Offenhauser, on April 5, 1973.

The highest average race lap speed for a closed circuit is over 195 m.p.h. during a 500-mile race by Richard Brickhouse (U.S.) driving a 1969 Dodge Daytona Charger powered by a 426-cu. in. 600-b.h.p. V8 engine on the 2.66-mile 33-degree banked turn tri-oval at Alabama International Motor Speedway, Talladega, Alabama, on September 14, 1969.

The fastest road circuit is the Francorchamps circuit near Spa, Belgium. It is 14.10 kilometers (8 miles 1,340 yards) in length and was lapped in 3 minutes 13.4 seconds (average speed of 163.086 m.p.h.) during the Francorchamps 1,000-kilometer sports car race on May 6, 1973, by Henri Pescarolo (b. Paris, France, September 25, 1942) driving a 2,933-c.c. V12 Matra-Simca MS 670 Group 5 sports car. The practice lap record is 3 minutes 12.7 seconds (average speed 163.678 m.p.h.) by Jacques-Bernard "Jacky" Ickx (b. Brussels, Belgium, January 1, 1945) driving a 2,998.5-c.c. flat-12 Ferrari 312 P Group 5 sports car on May 4, 1973.

Fastest Races. The fastest race in the world was the 50-mile event at the NASCAR Grand National meeting on the 2.50-mile 31-degree banked tri-oval at Daytona International Speedway on February 8, 1964. It was won by Richard Petty (b. July 2, 1937) of Randleman, North Carolina, in 17 minutes 27 seconds (average speed 171.920 m.p.h.), driving a 405-b.h.p. 1964 Plymouth V8.

The fastest road race is the 1,000-kilometer (621-mile) sports car race held on the Francorchamps circuit (8 miles 1,340 yards) near Spa, Belgium. The record time for this 71-lap (622.055-mile) race is 4 hours 1 minute 9.7 seconds (average speed 154.765 m.p.h.) by Pedro Rodriguez (1940–71) of Mexico and Keith Jack "Jackie" Oliver (b. Chadwell Heath, Essex, England, Aug. 14, 1942), driving a 4,998-c.c. flat-12 Porsche 917K Group 5 sports car on May 9, 1971.

Toughest Circuits. The Targa Florio (first run 1906) is widely acknowledged to be the most arduous race. Held on the Piccolo Madonie Circuit in Sicily, it now covers eleven laps (492.126 miles) and involves the negotiation of 9,350 corners, over severe mountain gradients, and narrow rough roads.

The record time is 6 hours 27 minutes 48.0 seconds (average speed 76.141 m.p.h.) by Arturo Francesco Merzario (b. Civenna, Italy, March 11, 1943) and Sandro Munari (Italy) driving a

FASTEST CIRCUIT is Francorchamps in Belgium and the fastest road race is held on it. Here Pedro Rodriguez, driving a BRM, is setting a record in June, 1970, which he himself broke in 1971, with partner, Jackie Oliver.

2,995-c.c. flat-12 Ferrari 312 P Group 5 sports car in the 56th race on May 21, 1972. The lap record is 33 minutes 36.0 seconds (average speed 79.890 m.p.h.) by Leo Juhani Kinnunen (born Tampere, Finland, Aug. 5, 1943) on lap 11 of the 54th race in a 2,997-c.c. flat-8 Porsche 908/3 Spyder Group 6 prototype sports car on May 3, 1970.

The most difficult Grand Prix circuit is generally regarded to be that for the Monaco Grand Prix (first run on April 14, 1929), run through the streets and harbor of Monte Carlo. It is 3,278 meters (2 miles 65 yards) in length and has 11 pronounced corners and several sharp changes of gradient. The race is run over 78 laps (158.875 miles) and involves on average more than 2,000 gear changes.

The record for the race is 1 hour 57 minutes 44.3 seconds (average speed 80.963 m.p.h.) by John Young "Jackie" Stewart, O.B.E. (b. Milton, Dunbartonshire, Scotland, June 11, 1939) driving a 2,933-c.c. Tyrrell-Cosworth V8 on June 3, 1973). The race lap record is 1 minute 28.1 seconds (average speed 83.231 m.p.h.) by Emerson Fittipaldi (b. São Paulo, Brazil, December 12, 1946) driving a 2,933-c.c. Lotus 72 John Player Special-Cosworth V8 on lap 78 of the above race. The practice lap record is 1 minute 27.5 seconds (average speed 83.802 m.p.h.) by Stewart on June 1, 1973.

HOLDER OF THE MONACO GRAND PRIX RECORD: Jackie Stewart of Scotland also holds the practice lap record for the same race, regarded as the most difficult Grand Prix circuit.

FASTEST PRODUCTION MODEL: The Porsche 917L.

Le Mans

The world's most important race for sports cars is the 24-hour *Grand Prix d'Endurance* (first held on May 26–27, 1923) on the Sarthe circuit (8 miles 650 yards) at Le Mans, France. The greatest distance ever covered is 3,315.210 miles (average speed 138.134 m.p.h.) by Dr. Helmut Marko (b. Graz, Austria, April 27, 1943) and Jonkheer Gijs van Lennep (b. Bloemendaal, Netherlands, March 16, 1942) driving a 4,907-c.c. flat-12 Porsche 917K Group 5 sports car on June 12–13, 1971. The race lap record is 3 minutes 18.7 seconds (151.632 m.p.h.) by Pedro Rodriguez (1940–71) driving a Porsche 917L on June 12, 1971. The practice lap record is 3 minutes 13.6 seconds (average speed 155.627 m.p.h.) by Jackie Oliver driving a similar car on April 18, 1971. The pre-war record average speed was 86.85 m.p.h. by a 3.3-liter Bugatti in 1939.

Most Wins. The race has been won by Ferrari cars nine times, in 1949, 1954, 1958 and 1960–61–62–63–64–65. The most wins by one man is four by Oliver Gendebien (Belgium), who won in 1958 and 1960–1–2.

Indianapolis 500

The Indianapolis 500-mile race (200 laps) was inaugurated on May 30, 1911. The most successful drivers have been Warren Wilbur Shaw (1902–1954), who won in 1937, 1939, and 1940; Louis Meyer, who won in 1928, 1933 and 1936, and Anthony Joseph "A.J." Foyt, Jr. (b. Houston, Texas, 1935), who won in 1961, 1964 and 1967. Mauri Rose won in 1947 and 1948 and was the co-driver with Floyd Davis in 1941.

MOST GRAND PRIX WINS IN A YEAR: The late Jim Clark of Scotland, shown here in his V8-Ford-engined Lotus, won a record seven in 1963.

The record time is 3 hours 4 minutes 5.54 seconds (average speed 162.962 m.p.h.) by Mark Donohue (b. Summit, New Jersey, March 18, 1937) driving a 2,595-c.c. 900-b.h.p. turbocharged Sunoco McLaren M16B-Offenhauser on May 27, 1972. He received $218,767.90 from a record prize fund of $1,011,845.94 for winning this, the 56th, race. The individual prize record is $271,697.72 by Al Unser (b. Albuquerque, New Mexico, May 29, 1939) on May 30, 1970.

The race lap record is 47.99 seconds (average speed 187.539 m.p.h.) by Mark Donohue on lap 150 of the above race. The practice lap record is 45.21 (average speed 199.07 m.p.h.) by Johnny Rutherford (b. 1938) of Fort Worth, Texas, driving a 2,595-c.c. 900-b.h.p. turbocharged Gulf-McLaren-Offenhauser on lap 3 of his 4-lap qualification run on May 12, 1973.

Fastest Pit Stop. A. J. Foyt, Jr.'s first fuel stop on lap 14 during the Indianapolis 500 on May 29, 1971, took 9 seconds. This equaled the time set just 20 days previously by Jackie Oliver in loading 100 liters of fuel during the Francorchamps 1000-kilometer sports car race.

Duration Record

The greatest distance ever covered in one year is 400,000 kilometers (248,548.5 miles) by Francois Lecot (1879–1949), an innkeeper from Rochetaillée, France, in a 11-c.v. Citroën (1,900 c.c., 66 b.h.p.), mainly between Paris and Monte Carlo, from July 22, 1935 to July 26, 1936. He drove on 363 of the 370 days allowed.

The world's duration record is 185,353 miles 1,741 yards in 133 days 17 hours 37 minutes 38.6 seconds (average speed 58.07 m.p.h.) by Marchand, Presalé and six others in a Citroën on the Montlhéry track near Paris, during March–July, 1933.

Most Successful Drivers

Based on the World Drivers' Championships, inaugurated in 1950, the most successful driver is Juan-Manuel Fangio y Cia (born Balcarce, Argentina, June 24, 1911), who won five times in 1951–54–55–56–57. He retired in 1958, after having won 24 Grand Prix races (2 shared).

The most successful driver in terms of race wins is Stirling Craufurd Moss (born London, England, September 17, 1929), with 167 (11 shared) races won, including 16 Grand Prix victories (1 shared), from September 18, 1948 to February 11, 1962. Moss was awarded the annual Gold Star of the British Racing Drivers' Club in 1950–51–52, 1954–55–56–57–58–59 and 1961, a record total of ten awards.

The most Grand Prix victories is 27 by Jackie Stewart of Scotland between September 12, 1965 and August 5, 1973. Jim Clark, O.B.E. (1936–1968) of Scotland holds the record of Grand Prix victories in one year with 7 in 1963. He won 61 Formula One and Formula Libre races between 1959 and 1968. The most Grand Prix starts is 160 (out of a possible 168) between May 18, 1958, and Jan. 13, 1974, by Norman Graham Hill, O.B.E. (b. London, England, February 15, 1929). He took part in 90 *consecutive* Grands Prix between November 20, 1960 and October 5, 1969.

MOST SUCCESSFUL DRIVER: Manuel Fangio of Argentina won the World Drivers' Championship five times and 24 Grand Prix races before retiring in 1958.

Oldest and Youngest Grand Prix Winners and Drivers.
The youngest Grand Prix winner was Bruce Leslie McLaren (1937–70) of New Zealand, who won the U.S. Grand Prix at Sebring, Florida, on December 12, 1959, aged 22 years 104 days. The oldest Grand Prix winner was Tazio Giorgio Nuvolari (1892–1953) of Italy, who won the Albi Grand Prix at Albi, France, on July 14, 1946, aged 53 years 240 days. The oldest Grand Prix driver was Louis Alexandre Chiron (born Monaco, August 3, 1899), who finished 6th in the Monaco Grand Prix on May 22, 1955, aged 55 years 292 days.

The youngest Grand Prix driver was Christopher Arthur Amon (b. Bulls, New Zealand, July 20, 1943) who took part in the Belgian Grand Prix on June 9, 1963, aged 19 years 324 days.

Land Speed Records

The highest speed ever recorded by a wheeled vehicle was achieved by Gary Gabelich (b. San Pedro, California, August 29, 1940), at Bonneville Salt Flats, Utah, on October 23, 1970. He drove the Reaction Dynamics *The Blue Flame*, weighing 4,950 lbs. and measuring 37 feet long, powered by a liquid natural gas-hydrogen peroxide rocket engine developing a maximum static thrust of 22,000 lbs. On his first run, at 11:23 a.m. (local time), he covered the measured kilometer in 3.543 seconds (average speed 631.367 m.p.h.) and the mile in 5.829 seconds (617.602 m.p.h.). On the second run, at 12:11 p.m. his times were 3.554 seconds for the kilometer (629.413 m.p.h.) and 5.739 seconds for the mile (627.287 m.p.h.). The average times for the two runs were 3.5485 seconds for

LAND SPEED RECORD-HOLDER: Gary Gabelich with "The Blue Flame," the car in which he set the official mark for the mile at 622.407 m.p.h. across the Bonneville Salt Flats, Utah, in 1970. The vehicle is 37 feet long.

the kilometer (630.388 m.p.h.) and 5.784 seconds for the mile (622.407 m.p.h.). During the attempt only 13,000 lbs. s.t. was used and a peak speed of 650 m.p.h. was momentarily attained.

The most successful land speed record breaker was Major Sir Malcolm Campbell (1885–1948) (U.K.). He broke the official record nine times between September 25, 1924, with 146.157 m.p.h. in a Sunbeam, and September 3, 1935, when he achieved 301.129 m.p.h. in the Rolls-Royce engined *Bluebird*.

The world speed record for compression-ignition-engined cars is 190.344 m.p.h. (average of two runs over measured mile) by Robert Havemann of Eureka, California, driving his *Corsair* streamliner, powered by a turbocharged 6,980-c.c. 6-cylinder GMC 6-71 diesel engine developing 746 b.h.p., at Bonneville Salt Flats, Utah, in August, 1971. The faster run was made at 210 m.p.h.

Dragging

Piston-Engined. The highest terminal velocity recorded by a piston-engined dragster is 243.90 m.p.h. (elapsed time 6.175 seconds) by Donald Glenn "Big Daddy" Garlits (born 1932) of Seffner, Florida, driving his rear-engined *Swamp Rat I-R* AA-F dragster, powered by a 473-cu. in. supercharged Dodge V8 engine during the National Hot Rod Association's 3rd Annual Gatornationals at Gainesville Dragway, Florida, on March 19, 1972. This record was equalled by Gary Beck of Edmonton, Alberta, Canada (elapsed time 6.04 seconds) driving his rear-engined AA-F dragster, powered by a 484-cu. in. supercharged Chrysler V8 engine during the National Hot Rod Association's U.S. Nationals at Indianapolis Raceway Park, Indiana, on Sept. 3, 1973.

Rocket or Jet-Engined. The highest terminal velocity recorded by any dragster is 377.754 m.p.h. (elapsed time 4.65 seconds) by Norman Craig Breedlove (b. March 23, 1938) of Los Angeles, California driving his *English Leather Special* rocket dragster at Bonneville Salt Flats, Utah, in Sept., 1973. The lowest elapsed time recorded by any dragster is 4.62 seconds (terminal velocity 344.82 m.p.h.) by Dave Anderson of the United States driving his *Pollution Packer*, powered by a hydrogen peroxide rocket engine, during the National Hot Rod Association's U.S. Nationals at Indianapolis Raceway Park, Indiana, on Sept. 3, 1973.

The lowest elapsed time recorded is 5.91 seconds (terminal velocity 231.95 m.p.h.) by Don Moody driving his rear-engined AA-F dragster, powered by a 7,931-c.c. supercharged Chrysler V8 engine, during the National Hot Rod Association's first All Pro Supernationals at Ontario Motor Speedway, Ontario, California, on Nov. 19, 1972.

Terminal velocity is the speed attained at the end of a 440-yard run made from a standing start and elapsed time is the time taken for the run.

Stock Car Racing

Richard Petty of Randleman, North Carolina, was the first stock car driver to attain $1,000,000 lifetime earnings on August 1, 1971.

WINNER OF FIRST RALLY (1907): The 40-h.p. Italian car, one of the five cars that left Peking on June 10, arriving in Paris exactly two months later.

Rallies

Earliest. The earliest long rally was promoted by the Parisian daily *Le Matin* in 1907 from Peking, China to Paris, over a route of about 7,500 miles. Five cars left Peking on June 10. The winner, Prince Scipione Borghese, arrived in Paris on August 10, 1907 in his 40 h.p. Itala.

Longest. The world's longest ever rally event was the £10,000 ($24,000) London *Daily Mirror* World Cup Rally run over 16,243 miles starting from London, England, on April 19, 1970, to Mexico City via Sofia, Bulgaria and Buenos Aires, Argentina, passing through 25 countries. It was won on May 27, 1970, by Hannu Mikkola (born Joensuu, Finland, May 24, 1942) and Gunnar Palm (b. Kristinehamn, Sweden, February 25, 1937) in an 1,834-c.c. Ford Escort RS1600. The longest held annually is the East African Safari (first run 1953), run through Kenya, Tanzania and Uganda, which is up to 3,874 miles long, as in the 17th Safari held on April 8–12, 1971.

Smallest Car. The smallest car to win the Monte Carlo rally (founded 1911) was an 841-c.c. Saab driven by Erik Carlsson (born Sweden, 1929) and Gunnar Häggbom of Sweden on January 25, 1962, and by Carlsson and Gunnar Palm on January 24, 1963.

Go-Kart Circumnavigation

The only recorded instance of a go-kart being driven around the world was a circumnavigation by Stan Mott, of New York, who drove a Lambretta-engined 175-c.c. Italkart with a ground clearance of two inches, 23,300 land miles through 28 countries from February 15, 1961, to June 5, 1964, starting and finishing in New York.

Pike's Peak Race

The Pike's Peak Auto Hill Climb, Colorado (instituted 1916) has been won by Bobby Unser 11 times between 1956 and 1969 (9 championship, 1 stock and 1 sports car title). On June 30, 1968, in the 46th race, he set a record of 11 minutes 54.9 seconds in his 5,506-c.c. Chevrolet championship car over the 12.42-mile course rising from 9,402 to 14,110 feet through 157 curves.

Badminton

MOST TITLES WON BY A WOMAN: Judy Hashman of the U.S. shares the record at 17 with 10 singles and 7 doubles victories in the All-England championship.

Origins. The game was devised *c.* 1863 at Badminton Hall in Gloucestershire, England, the seat of the Dukes of Beaufort.

International Championships. The International Championship or Thomas Cup (instituted 1948) has been won five times by Indonesia in 1957–58, 1960–61, 1963–64, 1970–71, and 1972–73.

The inaugural Ladies International Championship or Uber Cup (instituted 1956) has been most often won by Japan with a fourth victory in 1972.

Most Titles Won. The record number of All-England Championship (instituted 1899) titles won is 21 by Sir George Thomas (d. 1972) between 1903 and 1928. The record for men's singles is 7 by Erland Kops of Denmark (1958–67). The most, including doubles, by women is 17, a record shared by Miss M. Lucas (1899–1910) and Mrs. G. C. K. Hashman (*née* Judy Devlin) (U.S.) from 1954 to 1967, who won 10 singles titles.

Longest Hit. Frank Rugani drove a shuttlecock 79 feet 8½ inches in tests at San Jose, California, on February 29, 1964.

Baseball

Origins. Baseball is a totally American derivative of the English game of cricket (first recorded in the U.S. in 1747) and the now-little-played English game of rounders. The game evolved about the end of the eighteenth century; as early as 1786, "baste-ball" was banned at Princeton, N.J. Haphazard versions of the so-called Town Ball Game grew up in Boston, New York and Philadelphia during the period 1820–33. Rules were first codified in 1845 in New York by Alexander Cartwright.

On February 4, 1962, it was claimed in *Nedelya*, the weekly supplement to the Soviet newspaper *Izvestia*, that "Beizbol" was an old Russian game.

Earliest Games. The earliest game on record under the Cartwright rules was on June 19, 1846, in Hoboken, N.J., where the "New York Nine" defeated the Knickerbockers 23 to 1 in 4 innings. The earliest all-professional team was the Cincinnati Red Stockings in 1869.

Home Runs. Henry (Hank) Aaron (Atlanta NL) who hit 713 by the end of the 1973 season, passed Babe Ruth's record of 714 and set a new lifetime home run record in 1974, with 720 at the time this book went to press. An all-league record of 800 in a lifetime has been claimed for Josh Gibson (1912–47) of the Homestead Grays of the Negro League, who has been elected to the Baseball Hall of Fame in Cooperstown, New York. Gibson hit 84 round-trippers in one season.

Fastest Pitcher

In Army tests, it was learned that Bob Feller (Cleveland AL) threw a pitch which was traveling at a speed of 98.6 miles per hour as it crossed the plate.

Youngest Player

The youngest major league player of all time was the Cincinnati pitcher, Joe Nuxhall, who started his career in June, 1944, aged 15 years 10 months 11 days.

Highest Catch

Joe Spring (San Francisco Seals, Pacific Coast League) caught a baseball (on his fifth attempt) dropped from an airship at about 1,000 feet over Treasure Island, in San Francisco Bay in 1939. The force of catching the ball broke his jaw.

MAJOR LEAGUE ALL-TIME RECORDS
(including 1973 season)

Individual Batting

Highest percentage, lifetime (5,000 at-bats)
.367   Tyrus R. Cobb, AL: Det. 1905–26; Phil. 1927–28

Highest percentage, season (500 at-bats)
(Leader in each league)
.438   Hugh Duffy, NL: Bos. 1894
.422   Napoleon Lajoie, AL: Phil. 1901

Most games played
3,033   Tyrus R. Cobb, Det. (2,804) AL, 1905–26; Phil. (229) AL, 1927–28 (24 years)

Most consecutive games played
2,130   Henry Louis Gehrig, N.Y. AL, June 1, 1925 through Apr. 30, 1939

Most runs, lifetime
2,244   Tyrus R. Cobb, Det. AL, 1905–1926; Phil. AL, 1927–28; 24 years

Most runs, season
196   William R. Hamilton, Phil. NL, 131 games, 1894

IRON MAN: Lou Gehrig (New York AL) played in 2,130 consecutive games.

GREATEST BATTER of all time: Ty Cobb (Detroit AL) had highest lifetime batting average (.367), made most base hits (4,191) and scored most runs (2,244), as well as stealing the most bases (892).

Most base hits, consecutive, game
7 Wilbert Robinson, Balt. NL, June 10, 1892, 1st game (7-ab), 6-1b, 1-2b
Cesar Gutierrez, Det. AL, June 21, 1970, 2nd game (7-ab) 6-1b, 1-2b (extra-inning game)

Most hits in succession
12 M. Frank (Pinky) Higgins, Bos. AL, June 19–21 (4 games), 1938; Walter Dropo, Det. AL, July 14, July 15, 2 games, 1952

Most consecutive games batted safely, season
56 Joseph P. DiMaggio, N.Y. AL (91 hits—16-2b, 4-3b, 15 hr), May 15 to July 16, 1941

Most long hits, season
119 George H. (Babe) Ruth, N.Y. AL (44-2b, 16-3b, 59 hr), 152 games, 1921

Most total bases, lifetime
6,424 Henry Aaron, Mil. 1954–65, Atl. 1966–73 NL

Most total bases, season
457 George H. (Babe) Ruth, N.Y. AL, 152 g. (85 on 1b, 88 on 2b, 48 on 3b, 236 on hr), 1921

Most total bases, game
18 Joseph W. Adcock, Milw. NL (1-2b, 4-hr), July 31, 1954

Sluggers' percentage
(The percentage is obtained by dividing the "times at bat" into total bases.)
Highest slugging percentage, lifetime
.690 George H. (Babe) Ruth, Bos.-N.Y. AL, 1914–34; Bos. NL, 1935

Individual Batting Records (continued)

Most runs batted in, lifetime
2,133 Henry Aaron, Mil. 1954–65, Atl. 1966–73 NL

Most runs batted in, season
190 Lewis R. (Hack) Wilson, Chi. NL, 155 games, 1930

Most runs batted in, game
12 James L. Bottomley, St. L. NL, Sept. 16, 1924

Most runs batted in, inning
7 Edward Cartwright, St. L. AA, Sept. 23, 1890

Most base hits
4,191 Tyrus R. Cobb, Det. AL, 1905–26; Phil. AL, 1927–28; 24 years

Most base hits, season
257 George H. Sisler, St. L. AL, 154 games, 1920

LONGEST HOMER: Mickey Mantle (New York AL) hit the longest measured home run in a major league game (565 feet) in 1953. Babe Ruth hit a 587-foot measured homer in a pre-season game at Tampa, Florida, in 1919 for the Boston Red Sox against the New York Giants. The minor league record is 618 feet by Roy Carlyle at Emeryville, California, on July 4, 1929. Other homers may have been longer but went unmeasured.

HOME RUN KING: Henry Aaron (Mil., Atl. NL), who, in 1974, passed Babe Ruth's record of 714 homers in a lifetime, also holds the RBI record. He batted 2,133 runs in, to the end of 1973.

Individual Batting Records (continued)

Triple-Crown winners
(Most times leading league in batting, runs batted in and home runs.)
  2 Rogers Hornsby, St. L. NL, 1922, 1925
      Theodore S. Williams, Bos. AL, 1942, 1947

Most Valuable Player, as voted by Baseball Writers Association
3 times James E. Foxx, Phil. AL, 1932, 33, 38
      Joseph P. DiMaggio, N.Y. AL, 1939, 41, 47
      Stanley F. Musial, St. L. NL, 1943, 46, 48
      Lawrence P. (Yogi) Berra, N.Y. AL, 1951, 54, 55
      Roy Campanella, Bklyn. NL, 1951, 53, 55
      Mickey C. Mantle, N.Y. AL, 1956, 57, 62

Most one-base hits (singles), season
  202 William H. Keeler, Balt. NL, 128 games, 1898

Most two-base hits, season
  67 Earl W. Webb, Bos. AL, 151 games, 1931

Most three-base hits, season
  36 J. Owen Wilson, Pitts. NL, 152 games, 1912

Most home runs, lifetime
  714* George H. (Babe) Ruth, Bos. AL, 1915 (4), 1916 (3), 1917 (2), 1918 (11), 1919 (29); N.Y. AL, 1920 (54), 1921 (59), 1922 (35), 1923 (41), 1924 (46), 1925 (25), 1926 (47), 1927 (60), 1928 (54), 1929 (46), 1930 (49), 1931 (46), 1932 (41), 1933 (34), 1934 (22); Bos. NL, 1935 (6)

Most home runs, season (154-game schedule)
  60 George H. (Babe) Ruth, N.Y. AL (28 home, 32 away), 151 gs, 1927

*During 1974, this record was surpassed by Hank Aaron

RECORD SLUGGER: Babe Ruth (New York AL) still holds the record for 60 home runs in a 154-game season, most long hits (119), most total bases (457), and most bases on balls (170) in a season.

Most home runs, season (162-game schedule)
61   Roger E. Maris, N.Y. AL (30 home, 31 away), 161 gs. 1961

Most home runs, one month
18   Rudolph York, Det. AL, Aug. 1937

Most consecutive games hitting home runs
8-R Dale Long, Pitt. NL, May 19–28, 1956

Most home runs, one double header
5   Stanley F. Musial, St. L. NL, 1st game (3), 2nd game (2), May 2, 1954
     Nathan Colbert, S.D. NL, 1st game (2), 2nd game (3), Aug. 1, 1972

Most home runs bases filled, lifetime
23   Henry Louis Gehrig, N.Y. AL, 1927–1938

Most home runs with bases filled, season
5   Ernest Banks, Chi. NL, May 11, 19, July 17 (1st game), Aug. 2, Sept. 19, 1955
     James E. Gentile, Balt. AL, May 9 (2), July 2, 7, Sept. 22, 1961

Most home runs, with bases filled, same game
2   Anthony M. Lazzeri, N.Y. AL, May 24, 1936
     James R. Tabor, Bos. AL (2nd game), July 4, 1939
     Rudolph York, Bos. AL, July 27, 1946
     James E. Gentile, Balt. AL, May 9, 1961 (consecutive at-bats)
     Tony L. Cloninger, Atl. NL, July 3, 1966
     James T. Northrup, Det. AL, June 24, 1968 (consecutive at-bats)
     Frank Robinson, Balt. AL, June 26, 1970 (consecutive at-bats)

Most bases on balls, game
6   Walter Wilmot, Chi. NL, Aug. 22, 1891
     James E. Foxx, Bos. AL, June 16, 1938

Most bases on balls, season
170   George H. (Babe) Ruth, N.Y. AL, 152 games, 1923

Most consecutive pinch hits, lifetime
9   David E. Philley, Phil. NL, Sept. 9, 11, 12, 13, 19, 20, 27, 28, 1958; Apr. 16, 1959

LONGEST HITTING STREAK:
Joe Di Maggio (New York AL) hit safely in 56 consecutive games in 1941.

Base Running

Most stolen bases, lifetime since 1900
892   Tyrus R. Cobb. Det. AL, 1905–26; Phil. AL, 1927–28

Most stolen bases, season since 1900
104   Maurice M. Wills, L.A. NL, 165 games, 1962

Most stolen bases, game
7   George F. (Piano Legs) Gore, Chi. NL, June 25, 1881
     William R. (Sliding Billy) Hamilton, Phil. NL, 2nd game, 8 inn., Aug. 31, 1894

Most times stealing home, game
2   by 8 players

Most times stealing home, lifetime
34   Tyrus R. Cobb, Det.-Phil. AL, 1905–28

Fewest times caught stealing, season (50+ attempts)
2   Max Carey, Pitt. NL, 1922 (53 atts.)

Pitching

Most games, lifetime
1,070 J. Hoyt Wilhelm, N.Y.-St. L.-Atl.-Chi.-L.A. NL, 1952–57, 69–72; Clev.-Balt.-Chi.-Cal. (622) AL, 1957–69

Most complete games, lifetime
751 Denton T. (Cy) Young, Clev.-St. L.-Bos. NL (428); Bos.-Clev. AL (323), 1890–1911

Most complete games, season
74 William H. White, Cin. NL, 1879

Most innings pitched, game
26 Leon J. Cadore, Bklyn. NL, May 1, 1920
Joseph Oeschger, Bos. NL, May 1, 1920

Lowest earned run average, season
0.90 Ferdinand M. Schupp, N.Y. NL, 1916 (140 inn)
1.01 Hubert B. (Dutch) Leonard, Bos. AL, 1914 (222 inn)
1.12 Robert Gibson, St. L. NL, 1968 (305 inn)

Most games won, lifetime
511 Denton T. (Cy) Young, Clev. NL (239) 1890–98; St. L. NL (1899–1900; Bos. AL (193) 1901–08; Clev. AL (29) 1909–11; Bos. NL (4) 1911

Most games won, season
60 Charles Radbourne, Providence NL, 1884

Most consecutive games won, lifetime
24 Carl O. Hubbell, N.Y. NL, 1936 (16); 1937 (8)

Most shutout games, season
16 George W. Bradley, St. L. NL, 1876
Grover C. Alexander, Phil. NL, 1916

Most shutout games, lifetime
113 Walter P. Johnson, Wash. AL, 21 years, 1907–27

Most consecutive shutout games, season
6 Donald S. Drysdale, L.A. NL, May 14, 18, 22, 26, 31, June 4, 1968

CONSECUTIVE GRAND SLAMS: Jim Northrup (Detroit AL) in 1968 tied the record set by Jim Gentile (Baltimore AL) when he hit homers with bases loaded in two consecutive times at bat in consecutive innings. In 1970, Frank Robinson (Baltimore AL) performed the same feat. **MOST NO-HIT GAMES:** Sandy Koufax (Los Angeles NL), youngest player ever to be elected to the Baseball Hall of Fame, pitched 4 no-hit games in his career and had 31 strikeouts in two consecutive games.

LONGEST-LASTING PITCHER: Hoyt Wilhelm (left), knuckleball pitcher for 9 teams in both leagues, played in 1,070 major league games between 1952 and 1972, and had a lifetime ERA of 2.52. PERFECT GAME PITCHER: Jim Hunter (right) (Oakland AL), is the last one to have performed this feat (1968).

Most consecutive shutout innings
58 Donald S. Drysdale, L.A. NL, May 14–June 8, 1968

Most strikeouts, lifetime
3,508 Walter P. Johnson, Wash. AL, 1907–27

Most strikeouts, season
505 Matthew Kilroy, Balt. AA, 1886 (Distance 50 ft)
383 L. Nolan Ryan, Cal. AL, 1973 (Distance 60 ft 6 in)

Most strikeouts, game (9 inn) since 1900:
19 Steven N. Carlton, St. L. NL vs N.Y., Sept. 15, 1969 (lost)
     G. Thomas Seaver, N.Y. NL vs S.D., Apr. 22, 1970

Most strikeouts, extra-inning game
21 Thomas E. Cheney, Wash. AL vs Balt. (16 inns), Sept. 12, 1962 (night)

Special mention
1959 Harvey Haddix, Jr., Pitt. vs Milw. NL, May 26, pitched 12 "perfect" innings, allowed hit in 13th and lost

Most no-hit games, lifetime
4 Sanford Koufax, L.A. NL, 1962–63–64–65

PITCHING ACE: L. Nolan Ryan (California AL) set a new modern record with 383 strikeouts in the 1973 season.

Perfect game—9 innings

1880	John Lee Richmond, Worcester vs Clev. NL, June 12	1–0
	John M. Ward, Prov. vs Buff. NL, June 17 AM	5–0
1904	Denton T. (Cy) Young, Bos. vs Phil. AL, May 5	3–0
1908	Adrian C. Joss, Clev. vs Chi. AL, Oct. 2	1–0
†1917	Ernest G. Shore, Bos. vs Wash. AL, June 23 (1st g.)	4–0
1922	C. C. Robertson, Chi. vs Det. AL, April 30	2–0
*1956	Donald J. Larsen, N.Y. AL vs Bklyn. NL, Oct. 8	2–0
1964	James P. Bunning, Phil. NL vs N.Y., June 21 (1st g.)	6–0
1965	Sanford Koufax, L.A. NL vs Chi., Sept. 9	1–0
1968	James A. Hunter, Oak. AL vs Minn., May 8	4–0

Club Batting

Highest percentage, season
.343 Phil. NL, 132 games, 1894
.319 N.Y. NL, 154 games, 1930

Most runs, one club, game
36 Chi. NL (36) vs Louisville (7), June 29, 1897

Most runs, one club, inning
18 Chi. NL, 7th inning, Sept. 6, 1883

Most runs, both clubs, inning
19 Wash. AA (14), Balt. (5), 1st inn., June 17, 1891

Most hits, one club, 9-inning game
36 Phil. NL, Aug. 17, 1894

Most hits, one club, inning
18 Chi. NL, 7th inning, Sept. 6, 1883

Fewest hits, both clubs, game
1 Chi. NL (0) vs L.A. (1), Sept. 9, 1965

Most home runs, one club, season (154-game schedule)
221 N.Y. NL, 155 games, 1947
Cin. NL, 155 games, 1956

Most home runs, one club, season (162-game schedule)
240 N.Y. AL, 163 games, 1961

Fewest home runs (135 or more games), one club, season
3 Chi. AL, 156 games, 1908

Club Fielding

Highest percentage, one club, season
.985 Balt. AL, 1964

Fewest errors, season
95 Balt. AL, 163 games, 1964

Most double plays, club, season
217 Phil. AL, 154 games, 1949

Most double plays, club, game
7 N.Y. AL, Aug. 14, 1942
Houst. NL, May 4, 1969

Most stolen bases (1900 to date), one club, season
347 N.Y. NL, 154 games, 1911

Most stolen bases, one club, inning
8 Wash. AL, 1st inning, July 19, 1915
Phil. NL, 9th inning, 1st g., July 7, 1919

General Club Records

Shortest and longest game by time
51 minutes N.Y. NL (6), Phil. (1), 1st g., Sept. 28, 1919
7:23 S.F. NL (8) at N.Y. (6) 23 inn., 2nd g., May 31, 1964

Longest 9-inning game
4:18 S.F. NL (7) at L.A. (8), Oct. 2, 1962

Fewest times shutout, season
0 Bos. NL, 1894 (132 g.)
Phil. NL, 1894 (127 g.)
N.Y. AL, 1932 (155 g.)

Most consecutive innings shutting out opponets
56 Pitt. NL, June 1–9, 1903

Highest percentage games won, season
.798 Chi. NL (won 67, lost 17), 1880
.763 Chi. NL (won 116, lost 36), 1906
.721 Clev. AL (won 111, lost 43), 1954

Most games won, season (154-game schedule)
116 Chi. NL, 1906

Most consecutive games won, season
26 N.Y. NL, Sept. 7 (1st g.) to Sept. 30 (1 tie), 1916

---

†Starting pitcher, "Babe" Ruth, was banished from game by Umpire Owens after giving first batter, Morgan, a base on balls. Shore relieved and while he pitched to second batter, Morgan was caught stealing. Shore then retired next 26 batters to complete "perfect" game.

*World Series game.

Most pitchers used in a game, 9 innings, one club
9 St. L. AL vs Chi., Oct. 2, 1949

Managers' consecutive championship records
5 years Charles D. (Casey) Stengel, N.Y. AL, 1949–50–51–52–53

World Series Records

Most series played
14 Lawrence P. (Yogi) Berra, N.Y., AL, 1947, 49–53, 55–58, 60–63

Highest batting percentage (20 g. min.), total series
.391 Louis C. Brock, St. L. NL, 1964, 67–68 (g-21, ab-87, h-34)

Highest batting percentage, 4 or more games, one series
.625 4-game series, George H., (Babe) Ruth, N.Y. AL, 1928

Most runs, total series
42 Mickey C. Mantle, N.Y. AL, 1951–53, 55–58, 60–64

Most runs, one series
9 George H. (Babe) Ruth, N.Y. AL, 1928
   Henry Louis Gehrig, N.Y. AL, 1932

Most runs batted in, total series
40 Mickey C. Mantle, N.Y., AL, 1951–53, 55–58, 60–64

Most runs batted in, game
6 Robert C. Richardson, N.Y. AL, (4) 1st inn., (2) 4th inn., Oct. 8, 1960

Most runs batted in, consecutive times at bat
7 James L. (Dusty) Rhodes, N.Y. NL, first 4 times at bat, 1954

Most base hits, total series
71 Lawrence P. (Yogi) Berra, N.Y. AL, 1947, 49–53, 55–58, 60–61

Most home runs, total series
18 Mickey C. Mantle, N.Y. AL, 1952 (2), 53 (2), 55, 56 (3), 57, 58 (2), 60 (3), 63, 64 (3)

Most home runs, 4-game series
4 Henry Louis Gehrig, N.Y. AL, 1928

Most home runs, game
3 George H. (Babe) Ruth, N.Y. AL, Oct. 6, 1926; Oct. 9, 1928

Pitchers' Records

Pitching in most series
11 Edward C. (Whitey) Ford, N.Y. AL, 1950, 53, 55–58, 60–64

Most victories, total series
10 Edward C. (Whitey) Ford, N.Y. AL, 1950 (1), 55 (2), 56 (1), 57 (1), 60 (2), 61 (2), 62 (1)

All victories, no defeats
6 Vernon L. (Lefty) Gomez, N.Y. AL, 1932 (1), 36 (2), 37 (2), 38 (1)

Most games won, one series
3 games in 5-game series Christy Mathewson, N.Y. NL, 1905
J. W. Coombs, Phil. AL, 1910
Many others won 3 games in series of more games.

Most shutout games, total series
4 Christy Mathewson, N.Y. NL, 1905 (3), 1913

Most shutout games, one series
3 Christy Mathewson, N.Y. NL, 1905

Most strikeouts, one pitcher, total series
94 Edward C. (Whitey) Ford, N.Y. AL, 1950, 53, 55–58, 60–64

Most strikeouts, one series
23 in 4 games Sanford Koufax, L.A. NL, 1963
18 in 5 games Christy Mathewson, N.Y. NL, 1905
20 in 6 games C. A. (Chief) Bender, Phil. AL, 1911
35 in 7 games Robert Gibson, St. L. NL, 1968
28 in 8 games W. H. Dinneen, Bos. AL, 1903

Most strikeouts, one pitcher, game
17 Robert Gibson, St. L. NL, Oct. 2, 1968

World Series Winners

Most Series Won
20 New York AL, 1923, 1927, 1928, 1932, 1936, 1937, 1938, 1939, 1941, 1943, 1947, 1949, 1950, 1951, 1952, 1953, 1956, 1958, 1961, 1962

Highest attendance
420,784 L.A. NL, World Champions vs Chi. AL, 4–2, 1959

Baseball records from "The Book of Baseball Records" by Seymour Siwoff.

Basketball

Origins. *Ollamalitzli* was a 16th-century Aztec precursor of basketball played in Mexico. If the solid rubber ball was put through a fixed stone ring placed high on one side of the stadium, the player was entitled to the clothing of all the spectators. The captain of the losing team often lost his head (by execution). Another game played much earlier, in the 7th century B.C. by the Mayas in Mexico, called *Pok-ta-Pok*, also resembled basketball in its concept of a ring through which a round object was passed.

Modern basketball was devised by the Canadian-born Dr. James A. Naismith (1861–1939) at the Training School of the International Y.M.C.A. College at Springfield, Massachusetts, in December, 1891, and first played on January 20, 1892. The first public contest was on March 11, 1892. The game is now a global activity.

The International Amateur Basketball Federation (F.I.B.A.) was founded in 1932.

Olympic Champions

The U.S. won all seven Olympic titles from the time the sport was introduced to the Games in 1936 until 1968, without losing a single match. In 1972, in Munich, their run of 64 consecutive victories was broken when they lost 51–50 to the U.S.S.R. in a much-disputed final match, in which the officials ignored the rules.

World Champions

Brazil is the only country to win the World Championship (instituted 1950) on more than one occasion. They won the title in 1959 and again in 1963.

Greatest Attendances. The Harlem Globetrotters played an exhibition to 75,000 in the Olympic Stadium, West Berlin, Germany, in 1951. The largest indoor basketball crowd was at the Astrodome, Houston, Texas, where 52,693 watched a game on January 20, 1968, between the University of Houston and U.C.L.A.

The Harlem Globetrotters set unapproached attendance records in their silver jubilee season of 1951–52. They won 333 exhibitions and lost 8 before over 3,000,000 spectators and traveled over 75,000 miles. The team was founded by Abraham M. Saperstein (1903–66) of Chicago, and their first game was played at Hinckley, Illinois, on January 7, 1927.

BOXER CANNOT OUTREACH BASKETBALL PLAYER: Cassius Clay (who calls himself Muhammad Ali), dethroned heavyweight champion, is dwarfed by Wilt Chamberlain, who is 7 feet 1 inch tall.

WORLD'S TALLEST
BASKETBALL PLAYER:
At 7 feet 7.3 inches, the
Russian Vasiliy Akhtayev
played for Kazakhstan in
1956.

Tallest Players. The tallest player of all time was Vasiliy
Akhtayev (born 1935) of the U.S.S.R., who played for Kazakhstan
in 1956, when measuring 7 feet 7.3 inches. The tallest woman player
is Ulyana Semyonova (b. 1950), who plays for T.T.T. Riga, Latvia,
and stands 6 feet 9½ inches. The tallest N.B.A. player is Ferdinand
Lewis Alcindor (born April 16, 1947) now called Kareem Abdul-
Jabbar, who stands 7 feet 3⅜ inches in height.

Highest Scoring. Probably the most points scored by a college
basketball team in a single game of regulation length was 207 by
Bliss College (Columbus, Ohio) vs. Oberlin College of Commerce
(88) on March 5, 1966. Playing for Coach J. J. Redman, two
forwards scored 183 of the Bliss points—Ron Porter (96) and Jim
Marshall (87). In England, a team called Bestwood beat Meadow
Jets 242–20 at Nottingham on January 20, 1972.

The highest aggregate by any N.B.A. teams is 316, scored when the
Philadelphia Warriors beat the N.Y. Knickerbockers 169–147 at
Hershey, Pennsylvania, on March 2, 1962.

The highest score by an individual player occurred in a college
game when Clarence (Bevo) Francis of Rio Grande College, Rio
Grande, Ohio, scored 150 points in a game in 1954.

Marathon

The longest recorded marathon between two teams of five without
substitutes or rest breaks is 44 hours by Galt High School students,
Galt, California, ending April 18, 1973. A longer marathon, but with
rest breaks, of 46 hours 38 minutes, was achieved at H.M. Training
Prison, Beechworth, Victoria, Australia.

Most Accurate Shooting. The greatest goal-shooting demonstration was made by an amateur, Ted St. Martin of Riverdale, California, who sank 200 baskets in a row at the local high school gym in a demonstration in mid-1972. His average of 90.45 per cent accuracy in shooting from the foul line in a 24-hour demonstration period is also probably a record.

Bunny Levitt of Neptune, New Jersey, who once toured with the Harlem Globetrotters, claims to have sunk 499 consecutive free throws in Chicago in 1935, and 871 baskets with only a single miss. Neither record can be verified.

NATIONAL BASKETBALL ASSOCIATION
Regular Season Records
Including 1973–74 Season

The National Basketball Association's Championship series was established in 1947. Prior to 1949, when it joined with the National Basketball League, the professional circuit was known as the Basketball Association of America.

While the American Basketball Association has been in existence for 7 years, its records are not included for two reasons:
(1) career records are not yet of any significance;
(2) very few seasonal or game efforts now surpass existing N.B.A. records.

There has been talk of a merger between the two leagues. If this merger does occur, the respective league records will be merged. If no merger is forthcoming, the A.B.A. records will be published separately in future editions.

SERVICE

Most Games, Lifetime
1,122 Hal Greer, Syr. 1959–63; Phil. 1964–73

Most Games, Consecutive, Lifetime
844 John Kerr, Syr.-Phil.-Balt., Oct. 31, 1954–Nov. 4, 1965

Most Complete Games, Season
79 Wilt Chamberlain, Phil. 1962

Most Complete Games, Consecutive, Season
47 Wilt Chamberlain, Phil. 1962

Most Minutes, Lifetime
47,859 Wilt Chamberlain, Phil.-S.F.-L.A. 1960–73

Most Minutes, Season
3,882 Wilt Chamberlain, Phil. 1962

SCORING

Most Seasons Leading League
7 Wilt Chamberlain, Phil. 1960–62; S.F. 1963–64; S.F.-Phil. 1965; Phil. 1966

Most Points, Lifetime
31,419 Wilt Chamberlain, Phil.-S.F.-L.A. 1960–73

Most Points, Season
4,029 Wilt Chamberlain, Phil. 1962

Most Seasons 1000+ Points
13 Bob Cousy, Bos. 1951–63
Wilt Chamberlain, Phil. 1960–62; S.F. 1963–64; S.F.-Phil. 1965; Phil. 1966–68; L.A. 1969, 71–73
Oscar Robertson, Cin. 1961–70; Mil. 1971–73
Jerry West, L.A. 1961–73

Most Points, Game
100 Wilt Chamberlain, Phil. vs. N.Y., Mar. 2, 1962

Most Points, Half
59 Wilt Chamberlain, Phil. vs. N.Y., Mar. 2, 1962

Most Points, Quarter
31 Wilt Chamberlain, Phil. vs. N.Y., Mar. 2, 1962

Most Points, Overtime Period
13 Earl Monroe, Balt. vs. Det., Feb. 6, 1970
Joe Caldwell, Atl. vs. Cin., Feb. 18, 1970

Highest Scoring Average, Lifetime
30.5 Kareem Abdul-Jabbar, Mil. 1970–74

Highest Scoring Average, Season
50.4 Wilt Chamberlain, Phil. 1962

REBOUND RECORD-HOLDER: Wilton Norman (the Stilt) Chamberlain (b. August 21, 1936) who has played with various teams, is probably the greatest basketball player of all time. He made 55 rebounds in one game, 2,149 in a season. He also set records of 100 points in a game, 4,029 points in a season, most field goals (36 in a game, 35 in succession, 1,597 in a season), most free throws, made (28) in a game, and other records.

Basketball (N.B.A.) continued

Field Goals Made

Most Field Goals, Lifetime
12,681 Wilt Chamberlain, Phil.-S.F.-L.A. 1960–73
Most Field Goals, Season
1,597 Wilt Chamberlain, Phil. 1962
Most Field Goals, Consecutive, Season
35 Wilt Chamberlain, Phil. Feb. 17–28, 1967
Most Field Goals, Game
36 Wilt Chamberlain, Phil. vs. N.Y., Mar. 2, 1962
Most Field Goals, Half
22 Wilt Chamberlain, Phil. vs. N.Y., Mar. 2, 1962
Most Field Goals, Quarter
12 Cliff Hagan, St.L. vs. N.Y., Feb. 4, 1958
Wilt Chamberlain, Phil. vs. N.Y., Mar. 2, 1962

Field Goals Attempted

Most Field Goal Attempts, Lifetime
23,497 Wilt Chamberlain, Phil.-S.F.-L.A. 1960–73
Most Field Goal Attempts, Season
3,159 Wilt Chamberlain, Phil. 1962
Most Field Goal Attempts, Game
63 Wilt Chamberlain, Phil. vs. N.Y., Mar. 2, 1962
Most Field Goal Attempts, Half
37 Wilt Chamberlain, Phil. vs. N.Y., Mar. 2, 1962
Most Field Goal Attempts, Quarter
21 Wilt Chamberlain, Phil. vs. N.Y., Mar. 2, 1962

Field Goal Percentage

Most Seasons Leading League
9 Wilt Chamberlain, Phil. 1961; S.F. 1963; S.F.-Phil. 1965; Phil. 1966–68; L.A. 1969, 72–73
Highest Percentage, Lifetime
.553 Kareem Abdul-Jabbar, Mil. 1970–74
Highest Percentage, Season
.727 Wilt Chamberlain, L.A. 1973

Free Throws Made

Most Free Throws Made, Lifetime
7,694 Oscar Robertson, Cin.-Mil. 1961–74
Most Free Throws Made, Season
840 Jerry West, L.A. 1966
Most Free Throws Made, Consecutive, Season
55 Bill Sharman, Bos. Nov. 22–Dec. 27, 1956
Most Free Throws Made, Game
28 Wilt Chamberlain, Phil. vs. N.Y., Mar. 2, 1962
Most Free Throws Made (No Misses), Game
19 Bob Pettit, St.L. vs. Bos., Nov. 22, 1961
Most Free Throws Made, Half
19 Oscar Robertson, Cin. vs. Balt., Dec. 27, 1964
Most Free Throws Made, Quarter
14 Rick Barry, S.F. vs. N.Y., Dec. 6, 1966

Free Throws Attempted

Most Free Throw Attempts, Lifetime
11,862 Wilt Chamberlain, Phil.-S.F.-L.A. 1960–73

Most Free Throw Attempts, Season
1,363 Wilt Chamberlain, Phil. 1962

Most Free Throw Attempts, Game
34 Wilt Chamberlain, S.F. vs. N.Y., Nov. 27, 1963

Most Free Throw Attempts, Half
22 Oscar Robertson, Cin. vs. Balt., Dec. 27, 1964

Most Free Throw Attempts, Quarter
16 Oscar Robertson, Cin. vs. Balt., Dec. 27, 1964
Stan McKenzie, Phoe. vs. Phil., Feb. 15, 1970

Free Throw Percentage

Most Seasons Leading League
7 Bill Sharman, Bos. 1953–57, 59, 61

Highest Percentage, Lifetime
.884 Rick Barry, S.F.-G.S. 1966–67, 73–74

Highest Percentage, Season
.932 Bill Sharman, Bos. 1959

REBOUNDS

Most Seasons Leading League
11 Wilt Chamberlain, Phil. 1960–62; S.F. 1963; Phil. 1966–68; L.A. 1969, 71–73

Most Rebounds, Lifetime
23,924 Wilt Chamberlain, Phil.-S.F. L.A. 1960–73

Most Rebounds, Season
2,149 Wilt Chamberlain, Phil. 1961

Most Rebounds, Game
55 Wilt Chamberlain, Phil. vs. Bos., Nov. 24, 1960

Most Rebounds, Half
32 Bill Russell, Bos. vs. Phil., Nov. 16, 1957

Most Rebounds, Quarter
18 Nate Thurmond, S.F. vs. Balt., Feb. 28, 1965

Highest Average (per game), Lifetime
22.9 Wilt Chamberlain, Phil.-S.F.-L.A. 1960–73

Highest Average (per game), Season
27.2 Wilt Chamberlain, Phil. 1961

ASSISTS

Most Seasons Leading League
8 Bob Cousy, Bos. 1953–60

Most Assists, Lifetime
9,887 Oscar Robertson, Cin.-Mil. 1961–74

Most Assists, Season
910 Nate Archibald, K.C.-Omaha 1973

Most Assists, Game
28 Bob Cousy, Bos. vs. Minn., Feb. 27, 1959
Guy Rodgers, S.F. vs. St.L., Mar. 14, 1963

Most Assists, Half
19 Bob Cousy, Bos. vs. Minn., Feb. 27, 1959

Most Assists, Quarter
12 Bob Cousy, Bos. vs. Minn., Feb. 27, 1959

Highest Average (per game), Lifetime
9.5 Oscar Robertson, Cin.-Mil. 1961–74

Highest Average (per game), Season
11.5 Oscar Robertson, Cin. 1965

PERSONAL FOULS

Most Personal Fouls, Lifetime
3,855 Hal Greer, Syr.-Phil. 1959–73

Most Personal Fouls, Season
366 Bill Bridges, St.L. 1968

Most Personal Fouls, Game
8 Don Otten, T.C. vs. Sheb., Nov. 24, 1949

Most Personal Fouls, Half
6 By many. Last:
Don Smith, Hou. vs. Clev., Feb. 8, 1974

Most Personal Fouls, Quarter
6 Connie Dierking, Syr vs Cin., Nov. 17, 1959
Henry Akin, Seattle vs Phil., Dec. 20, 1967
Bud Ogden, Phil. vs Phoe., Feb. 15, 1970
Don Smith, Hou. vs. Clev., Feb. 8, 1974

ASSIST SPECIALIST: Oscar Robertson holds the record for setting up plays with 9,887 assists in his lifetime, highest average (9.5) per game lifetime and highest average (11.5) in one season.

MOST ASSISTS IN ONE GAME:
Bob Cousy, star of the Boston Celtics, made a record 28 assists in 1959.

FIELD GOAL LEADER: Kareem Abdul-Jabbar has a shooting percentage of .553 in his 4 years in pro basketball.

DISQUALIFICATIONS

(Fouling Out of Game)
Most Disqualifications, Lifetime
   127 Vern Mikkelsen, Minn., 1950–59
Most Disqualifications, Season
   26 Don Meineke, Ft. W. 1953
Most Games, No Disqualifications, Lifetime
  1,045 Wilt Chamberlain, Phil.-S.F.-L.A. 1960–73 (Entire Career)

TEAM RECORDS

(OT=Overtime)
Most Seasons, League Champion
   12 Boston 1957, 59–66, 68–69, 74
Most Seasons, Consecutive, League Champion
   8 Boston 1959–66
Most Seasons, Division Champion
   12 Boston 1957–65, 72–74
Most Seasons, Consecutive, Division Champion
   9 Boston 1957–65
Most Games Won, Season
   69 Los Angeles, 1972
Most Games Won Consecutive, Season
   33 Los Angeles Nov. 5, 1971–Jan. 7, 1972
Most Games Won, Consecutive, Start of Season
   15 Washington Nov. 3–Dec. 4, 1948
Most Games Won, Consecutive, End of Season
   14 Milwaukee Feb. 28–Mar. 27, 1973
Most Games Lost, Season
   73 Philadelphia 1973
Most Games Lost, Consecutive, Season
   20 Philadelphia Jan. 9–Feb. 11, 1973
Most Games Lost, Consecutive, Start of Season
   15 Denver Oct. 29–Dec. 25, 1949
       Cleveland Oct. 14–Nov. 10, 1970
       Philadelphia Oct. 10–Nov. 10, 1973
Highest Percentage, Games Won, Season
  .841 Los Angeles 1972
Lowest Percentage, Games Won, Season
  .110 Philadelphia 1973

Team Scoring

Most Points, Season
10,143 Philadelphia 1967
Most Games, 100+ Points, Season
   81 Los Angeles 1972
Most Games, Consecutive, 100+ Points, Season
   77 New York 1967
Most Points, Game
  173 Boston vs Minn. Feb. 27, 1959

Most Points, Both Teams, Game
316 Phil. (169) vs N.Y. (147) Mar. 2, 1962
Cin. (165) vs San Diego (151) Mar. 12, 1970
Most Points, Half
97 Atlanta vs San Diego Feb. 11, 1970
Most Points, Quarter
58 Buffalo vs Bos. Oct. 20, 1972
Widest Victory Margin, Game
63 Los Angeles (162) vs Golden State (99) Mar. 19, 1972

Field Goals Made

Most Field Goals, Season
3,972 Milwaukee 1971
Most Field Goals, Game
72 Boston vs Minn. Feb. 27, 1959
Most Field Goals, Both Teams, Game
134 Cin. (67) vs San Diego (67) Mar. 12, 1970
Most Field Goals, Half
40 Boston vs Minn. Feb. 27, 1959
Syracuse vs Det. Jan. 13, 1963
Most Field Goals, Quarter
23 Boston vs Minn. Feb. 27, 1959
Buffalo vs Bos. Oct. 20, 1972

Field Goals Attempted

Most Field Goal Attempts, Season
9,295 Boston 1961
Most Field Goal Attempts, Game
153 Philadelphia vs. L.A. Dec. 8, 1961 (3 ot)
150 Boston vs Phil. Feb. 3, 1960

BIG SCORER: Jerry West of the Los Angeles Lakers, along with Cousy, Chamberlain and Robertson, has scored 1,000 or more points in 13 seasons.

Most Field Goal Attempts, Both Teams, Game
291 Phil. (153) vs L.A. (138) Dec. 8, 1961 (3 ot)
274 Bos. (149) vs Det. (125) Jan. 27, 1961
Most Field Goal Attempts, Half
83 Philadelphia vs Syr. Nov. 4, 1959
Boston vs Phil. Dec. 27, 1960
Most Field Goal Attempts, Quarter
47 Boston vs Minn. Feb. 27, 1959
Highest Field Goal Percentage, Season
.509 Milwaukee 1971

Free Throws Made

Most Free Throws Made, Season
2,434 Phoenix 1970
Most Free Throws Made, Game
59 Anderson vs Syr. Nov. 24, 1949 (5 ot)
Most Free Throws Made, Both Teams, Game
116 And. (59) vs Syr. (57) Nov. 24, 1949 (5 ot)
Most Free Throws Made, Half
36 Chicago vs Phoe. Jan. 8, 1970
Most Free Throws Made, Quarter
24 St. Louis vs Syr. Dec. 21, 1957

Free Throws Attempted

Most Free Throw Attempts, Season
3,411 Philadelphia 1967
Most Free Throw Attempts, Game
86 Syracuse vs And. Nov. 24, 1949 (5 ot)
71 Chicago vs Phoe. Jan. 8, 1970

MOST GAMES: Hal Greer, with Syracuse for 5 seasons and Philadelphia for 10, has played in more games (1,122) than any other player.

Most Free Throw Attempts, Both
    Teams, Game
    160 Syr. (86) vs And. (74) Nov. 24,
         1949 (5 ot)
    127 Ft.W. (67) vs Minn. (60) Dec.
         31, 1954
Most Free Throw Attempts, Half
    48 Chicago vs. Phoe. Jan. 8, 1970
Most Free Throw Attempts, Quarter
    30 Boston vs Chi. Jan. 9, 1963
Highest Free Throw Percentage, Season
.812 Houston 1974

Rebounds

Most Rebounds, Season
6,131 Boston 1961
Most Rebounds, Game
    112 Philadelphia vs Cin. Nov. 8,
         1959
         Boston vs Det. Dec. 24, 1960
Most Rebounds, Both Teams, Game
    215 Phil. (110) vs L.A. (105) Dec. 8,
         1961 (3 ot)
    196 Bos. (106) vs Det. (90) Jan. 27,
         1961
Most Rebounds, Half
    62 Boston vs Phil. Nov. 16, 1957
        New York vs Phil. Nov. 19, 1960
        Philadelphia vs Syr. Nov. 9,
        1961
Most Rebounds, Quarter
    40 Philadelphia vs Syr. Nov. 9,
        1961

Assists

Most Assists, Season
2,320 Boston 1973
Most Assists, Game
    60 Syracuse vs Balt. Nov. 15, 1952
        (1 ot)
    52 Chicago vs Atl. Mar. 20, 1971
Most Assists, Both Teams, Game
    89 Det. (48) vs Clev. (41) Mar. 28,
        1973 (1 ot)
    88 Phoe. (47) vs San Diego (41)
        Mar. 15, 1969
Most Assists, Half
    29 Chicago vs Atl. Mar. 20, 1971
Most Assists, Quarter
    16 Boston vs Minn. Feb. 27, 1959
        Chicago vs Atl. Mar. 20, 1971

FREE THROW RECORD HOLDER:
Bill Sharman (now a coach) wears the
crown with a .932 percentage in the
1959 season.

Personal Fouls

Most Personal Fouls, Season
2,372 Seattle 1968
Most Personal Fouls, Game
    66 Anderson vs Syr. Nov. 24, 1949
        (5 ot)
Most Personal Fouls, Both Teams,
    Game
    122 And. (66) vs Syr. (56) Nov. 24,
         1949 (5 ot)
    97 Syr. (50) vs N.Y. (47) Feb. 15,
        1953
Most Personal Fouls, Half
    30 Rochester vs Syr. Jan. 15, 1953
Most Personal Fouls, Quarter
    16 Syracuse vs Bos. Dec. 26, 1950
        Rochester vs Syr. Jan. 15, 1953
        Chicago vs Bos. Jan. 9, 1963
        Philadelphia vs San Diego Nov.
        19, 1969
        Portland vs. Atl. Mar. 8, 1973
        New York vs. Chi. Nov. 30, 1973

Bicycling

Earliest Race. The earliest recorded bicycle race was a veloci-pede race over two kilometers (1.24 miles) at the Parc de St. Cloud, Paris, on May 31, 1868 won by James Moore (G.B.).

Slow Cycling. Slow cycling records came to a virtual end in 1965 when Tsugunobu Mitsuishi, aged 39, of Tokyo, Japan, stayed stationary for 5 hours 25 minutes.

Highest Speed. The highest speed ever achieved on a bicycle is 140.5 m.p.h. by Dr. Allan V. Abbott, 29, of San Bernardino, Cali-fornia, behind a windshield mounted on a 1955 Chevrolet over $\frac{3}{4}$ of a mile at Bonneville Salt Flats, Utah, on August 25, 1973. His speed over a mile was 138.674 m.p.h.

Antonio Maspes (Italy) recorded an unofficial unpaced 10.6 sec. for 200 meters (42.21 m.p.h.) at Milan on August 28, 1962.

The greatest distance ever covered in one hour is 76 miles 604 yards by Leon Vanderstuyft (Belgium) on the Montlhéry Motor Circuit, France, on September 30, 1928. This was achieved from a standing start paced by a motorcycle. The 24-hour record behind pace is 860 miles 367 yards by Hubert Opperman in Australia in 1932.

Most Olympic Titles. Cycling has been on the Olympic program since the revival of the Games in 1896. The greatest number of gold medals ever won is four by Marcus Hurley (U.S.) over the $\frac{1}{4}$, $\frac{1}{3}$, $\frac{1}{2}$ and 1 mile in 1904.

Tour de France

The greatest number of wins in the Tour de France (inaugurated 1903) is five by Jacques Anquetil (born Janaury 8, 1934) of France, who won in 1957, 1961, 1962, 1963, and 1964. The closest race ever was that of 1968 when after 2,898.7 miles over 25 days (June 27–July 21) Jan Jannssen (Netherlands) (born 1940) beat Herman van Springel (Belgium) in Paris by 38 seconds. The longest course was 3,569 miles on June 20–July 18, 1926.

World Titles

The only three cyclists to have won 7 world titles in any of the world championship events are Leon Meredith (G.B.) who won the Amateur 100-kilometer paced event in 1904–05–07–09–11–13; Jeff Scherens (Belgium) and Antonio Maspes (Italy) who won the Professional sprint title in 1932–33–34–35–36–37 and 1947 and in 1955–56–59–60–62–64–65.

One Hour and 24 Hour Records

The greatest distance covered in 60 minutes unpaced is 30 miles 214 yards by Ole Ritter (Denmark) at Mexico City, Mexico, on October 10, 1968. The 24-hour record on the road is 507.00 miles by Roy Cromock in Cheshire, England, on July 26–27, 1969.

WINNER OF MOST TOUR DE FRANCE VICTORIES: Jacques Anquetil of France has retained the yellow jersey as overall leader in the 2,861-mile race five times.

Coast to Coast

The youngest cyclist to achieve this feat is Becky Gorton, aged 11 years 5 months, who arrived at Boston, Massachusetts, on July 22, 1973, having set out from Olympia, Washington, on June 6, 1973.

Billiards

Earliest Mention. The earliest recorded mention of billiards was in France in 1429, and it was mentioned in England in 1588 in inventories of the Duke of Norfolk's Howard House and the Earl of Leicester's property in Essex. The first recorded public room for billiards in England was the Piazza, Covent Garden, London, in the early part of the 19th century.

Rubber cushions were introduced in 1835 and slate beds in 1836.

Highest Breaks. Tom Reece (England) made an unfinished break of 499,135, including 249,152 cradle cannons (2 points each), in 85 hours 49 minutes against Joe Chapman at Burroughes' Hall, Soho Square, London, between June 3 and July 6, 1907. This was not recognized because press and public were not continuously present. The highest certified break made by the anchor cannon is 42,746 by W. Cook (England) from May 29 to June 7, 1907. The official world record under the then baulk-line rule is 1,784 by Joe Davis (born April 15, 1901), in the United Kingdom Championship on May 29, 1936. Walter Lindrum (Australia) made an official break of 4,137 in 2 hours 55 minutes against Joe Davis at Thurston's, London, on January 19–20, 1932, before the baulk-line rule was in force. The amateur record is 859 by Mohammed Lafir (Sri Lanka) versus Eric Simons (New Zealand) in the World Amateur Championship in Bombay, India, on December 5, 1973. Davis has an unofficial personal best of 2,502 (mostly pendulum cannons) in a match against Tom Newman in Manchester, England, in 1930.

Fastest Century. Walter Lindrum (1898–1960) of Australia made an unofficial 100 break in 27.5 seconds in Australia on October 10, 1952. His official record is 100 in 46.0 seconds, set in Sydney, 1941.

Most World Titles. The greatest number of world championship titles (instituted 1870) won by one player is eight by John Roberts, Jr. (England) in 1870 (twice), 1871, 1875 (twice), 1877 and 1885 (twice). Willie Hoppe (U.S.) won 51 "world" titles in the U.S. variants of the game between 1906 and 1952.

Most Amateur Titles. The record for world amateur titles is four by Robert Marshall (Australia) in 1936–38–51–62.

Bobsledding

Origins. The oldest known sled is dated *c.* 6500 B.C. and came from Heinola, southern Finland. The word toboggan comes from the Micmac American Indian word *tobaakan*. The oldest bobsledding club in the world is at St. Moritz, Switzerland, home of the Cresta Run, founded in 1887. Modern world championships were inaugurated in 1924. Four-man bobs were included in the first Winter Olympic Games at Chamonix, France, in 1924 and two-man boblets from the third Games at Lake Placid, New York, in 1932.

Olympic and World Titles. The Olympic four-man bob has been won four times by Switzerland (1924–36–56–72). The U.S. (1932, 1936), Italy (1956, 1968) and West Germany (1952 and 1972) have won the Olympic boblet event twice.

The world four-man bob has been won 11 times by Switzerland (1924–36–39–47–54–55–56–57–71–72–73). Italy won the two-man title 13 times (1954–56–57–58–59–60–61–62–63–66–68–69–71). Eugenio Monti (Italy) (b. January 23, 1928) has been a member of 11 world championship crews.

Tobogganing

The skeleton one-man toboggan dates, in its present form, from 1892. On the 1,325-yard-long Cresta Run at St. Moritz, Switzerland, dating from 1884, the record from the Junction (2,868 feet) is 43.45 seconds by Bruno Bischofberger (Switzerland) in February, 1973. The record from Top (3,981 feet) is 54.21 seconds by Paul Maroli (Italy) reaching 85 m.p.h. near the finish.

The greatest number of wins in the Cresta Run Grand National (instituted 1885) is eight by the 1948 Olympic champion Nino Bibbia (Italy) (b. September 9, 1924) in 1960–61–62–63–64–66–68–73. The greatest number of wins in the Cresta Run Curzon Cup (instituted in 1910) is eight by Bibbia in 1950–57–58–60–62–63–64–69 who hence won the Double in 1960–62–63–64.

Lugeing

In lugeing the rider adopts a sitting, as opposed to a prone position. It was largely developed by British tourists at Klosters, Switzerland, from 1883. The first European championships were at Reichenberg, (now East) Germany, in 1914 and the first world championships at Oslo, Norway, in 1953. The International Luge Federation was formed in 1957. Lugeing attracts more than 15,000 competitors in Austria.

Most World Titles. The most successful rider in the world championships is Thomas Köhler (East Germany) (b. June 25, 1940), who won the single-seater title in 1962, 1964 (Olympics), and 1967, and shared in the two-seater title in 1967 and 1968 (Olympics). Miss Otrum Enderlein (East Germany) (b. January 12, 1943) has won 3 times—1964 (Olympics), 1965 and 1967.

Highest Speed. The fastest luge run is at Krynica, Poland, where speeds of more than 80 m.p.h. have been recorded.

Bowling

Origins. Bowling can be traced to articles found in the tomb of an Egyptian child of 5200 B.C. where there were nine pieces of stone to be set up as pins at which a stone "ball" was rolled. The ball first had to roll through an archway made of three pieces of marble. There is also resemblance to a Polynesian game called *ula maika* which utilized pins and balls of stone. The stones were rolled a distance of 60 feet. In the Italian Alps about 2,000 years ago, the underhand tossing of stones at an object is believed the beginnings of *bocci*, a game still widely played in Italy and similar to bowling. Bowling at pins probably originated in ancient Germany as a religious ceremony. Martin Luther is credited with the statement that nine was the ideal number of pins. In the British Isles, lawn bowls was preferred to bowling at pins. In the 16th century, bowling at pins was the national sport in Scotland. How bowling at pins came to the United States is a matter of controversy. Early British settlers probably brought lawn bowls and set up what is known as Bowling Green at the tip of Manhattan Island in New York but perhaps the Dutch under Henry Hudson were the ones to be credited. Some historians say that in Connecticut the tenth pin was added to evade a legal ban against the nine-pin game in 1845 but others say that ten pins was played in New York City before this and point to Washington Irving's "Rip Van Winkle" written about 1818 as evidence.

Lanes. In the U.S. there are 8,674 bowling establishments with 138,562 lanes in 1972 and about 52,000,000 bowlers. The world's largest bowling hall is the Tokyo World Lanes Bowling Center in Tokyo, Japan, with 504 lanes.

Organizations. The American Bowling Congress (ABC) comprises 4,200,000 men who bowl in leagues and tournaments. The Woman's International Bowling Congress (WIBC) has a membership of 3,300,000. An estimated 52,000,000 men, women and children bowl in either leagues or on a recreational basis in the U.S.

World Championships

The Federation Internationale des Quilleurs world championships were instituted in 1954. The highest pinfall in the individual men's event is 5,963 for 28 games by Ed Luther (U.S.) at Milwaukee, Wisconsin, in 1971.

Highest Game. The greatest altitude at which a game has taken place is 25,000 feet, when Dick Weber played Sylvia Wene in a Boeing 707 "Starstream Astrojet" freighter of American Airlines on January 7, 1964.

League Scores

Highest Men's. The highest individual score for three games is 886 by Allie Brandt of Lockport, New York, in 1939. Maximum possible is 900 (three perfect games). Highest team score is 3,858 by Budweisers of St. Louis in 1958.

Highest Women's. The highest individual score for three games is 818 by Bev Ortner, Galva, Iowa in 1968. Highest team score is 3,379 by Freeway Washer of Cleveland in 1960. (Highest in WIBC tournament play is 737 by D. D. Jacobson in 1972.)

Consecutive Strikes. The record for consecutive strikes in sanctioned match play is 29 by Frank Caruna at Buffalo, New York, on March 5, 1924, and 29 by Max Stein at Los Angeles, on October 8, 1939.

Most Perfect Scores. The highest number of sanctioned 300 games is 25 (to 1974) by Elvin Mesger of Sullivan, Missouri. The maximum 900 for a three-game series has been recorded three times in unsanctioned games—by Leo Bentley at Lorain, Ohio, on March 26, 1931; by Joe Sargent at Rochester, New York, in 1934; and by Jim Murgie in Philadelphia, on February 4, 1937.

FIRST TEAM EVENT PERFECT GAME: Les Schissler of Denver claps his hands as his 12th ball scatters the pins for the only 300 game in the team event in the 67-year history of the American Bowling Congress Tournament, at Miami Beach, Florida, in 1967.

ABC Tournament Scores

Highest Individual. Highest three-game series in singles is 775 by Lee Jouglard of Detroit in 1951. Best three-game total in any ABC event is 792 by Jack Winters of Philadelphia in doubles in 1962. Winters also holds the record of 2,147 (679–792–676) for a nine-game All-Events total. Jim Stefanich of Joliet, Illinois, has won the most championships with 6 (team in 1963 and 1968; doubles in 1966 and 1969; singles in 1969; All-Events in 1968). This record was tied by Bill Lillard of Houston, Texas, with 6 (team in 1955, 1956, 1962 and 1971; doubles in 1956 and All-Events in 1956).

Highest Doubles. The ABC record of 544 was set in 1946 by Joseph Gworek (279) and Henry Kmidowski (265) of Buffalo. The record score in a doubles series is 1,453, set in 1952 by John Klares (755) and Steve Nagy (698) of Cleveland.

Perfect Scores. Les Schissler of Denver scored 300 in the team event in 1967, the only one in that event. In all, there have been only twenty-three 300 games in the ABC tournament. (See photo.)

There have been 14 perfect games in singles, eight in doubles, and only one in team play.

Best Finishes in One Tournament. Les Schissler of Denver won the singles, All-Events, and was on the winning team in 1966 to tie Ed Lubanski of Detroit and Bill Lillard of Dallas as the only man to win three ABC crowns in one year. The best four finishes in one ABC tournament were third in singles, second in doubles, third in team and first in All-Events by Bob Strampe, Detroit, in 1967, and first in singles, third in team and doubles and second in All-Events by Paul Kulbaga, Cleveland, in 1960.

Attendance. Largest attendance on one day for an ABC tournament was 5,257 in Milwaukee in 1952. Total attendance record was also set at that tournament with 147,504 in 85 days.

Prize Winnings

Largest individual prize winner in an ABC tournament was Tom Hennessey of St. Louis, with $4,000 in 1965. Highest prize fund in one tournament was $756,721 in Detroit in 1971.

Youngest and Oldest Winners. The youngest champion was Harold Allen of Detroit who was a 1915 doubles winner at the age of 18. The oldest champion was E.D. (Sarge) Easter of Detroit, who, at the age of 67, was a winner in the 1950 team event. The oldest doubles team in ABC competition totaled 165 years in 1955: Jerry Ameling (83) and Joseph Lehnbeutter (82), both from St. Louis.

Strikes and Spares in a Row

In the greatest finish to win an ABC title, Ed Shay set a record of 12 strikes in a row in 1958, when he scored a perfect game for a total of 733 in the series.

The most spares in a row is 23, a record set by Lt. Hazen Sweet of Battle Creek, Michigan, in 1950.

Marathon

Bob W. Petersen (U.S.) bowled 1,252 games (knocked down 104,552 pins), scoring 1,228 strikes, walked 192 miles and lifted $12\frac{1}{2}$ tons in 82 hours 20 minutes of consecutive bowling at Sacramento, California, on June 7–10, 1973.

Boxing

Earliest References. Boxing with gloves was depicted on a fresco from the Isle of Thera, Greece, which has been dated 1520 B.C. The earliest prize-ring code of rules was formulated in England on August 16, 1743, by the champion pugilist Jack Broughton (1704–89), who reigned from 1729 to 1750. Boxing, which had in 1867 come under the Queensberry Rules, formulated for John Sholto Douglas, 8th Marquess of Queensberry, was not established as a legal sport in Britain until after a ruling of Mr. Justice Grantham on April 24, 1901, following the death of Billy Smith (Murray Livingstone) at Covent Garden, London.

Longest Fight. The longest recorded fight with gloves was between Andy Bowen and Jack Burke in New Orleans, on April 6–7, 1893. The fight lasted 110 rounds and 7 hours 19 minutes from 9:15 p.m. to 4:34 a.m., but was declared a no contest when both men were unable to continue. The longest recorded bare knuckle fight was one of 6 hours 15 minutes between James Kelly and Jonathan Smith at Melbourne, Australia, on October 19, 1856. The greatest recorded number of rounds is 278 in 4 hours 30 minutes, when Jack Jones beat Patsy Tunney in Cheshire, England, in 1825.

Shortest Fight. There is a distinction between the quickest knockout and the shortest fight. A knockout in 10½ seconds (including a 10-second count) occurred on September 29, 1946, when Al Couture struck Ralph Walton while the latter was adjusting a gum shield in his corner at Lewiston, Maine. If the time was accurately taken it is clear that Couture must have been more than half-way across the ring from his own corner at the opening bell.

The shortest fight on record appears to be one at Palmerston, New Zealand, on July 8, 1952, when Ross Cleverley floored D. Emerson with the first punch and the referee stopped the contest with a count 7 seconds from the bell.

Teddy Barker (U.K.) scored a technical knockout over Bob Roberts (Nigeria) at the first blow in a welterweight fight at Maesteg,

ONE-BLOW FIGHT was won by technical K.O. in the first seconds in 1957 by Teddy Barker (U.K.), shown here in another bout. The referee stopped the fight without a count.

Glamorganshire, Wales, on September 2, 1957. The referee stopped the fight without a count 10 seconds from the bell.

The shortest world heavyweight title fight occurred when Tommy Burns (1881–1955) (*né* Noah Brusso) of Canada knocked out Jem Roche in 1 minute 28 seconds in Dublin, Ireland, on March 17, 1908. The duration of the Clay *vs.* Liston fight at Lewiston, Maine, on May 25, 1965, was 1 minute 57 seconds (including the count) as timed from the video tape recordings despite a ringside announcement giving a time of 1 minute. The shortest world title fight was when Al McCoy knocked out George Chip in 45 seconds for the middleweight crown in New York on April 6, 1914.

Tallest and Heaviest. The tallest and heaviest boxer to fight professionally was Gogea Mitu (born 1914) of Rumania in 1935. He was 7 feet 4 inches and weighed 327 lbs. John Rankin, who won a fight in New Orleans, in November, 1967, was reputedly also 7 feet 4 inches.

World Heavyweight Champions

Longest and Shortest Reigns. The longest reign of any world heavyweight champion is 11 years 8 months and 7 days by Joe Louis (born Joseph Louis Barrow, at Lafayette, Alabama, May 13, 1914), from June 22, 1937, when he knocked out James J. Braddock in the 8th round at Chicago until announcing his retirement on March 1, 1949. During his reign Louis made a record 25 defenses of his title. The shortest reign was by Primo Carnera (Italy) for 350 days from June 29, 1933 to June 14, 1934. However, if the disputed title claim of Marvin Hart is allowed, his reign from July 3, 1905, to February 23, 1906, was only 235 days.

Heaviest and Lightest. The heaviest world champion was Primo Carnera (Italy) (1906–67), the "Ambling Alp," who won the title from Jack Sharkey in 6 rounds in New York City, on June 29, 1933. He scaled 267 lbs. for this fight but his peak weight was 270 lbs. He had the longest reach at 85½ inches (fingertip to fingertip) and also the largest fists with a 14¾-inch circumference. He had an expanded chest measurement of 53 inches. The lightest champion was Robert Prometheus Fitzsimmons (1862–1917), who was born at Helston, Cornwall, England, and, at a weight of 167 lbs., won the title by knocking out James J. Corbett in 14 rounds at Carson City, Nevada, on March 17, 1897.

The greatest differential in a world title fight was 86 lbs. between Carnera (270 lbs.) and Tommy Loughran (184 lbs.) of the U.S., when the former won on points at Miami, Florida, on March 1, 1934.

Tallest and Shortest. The tallest world champion was the 6-feet-5.4-inch-tall Carnera, who was measured by the Physical Education Director at the Hemingway Gymnasium of Harvard. Jess Willard (1881–1968), who won the title in 1915, often stated as 6 feet 6¼ inches tall, and widely reported and believed to be up to 6 feet 8½ inches, was in fact 6 feet 5.25 inches. The shortest was Tommy Burns (1881–1955) of Canada, world champion from February 23, 1906, to December 26, 1908, who stood 5 feet 7 inches, and weighed 179 lbs.

Oldest and Youngest. The oldest man to win the heavyweight crown was Jersey Joe Walcott (born Arnold Raymond Cream, January 31, 1914, at Merchantville, New Jersey), who knocked out Ezzard Charles on July 18, 1951, in Pittsburgh, when aged 37 years 5 months 18 days. The youngest age at which the world title has been won is 21 years 331 days by Floyd Patterson (born Waco, North Carolina, January 4, 1935). After the retirement of Rocky Marciano, Patterson won the vacant title by beating Archie Moore in 5 rounds in Chicago, on November 30, 1956. He is also the only man ever to regain the heavyweight championship. He lost to Ingemar Johansson (Sweden) on June 26, 1959, but defeated him in a rematch on June 20, 1960, at the Polo Grounds, New York City.

Undefeated. Only James Joseph (Gene) Tunney (1926–28) and Rocky Marciano (1952–56) *finally* retired as undefeated champions.

Cassius Marcellus Clay 7th (later Muhammad Ali Haj) (born Louisville, Kentucky, January 17, 1942) was undefeated in 29 fights during a professional career of 6 years and 5 months when stripped of his heavyweight title on March 22, 1967, for refusing to be inducted into the U.S. Army. On March 8, 1971, he fought and lost against Joe Frazier (b. Beaumont, S.C. January 14, 1944) at Madison Square Garden, New York City. (See photo on page 54.)

Earliest Title Fight. The first world heavyweight title fight, with gloves and 3-minute rounds, was between John L. Sullivan (1858–1918) and "Gentleman" James J. Corbett (1866–1933) in New Orleans, on September 7, 1892. Corbett won in 21 rounds.

World Champions (any weight)

Longest and Shortest Reign. Joe Louis's heavyweight duration record stands for all divisions. The shortest reign has been 54 days by the French featherweight Eugène Criqui from June 2 to July 26, 1923. The disputed flyweight champion Emile Pladner (France) reigned only 47 days from March 2, to April 18, 1929, as did the disputed featherweight champion Dave Sullivan from September 26, to November 11, 1898.

Youngest and Oldest. The youngest at which any world championship has been claimed is 19 years 6 days by Pedlar Palmer (born November 19, 1876), who won the bantamweight title in London on November 26, 1895. Willie Pep (born William Papaleo, November 22, 1922), of the U.S., won the featherweight crown in New York on his 20th birthday, November 22, 1942. After Young Corbett III knocked out Terry McGovern (1880–1918) in two rounds at Hartford, Connecticut, on November 28, 1901, neither was able to get his weight down to 126 lbs., and the title was claimed by Abe Attell, when aged only 17 years 251 days. The oldest world champion was Archie Moore (b. Archibald Lee Wright, Collinsville, Illinois, December 13, 1913 or 1916), who was recognized as a light-heavyweight champion up to early 1962, when his title was removed.

RETIRED UNDEFEATED HEAVYWEIGHT CHAMPION: Rocky Marciano (left) shares this honor with Gene Tunney.

He was then between 45 and 48. Bob Fitzsimmons (1872–1917) had the longest career of any official world titleholder with over 32 years from 1882 to 1914. He won his last world title aged 41 years 174 days in San Francisco on November 25, 1903. He was an amateur from 1880 to 1882.

Longest Fight. The longest world title fight (under Queensberry Rules) was between the lightweights Joe Gans (1874–1910), of the U.S., and Oscar "Battling" Nelson (1882–1954), the "Durable Dane," at Goldfield, Nevada, on September 3, 1906. It was terminated in the 42nd round when Gans was declared the winner on a foul.

Most Recaptures. The only boxer to win a world title five times is Sugar Ray Robinson (b. Walker Smith, Jr., in Detroit, May 3, 1920) who beat Carmen Basilio (U.S.) in the Chicago Stadium on March 25, 1958, to regain the world middleweight title for the fourth time. The other title wins were over Jake LaMotta (U.S.) in Chicago on February 14, 1951, Randy Turpin (U.K.) in New York on September 12, 1951, Carl "Bobo" Olson (U.S.) in Chicago on December 9, 1955, and Gene Fullmer (U.S.) in Chicago on May 1, 1957. The record number of title bouts in a career is 33 or 34 (at bantam and featherweight) by George Dixon (1870–1909), *alias* Little Chocolate, of the U.S., between 1890 and 1901.

CHAMPION BARE KNUCKLE FIGHT: $22,500 was the largest purse in the pre-glove era. This scene from Port Elizabeth, South Africa, occurred in a 27-round fight between Jack Cooper and Wolf Bendoff on July 29, 1889.

Most Titles Simultaneously. The only man to hold world titles at three weights simultaneously was Henry ("Homicide Hank") Armstrong (born December 22, 1912), now the Rev. Harry Jackson, of the U.S., at featherweight, lightweight and welterweight from August to December, 1938.

Greatest "Tonnage." The greatest "tonnage" recorded in any fight is 700 lbs., when Claude "Humphrey" McBride of Oklahoma at 340 lbs. knocked out Jimmy Black of Houston at 360 lbs. in the 3rd round at Oklahoma City on May 4, 1971.

The greatest "tonnage" in a world title fight was 488¾ lbs. when Carnera (259¼ lbs.) fought Paulino Uzcudum (229½ lbs.) of Spain in Rome, Italy, on October 22, 1933.

Smallest Champions. The smallest man to win any world title has been Pascual Perez (b. Mendoza, Argentina, on March 4, 1926) who won the flyweight title in Tokyo on November 26, 1954, at 107 lbs. and 4 feet 11½ inches tall. Jimmy Wilde (b. Merthyr Tydfil, 1892, d. 1969, U.K.) who held the flyweight title from 1916 to 1923 was reputed never to have fought above 108 lbs.

Most Knockdowns in Title Fights. Vic Toweel (South Africa) knocked down Danny O'Sullivan of London 14 times in 10 rounds in their world bantamweight fight at Johannesburg, on December 2, 1950, before the latter retired.

All Fights

Largest Purse. The greatest purse has been $2,500,000 each guaranteed to Joe Frazier and Muhammad Ali Haj (formerly Cassius Marcellus Clay) for their 15-round fight at Madison Square Garden, New York City, on March 8, 1971.

Highest Attendances. The greatest paid attendance at any boxing fight has been 120,757 (with a ringside price of $27.50) for the Tunney vs. Dempsey world heavyweight title fight at the Sesquicentennial Stadium, Philadelphia, on September 23, 1926. The indoor record is 37,321 at the Clay vs. Terrell fight in the Astrodome, Houston, Texas, on February 6, 1967. The highest non-paying attendance is 135,132 at the Tony Zale vs. Billy Prior fight at Juneau Park, Milwaukee, Wisconsin, on August 18, 1941.

Lowest. The smallest attendance at a world heavyweight title fight was 2,434 at the Clay vs. Liston fight at Lewiston, Maine, on May 25, 1965.

Greatest Receipts. The greatest total receipts from any boxing fight have been those from the Frazier-Ali fight in Madison Square Garden, New York City, on March 8, 1971. The gate was $1,352,951 (20,455 paid attendance) but the total gross, including T.V. closed circuit transmissions and all other rights have been estimated at more than $20,000,000. The highest *gate* receipts were those for the

UNDEFEATED IN 29 FIGHTS: Muhammad Ali Haj (born Cassius Clay), on the canvas, finally lost to Joe Frazier in 1971.

Tunney-Dempsey fight of 1927 (see previous page) when 104,943 paid $2,658,660 with a ringside price of $40.

Highest Earnings in Career. The largest known fortune ever made in a fighting career is an estimated $8,000,000 amassed by Cassius Clay (Muhammad Ali). This sum includes $2,500,000 guaranteed to him from his losing fight with Joe Frazier on March 8, 1971.

Including earnings for refereeing and promoting, Jack Dempsey had grossed over $10,000,000 to 1967.

Most Knockouts. The greatest number of knockouts in a career is 136 by Archie Moore (1936 to 1943). The record for consecutive K.O.'s is 44, set by Lamar Clark of Utah at Las Vegas, Nevada, on January 11, 1960. He knocked out 6 in one night (5 in the first round) in Bingham, Utah, on December 1, 1958.

Most Fights. The greatest recorded number of fights in a career is 1,309 by Abraham Hollandersky, *alias* Abe the Newsboy (U.S.), in the fourteen years from 1905 to 1918. He filled in the time with 387 wrestling bouts (1905–16).

Most Fights Without Loss. Hal Bagwell, a lightweight, of Gloucester, England, was reputedly undefeated in 183 consecutive fights, of which only 5 were draws, between August 10, 1938, and November 29, 1948. His record of fights in the wartime period (1939–46) is very sketchy, however.

Greatest Weight Difference. The greatest weight difference recorded in a major bout is 140 lbs., between Bob Fitzsimmons (172 lbs.) and Ed Dunkhorst (312 lbs.) at Brooklyn, New York City, on April 30, 1900. Fitzsimmons won in two rounds.

Longest Career. The heavyweight Jem Mace, known as "the gypsy" (born at Norwich, England, April 8, 1831), had a career lasting 35 years from 1855 to 1890, but there were several years in which he had only one fight. He died, aged 79, in Jarrow on November 30, 1910. Walter Edgerton, the "Kentucky Rosebud," knocked out John Henry Johnson, aged 45, in 4 rounds at the Broadway A.C., New York City, on February 4, 1916, when aged 63.

Most Olympic Gold Medals. The only amateur boxer ever to win three Olympic gold medals is the southpaw László Papp (born 1926 in Hungary), who took the middleweight (1948) and the light-middleweight titles (1952 and 1956). The only man to win two titles in one meeting was O. L. Kirk (U.S.), who took both the bantam and featherweight titles at St. Louis, Missouri, in 1904, when the U.S. won all the titles.

Bridge (Contract)

Earliest References. Bridge (a corruption of Biritch) is of Levantine origin, having been played in Greece in the early 1880's. The game was known in London in 1886 under the title of "Biritch or Russian Whist." Whist, first referred to in 1529, was the world's premier card game until 1930. Its rules had been standardized in 1742.

Auction bridge (highest bidder names trump) was introduced in 1904, but was swamped by contract bridge, which was devised by Harold S. Vanderbilt (U.S.) on a Caribbean voyage in November, 1925. The new version became a world-wide craze after the U.S. vs. Great Britain challenge match between Ely Culbertson (born in Rumania, 1891) and Lt.-Col. Walter Thomas More Buller (1886–1938) at Almack's Club, London, on September 15, 1930. The U.S. won the 54-hand match by 4,845 points.

Highest Possible Scores (excluding penalties for rules infractions)

Opponents bid 7 of any suit or no trump, doubled and redoubled and vulnerable. Opponents make no trick.		Bid 1 no trump, doubled and redoubled, vulnerable	
Above Line 1st undertrick	400	*Below Line* 1st trick (40 × 4)	160
12 subsequent under-tricks at 600 each	7,200	*Above Line* 6 overtricks (400 × 6)	2,400
All Honors	150	2nd game of 2-Game Rubber	*350
		All Honors (4 aces)	150
		Bonus for making redoubled contract	50
	7,750	(Highest Possible Positive Score)	3,110

* In practice, the full bonus of 700 points is awarded after the completion of the second game, rather than 350 after each game.

Perfect Deals. The mathematical odds against dealing 13 cards of one suit are 158,753,389,899 to 1, while the odds against receiving a "perfect deal" consisting of all 13 spades are 635,013,559,596 to 1. The odds against each of the 4 players receiving a complete suit are 2,235,197,406,895,366,368,301,559,999 to 1. Instances of this are reported frequently but the chances of it happening genuinely are extraordinarily remote—in fact if all the people in the world were grouped in bridge fours, and each four were dealt 120 hands a day, it would require 62×10^{12} years before one "perfect" deal could be expected to recur.

A "perfect" perfect deal with the dealer (South) with 13 clubs, round to East with 13 spades was the subject of affidavits by Mrs. E. F. Gyde (dealer), Mrs. Hennion, David Rex-Taylor and Mrs. P. Dawson at Richmond Community Centre, Surrey, England, on August 25, 1964. This deal, 24 times more remote than a "perfect deal," the second of the rubber, was with a pack not used for the first deal.

In view of the fact that there should be 31,201,794 deals with two perfect hands for each deal with four perfect hands, and that reports of the latter far outnumber the former, it can be safely assumed that reported occurrences of perfect deals are, almost without exception, phony.

A recent claim of a perfect deal was in a women's bridge game at the Cocoa-Rockledge Country Club in Cocoa, Florida, reported by the Associated Press in February, 1970. Upon investigation it turned out that the deck had been separated into suits just prior to shuffling and cutting.

World Titles. The World Championship (Bermuda Bowl) has been won most often by Italy's "Blue Team" (Squadron Azzura) (1957–58–59, 1961–62–63, 1965–66–67, 1969, 1973), whose team also won the Olympiad in 1964 and 1968. Two of the Italian players, Giorgio Belladonna (b. 1923) and Pietro Forquet, were on 13 of these winning teams. The team retired in 1969, but came back to defeat the Dallas Aces (1970–71 World Champions) 338–254 in Las Vegas in December, 1971, and take the Olympiad in Miami in June, 1972.

Longest Session. The longest recorded session is one of 180 hours by four students at Edinburgh University, Scotland, on April 21–28, 1972.

Most Master Points. In 1971, a new World Ranking List, based on Master Points was instituted. The leading male player was Georgio Belladonna (see above) with 1,333 points, followed by 5 more Italians.

The world's leading woman player was Mrs. Rixi Markus (G.B.) with 195 points.

HIGHEST-PAID BULLFIGHTER: El Cordobés became a multi-millionaire in 1966. In 1970 alone he received $1,800,000 for 121 ring battles.

Bull Fighting

The first renowned professional *espada* (bull fighter) was Francisco Romero of Ronda, in Andalusia, Spain, who introduced the *estoque* and the red muleta *c*. 1700. Spain now has some 190 active matadors. Since 1700, 42 major matadors have died in the ring.

Largest Stadiums and Gate. The world's largest bull-fighting ring is the Plaza, Mexico City, with a capacity of 48,000. The largest of Spain's 312 bullrings is Las Ventas, Madrid, with a capacity of 28,000.

Most Successful Matadors. The most successful matador measured by bulls killed was Lagartijo (1841–1900), born Rafael Molina, whose lifetime total was 4,867.

The longest career of any 20th century *espada* was that of Juan Belmonte (1892–1962) of Spain, who survived 29 seasons from 1909 to 1937 killing 3,000 bulls and being gored 50 times. In 1919, he killed 200 bulls in 109 *corridas*. (Recent Spanish law requires compulsory retirement at age 55.) Currently, Antonio Bienvenida is the *doyen* at 51.

Most Kills in a Day. In 1884, Romano set a record by killing 18 bulls in a day in Seville, and in 1949 El Litri (Miguel Báes) set a Spanish record with 114 *novilladas* in a season.

Highest Paid Matadors. The highest paid bull fighter in history is El Cordobés (born Manolo Benitez Pérez, probably on May 4, 1936, in Palma del Rio, Spain), who became a multi-millionaire in 1966, during which year he fought 111 *corridas* up to October 4, receiving over $15,000 for each half-hour in the ring. On May 19, 1968, he received $25,000 for a *corrida* in Madrid and in 1970 an estimated $1,800,000 for 121 fights.

Canoeing

Origins. The acknowledged pioneer of canoeing as a sport was John Macgregor, a British barrister, in 1865. The Canoe Club was formed on July 26, 1866.

Most Olympic Gold Medals. Gert Frederiksson (b. November 21, 1919) of Sweden has won the 1,000-meter Kayak singles in 1948, 1952 and 1956, the 10,000-meter Kayak singles in 1948 and 1956, and the 1,000-meter Kayak doubles in 1960. In addition to his 6 Olympic titles he has won 3 other world titles in non-Olympic years: 1,000-meter K.1 in 1950 and 1954, and 500-meter K.1 in 1954.

The Olympic 1,000-meter best performance of 3 minutes 14.02 seconds represents an average speed of 11.53 m.p.h. and a striking rate of about 125 strokes per minute.

Longest Journey

The longest canoe journey in history was one of 7,165 miles from New York City to Nome, Alaska, by Geoffrey W. Pope, aged 24, and Sheldon P. Taylor, 25, from April 25, 1936 arriving on August 11, 1937. The journey was made entirely on the North American river system by paddle and portage.

Eskimo Rolls. The record for Eskimo rolls is 400 in 27 minutes 29 seconds by Terence Russell, 15, of Swanley, Kent, England, at Eltham Baths, Greater London, on December 18, 1971. A "hand-rolling" record of 100 rolls in 5 minutes 52 seconds was set in Portsmouth, England, by Peter Mooney on November 26, 1972.

Transatlantic. In 1928 E. Romer (Germany) crossed the North Atlantic from Lisbon to the West Indies in a 19½-foot canvas sailing Kayak named *Deutsches Spart* in 58 days.

Downstream Canoeing

River	Miles	Canoers	Location	Duration
Rhine	708	Sgt. Charles Kavanagh	Chur, Switzerland to Willemstadt, Neths., Feb. 13, 1961	17½ days
Rhine	726*	L. Cpl. Peter Salisbury and Spr. Simon Chivers	Chur to Hook of Holland, April 17–May 9, 1972	21½ days
Murray	1,300	Philip Davis and Robert S. Lodge (15½-foot canoe)	Albury, N.S.W. to Murray Bridge, Dec. 27, 1970–Feb. 1, 1971	36 days
Amazon	3,900	Stephan Z. Bezak (U.S.) (kayak)	Atalaya to Belem, June 21–Nov., 1970	4½ mths.
Nile (Egypt)	4,000	John Goddard (U.S.), Jean Laporte and André Davy (France)	Kagera to the Delta, Nov., 1954–July, 1955	9 months

* With greater portages.

463 DAYS IN A CAVE:
This young Yugoslav,
Milutin Veljkovic, set the
endurance record.

Cave Exploration *(Spelunking)*

World's Deepest Caves

There are few caves the depth of which are internationally agreed.

Feet	Cave	Location
3,850*	Resea de la Pierre St. Martin	Western Pyrenees, France
3,743	Gouffre Berger	Dauphin Alps, France
3,149	Choroum des Aguilles	Dauphin Alps, France
3,018	Abisso Michele Gortani	Julian Alps, Italy
2,979	Gouffre de Cambou de Liard	Central Pyrenees, France
2,952	Reseau Felix Trombe	Eastern Pyrenees, France

Note: El Sotano Cave, Mexico, has the world's longest vertical pitch of 1,345 feet.
The highest known cave entrance in the world is that of the Rakhiot Cave, Nanga
Parbat, Kashmir, at 21,860 feet.

* An Austrian source gives 4,461 feet.

Feet	Cave	Cavers	Date
210	Lamb Lair, Somerset, England	John Beaumont (explored)	c. 1676
454	Macocha, Moravia	Nagel	May, 1748
742	Grotta di Padriciano, Trieste, Italy	Antonio Lindner, Svetina	1839
1,079	Grotta di Trebiciano, Trieste	Antonio Lindner	April 6, 1841
1,293	Nidlenloch, Switzerland	—	1909
1,433	Geldloch, Austria	—	1923
1,476	Abisso Bertarelli, Yugoslavia	R. Battelini, G. Cesca	Aug. 24, 1925
1,491	Spluga della Preta, Venice, Italy	*L. de Battisti	Sept. 18, 1927
1,775	Antro di Corchia, Tuscany, Italy	E. Fiorentino Club	1934
1,980	Trou de Glaz, Isère, France	F. Petzl, C. Petit-Didier	May 4, 1947
2,389	Gouffre de la Pierre St. Martin, Basses-Pyrénées, France	*Georges Lépineux	Aug. 15, 1953
2,428	Gouffre Berger, Isère, France	J. Cadoux, G. Garby	Sept. 11, 1954
2,963	Gouffre Berger, Isère, France	*F. Petzl and 6 men	Sept. 25, 1954
3,230	Gouffre Berger, Isère, France	L. Potié, G. Garby et al.	July 29, 1955
>3,600	Gouffre Berger, Isère, France	Jean Cadoux and 2 others	Aug. 11, 1956
>3,600	Gouffre Berger, Isère, France	*Frank Salt and 7 others	Aug. 23, 1962
3,743	Gouffre Berger, Isère, France	Kenneth Pearce	Aug. 4, 1963
3,850	Gouffre de la Pierre Saint Martin	C. Queffelec and 3 others	Aug., 1966
3,850	Gouffre de la Pierre Saint Martin	C. Queffelec and 10 others	Aug., 1968
3,850	Gouffre de la Pierre Saint Martin	Ass. de Rech. Spéléo Internationale	Nov. 8–11, 1969

* Leader

Duration. The endurance record for staying in a cave is 463 days by Milutin Veljkovic (b. 1935) (Yugoslavia) in the Samar Cavern, Svrljig Mountains, northern Yugoslavia from June 24, 1969 to September 30, 1970. (See photo, previous page.)

Checkers

Origins. Checkers, known as draughts in some countries, has origins earlier than chess. It was played in Egypt in the first millenium B.C. The earliest book on the game was by Antonio Torquemada of Valencia, Spain in 1547.

The earliest U.S. vs. Great Britain international match was in 1905, and was won by the Scottish Masters, 73–34, with 284 draws. The U.S. won in 1927 in New York, 96–20 with 364 draws.

The only man to win 5 titles has been J. Marshall (Fife, Scotland) in 1948–50–52–54–66. The longest tenure of invincibility in freestyle play was that of Melvin Pomeroy (U.S.), who was internationally undefeated from 1914 until his death in 1933.

Longest Game. In competition, the prescribed rate of play is not less than 30 moves per hour with the average game lasting about 90 minutes. In 1958 a match between Dr. Marian Tinsley (U.S.) and Derek Oldbury (G.B.) lasted 7½ hours.

Most Opponents. Newell W. Banks (b. Detroit, October 10, 1887) played 140 games simultaneously, winning 133 and drawing 7 in Chicago in 1933. His playing time was 145 minutes so averaging about one second per move.

Chess

Origins. The name chess is derived from the Persian word *shah*. It is a descendant of the game *Chaturanga*. The earliest reference is from the Middle Persian Karnamak (*c.* 590–628), though there are grounds for believing its origins are from the 2nd century, owing to the discovery, announced in March, 1973, of two ivory chessmen in the Uzbek Soviet Republic, datable to that century. The game reached Britain in *c.* 1255. The *Fédération Internationale des Echecs* was established in 1924. There were an estimated 7,000,000 registered players in the U.S.S.R. in 1973.

It has been calculated that the four opening moves can be made in 197,299 ways, leading to some 72,000 different positions. The approximate number of different games possible is 25×10^{116}—a number astronomically higher than the number of atoms in the observable universe.

World Champions. François André Danican, *alias* Philidor (1726–95), of France claimed the title of "world champion" from 1747 until his death. World champions have been generally recognized since 1886. The longest tenure has been 27 years by Dr. Emanuel Lasker (1868–1941) of Germany, from 1894 to 1921. Robert J. (Bobby) Fischer (b. Chicago, March 9, 1943) is reckoned on the officially adopted Elo system to be the great Grandmaster of all time. He has an I.Q. of 187 and became at 15 the youngest ever International Grandmaster.

The women's world championship has been most often won by Nona Gaprindashvili (U.S.S.R.) in 1963–66–69–72.

Longest Games. The most protracted chess game on record was one drawn on the 191st move between H. Pilnik (Argentina) and Moshe Czerniak (Israel) at Mar del Plata, Argentina, in April, 1950. The total playing time was 20 hours. A game of 21½ hours, but drawn on the 171st move (average over 7½ minutes per move), was played between Makagonov and Chekover at Baku, U.S.S.R., in 1945. A game of 221 moves between Kenneth Rogoff (U.S.) and Arthur Williams (U.K.) was played in Stockholm, Sweden, in August, 1969, but required only 4 hours 25 mins.

Marathon. The longest recorded session is one of 101 hours between John P. Cameron and Jon Stevens at Ipswich, Suffolk, England, March 21–25, 1970.

The longest game at "lightning chess" (*i.e.* all moves completed by a player in five minutes) is 81 hours 32 minutes by Nigel Williams, 16, and Michael Ashton, 15, at the Hurstbourne Tarrant Church Hall, Hants., England, on May 28–31, 1973.

The slowest recorded game (before modern rules) was one of 11 hours between Paul Morphy, the U.S. champion of 1852–62, and a chessmaster named Paulsen.

Shortest Game. The shortest recorded game between masters was one of four moves when Lazard (Black) beat Gibaud in a Paris chess café in 1924. The moves were: 1. P–Q4, N–KB3; 2. N–Q2, P–K4; 3. PxP, N–N5; 4. P–KR3, N–K6. White then resigned because if he played 5. PxN there would have followed Q–KR5 check and the loss of his Queen for a Knight by any other move.

Most Opponents. Records by chessmasters for numbers of opponents tackled simultaneously depend very much on whether or not the opponents are replaced as defeated, are in relays, or whether they are taken on in a simultaneous start. The greatest number tackled on a replacement basis is 400 (379 defeated) by the Swedish master Gideon Ståhlberg (died May 26, 1967), in 36 hours of play in Buenos Aires, Argentina, in 1940. Georges Koltanowski (Belgium, now of U.S.) tackled 56 opponents "blindfold" and won 50, drew 6, lost 0 in 9¾ hours at the Fairmont Hotel, San Francisco, on December 13, 1960.

Curling

Origins. An early form of the sport is believed to have originated in the Netherlands about 450 years ago. The first club was formed at Kilsyth, Scotland, in 1510. Organized administration began in 1838 with the formation of the Royal Caledonian Curling Club, the international legislative body based in Edinburgh. The first indoor ice rink to introduce curling was at Southport, England, in 1879.

The U.S. won the first Gordon International Medal series of matches, between Canada and the U.S., at Montreal in 1884. The first Strathcona Cup match between Canada and Scotland was won by Canada in 1903. Although demonstrated at the Winter Olympics of 1924, 1932 and 1964, curling has never been included in the official Olympic program.

Largest Rink. The world's largest curling rink is the Big Four Curling Rink, Calgary, Alberta, Canada, opened in 1959 at a cost of Can. $2,250,000. Each of the two floors has 12 rinks, accommodating 48 teams and 192 players.

Most Titles. The record for international team matches for the Scotch Cup and Air Canada Silver Broom (instituted 1959) is 12 wins by Canada, in 1959–60–61–62–63–64–66–68–69–70–71–72. The most Strathcona Cup wins is seven by Canada (1903–09–12–23–38–57–65) against Scotland.

Marathon. The longest recorded curling match is one of 37 hours 9 minutes by the Schwarzwald Curling Club at Baden-Baden, West Germany, on February 22–23, 1973.

Most Durable Player. In 1972, Howard "Pappy" Wood competed in his 65th consecutive annual *bonspiel* since 1908 at the Manitoba Curling Association.

MOST OLYMPIC GOLD MEDALS: The only 3-day event rider to win 3 gold medals, Richard Meade (G.B.) captured the individual title in 1972 and the team title in 1968 and 1972.

Equestrian Sports

Origin. Evidence of horse riding dates from an Anatolian statuette dated *c*. 1400 B.C. Pignatelli's academy of horsemanship at Naples dates from the sixteenth century. The earliest show jumping was in Paris in 1886. Equestrian events have been included in the Olympic Games since 1912.

Most Olympic Medals. The greatest number of Olympic gold medals is 5 by Hans Günter Winkler (West Germany), who won 4 team gold medals as captain in 1956, 1960, 1964 and 1972, and won the individual Grand Prix in 1956. The most team wins in the Prix de Nations is 5 by Germany in 1936, 1956, 1960, 1964, and 1972.

The lowest score obtained by a winner was no faults, by Frantisek Ventura (Czechoslovakia) in 1928. Pierre Jonqueres d'Oriola (France), is the only two-time winner of the individual gold medal, in 1952 and 1964. Richard John Hunnay Meade (G.B.) (b. December 4, 1938) is the only 3-day event rider to win 3 gold medals—the individual in 1972 and the team in 1968 and 1972.

Jumping Records. The official *Fédération Equestre Internationale* high jump record is 8 feet 1¼ inches by *Huasó*, ridden by Capt. A. Larraguibel Morales (Chile) at Santiago, Chile, on February 5, 1949, and 27 feet 2¾ inches for long jump over water by *Amado Mio* ridden by Col. Lopez del Hierro (Spain), at Barcelona, Spain, on November 12, 1951. *Heatherbloom*, ridden by Dick Donnelly was reputed to have covered 37 feet in clearing an 8-foot-3-inch *puissance* jump at Richmond, Virginia, in 1903. *Solid Gold* cleared 36 feet 3 inches over water at the Wagga Show, N.S.W., Australia, in August, 1936, for an Australian record. *Jerry M* allegedly cleared 40 feet over water at Aintree, Liverpool, England, in 1912.

At Cairns, Queensland, *Golden Meade* ridden by Jack Martin cleared an unofficially measured 8 feet 6 inches on July 25, 1946. *Ben Bolt* was credited with clearing 9 feet 6 inches at the 1938 Royal Horse Show, Sydney, Australia. The Australian record however is 8 feet 4 inches by C. Russell on *Flyaway* in 1939 and A. L. Payne on *Golden Meade* in 1946. The world's unofficial best for a woman is 7 feet 5½ inches by Miss B. Perry (Australia) on *Plain Bill* at Cairns, Queensland, Australia, in 1940.

The greatest recorded height reached bareback is 6 feet 7 inches by *Silver Wood* at Heidelberg, Victoria, Australia, on December 10, 1938.

Marathon. The longest continuous period spent in the saddle is 42 hours 20 minutes by Joseph Roberts of Newport Pagnell, Buckinghamshire, England, from Brighton to Bletchley, on July 6–8, 1972.

HIGHEST EQUESTRIAN JUMP: Captain Morales leaped 8 feet 1¼ inches on "Huasó" at Santiago, Chile, in 1949.

CHAMPION FENCER: Christian d'Oriola of France (right) won most men's titles with the foil.

Fencing

Origins. Fencing (fighting with single sticks) was practiced as a sport in Egypt as early as *c.* 1360 B.C. The first governing body for fencing in Britain was the Corporation of Masters of Defence founded by Henry VIII before 1540 and fencing was practiced as sport, notably in prize fights, since that time. The foil was the practice weapon for the short court sword from the 17th century. The épée was established in the mid-19th century and the light saber was introduced by the Italians in the late 19th century.

Most Olympic Titles. The greatest number of individual Olympic gold medals won is three by Ramón Fonst (Cuba) (b. 1883) in 1900 and 1904 (2) and Nedo Nadi (Italy) (b. June 9, 1894) in 1912 and 1920 (2). Nadi also won three team gold medals in 1920 making an unprecedented total of five gold medals at one Olympic meet.

Aladar Gerevich (Hungary) (b. March 16, 1910) was on the winning saber team, 1932–36–48–52–56–60. He also holds the record of 10 Olympic medals (7 gold, 1 silver, 2 bronze).

The women's record is 6 medals (2 gold, 3 silver, 1 bronze) by Ildiko Rejto Sagine (formerly Ujlaki-Rejto) (Hungary) (b. May 11, 1937) from 1960 to 1972.

Most World Titles. The greatest number of individual world titles won is four; this record is shared by d'Oriola and Pawlowski (see table, next page), but note that d'Oriola also won 2 individual Olympic titles. Likewise, of the three women foilists with 3 world titles, only Elek also won 2 individual Olympic titles.

Ellen Müller-Preiss (Austria) won the women's foil in 1947 and 1949 and shared it in 1950. She also won the Olympic title in 1932.

Italy won the men's foil team 13 times; Hungary the ladies' foil teams 11 times; Italy the épée teams 10 times and Hungary the saber teams 13 times.

Most Olympic and Most World Titles

Event	Olympic Gold Medals	World Championships (not held in Olympic years)
Men's Foil, Individual	2 Christian d'Oriola (France) b. Oct. 3, 1928 (1952, 56)	4 Christian d'Oriola (France) (1947, 49, 53, 54)
Men's Foil, Team	5 France (1924, 32, 48, 52, 68)	12 Italy (1929–31, 33–35, 37, 38, 49, 50, 54, 55)
Men's Epée, Individual	2 Ramón Fonst (Cuba) b. 1883 (1900, 04)	3 Georges Buchard (France) b. Dec. 21, 1893 (1927, 31, 33) 3 Aleksey Nikanchikov (U.S.S.R.) b. July 30, 1940 (1966, 67, 70)
Men's Epée, Team	6 Italy (1920, 28, 36, 52, 56, 60)	10 Italy (1931, 33, 37, 49, 50, 53–55, 57, 58)
Men's Sabre, Individual	2 Dr. Jenö Fuchs (Hungary) b. Oct. 29, 1882 (1908, 12) 2 Rudolf Kárpáti (Hungary) b. July 17, 1920 (1956, 60)	4 Jerzy Pawlowski (Poland) b. Oct. 25, 1932 (1957, 65, 66, 68)
Men's Sabre, Team	9 Hungary (1908, 12, 28, 32, 36, 48, 52, 56, 60)	13 Hungary (1930, 31, 33–35, 37, 51, 53–55, 57, 58, 66)
Women's Foil, Individual	2 Ilona Schacherer-Elek (Hungary) b. 1907 (1936, 48)	3 Helene Mayer (Germany) 1910–53 (1929, 31, 37) 3 Ilona Schacherer-Elek (Hungary) b. 1907 (1934, 35, 51) 3 Ellen Müller-Preiss (Austria) (1947, 49, 50 (shared))
Women's Foil, Team	3 U.S.S.R. (1960, 68, 72)	11 Hungary (1933–35, 37, 53–55, 59, 62, 65, 67)

Field Hockey

Origin. A representation of two hoop players with curved snagging sticks apparently in an orthodox "bully" position was found in Tomb No. 17 at Beni Hasan, Egypt, and has been dated to c. 2050 B.C. There is a reference to the game in Lincolnshire, England, in 1277. The first country to form a national association was England (The Hockey Association) in 1886.

Earliest International. The first international match was the Wales vs. Ireland match on January 26, 1895. Ireland won 3–0.

Highest International Score. The highest score in international field hockey was when India defeated the U.S. 24–1 at Los Angeles, in the 1932 Olympic Games. The Indians were Olympic Champions from the re-inception of Olympic hockey in 1928 until 1960, when Pakistan beat them 1–0 at Rome. They had their seventh win in 1964. Four Indians have won 3 Olympic gold medals—Dhyan Chand and R. J. Allen (1928, 1932, 1936), Randhir Gentle (1948, 1952, 1956), and Leslie Claudius (1948, 1952 and 1956).

The highest score in a women's international match occurred when England defeated France 23–0 at Merton, Surrey, on February 3, 1923.

The 1971 World Cup was won by Pakistan at Barcelona.

Longest Game. The longest international game on record was one of 145 minutes (into the sixth period of extra time), when Netherlands beat Spain 1–0 in the Olympic tournament at Mexico City on October 25, 1968.

Attendance. The highest attendance at a women's hockey match was 65,000 for the match between England and Wales at the Empire Stadium, Wembley, Greater London, on March 8, 1969.

Fishing

Largest Catches. The largest fish ever caught on a rod is an officially ratified man-eating great white shark (*Carcharodon carcharias*) weighing 2,664 lbs., and measuring 16 feet 10 inches long, caught by Alf Dean at Denial Bay, near Ceduna, South Australia, on April 21, 1959. Capt. Frank Mundus (U.S.) harpooned and landed a 17-foot-long 4,500-lb. white shark, after a 5-hour battle, off Montauk Point, Long Island, New York, in 1964.

The largest marine animal ever killed by *hand* harpoon was a blue whale 97 feet in length, killed by Archer Davidson in Twofold Bay, New South Wales, Australia, in 1910. Its tail flukes measured 20 feet across and its jaw bone 23 feet 4 inches. To date this has provided the ultimate in "fishing stories."

The largest fish ever taken spearfishing underwater was an 804-lb. giant black grouper or Jewfish by Don Pinder of the Miami Triton Club, Florida, in 1955.

Smallest Catch. The smallest full-grown fish ever caught is the *Schindleria praematurus*, weighing 1/14,000th of an ounce found near Samoa, in the central Pacific.

The smallest mature shark is the rare *Squalidus laticaudus*, found off the Philippines, which measures only 6 inches in length.

Freshwater Casting. The longest freshwater cast ratified under I.C.F. (International Casting Federation) rules is 574 feet 2 inches by Walter Kummerow (West Germany), for the Bait Distance Double-Handed 30-gramme event held at Lenzerheide, Switzerland, in the 1968 Championships.

Surf Casting. The longest surf casting distance ever reported is one of 1,000 feet achieved on a beach in South Africa.

Longest Fight. The longest recorded fight with a fish is 32 hours 5 minutes by Donal Heatley (b. 1938) (New Zealand) with a broad-bill (estimated length 20 feet and weight 1,500 lbs.) off Mayor Island off Tauranga, New Zealand, January 21–22, 1968. It towed the 12-foot launch 50 miles before breaking the line.

Fishing

(Sea fish records taken by tackle as ratified by the International Game Fish Association to January 1, 1973. Freshwater fish are marked *)

Species	Weight in lbs. oz.		Name of Angler	Location	Date
Amberjack	149	0	Peter Simons	Bermuda	June 21, 1964
Barracuda	83	0	K. J. W. Hackett	Lagos, Nigeria	Jan. 13, 1952
Bass (Californian Black Sea)	563	8	James D. McAdam	Anacapa Island, California	Aug. 20, 1968
Bass (Giant Sea)	680	0	Lynn Joyner	Fernandina Beach, Florida	May 20, 1961
*Carp†	55	5	Frank J. Ledwein	Clearwater Lake, Minnesota	July 10, 1952
Cod	98	12	Alphonse J. Bielevich	Isle of Shoals, Massachusetts	June 8, 1969
Marlin (Black)	1,560	0	Alfred C. Glassell, Jr.	Cabo Blanco, Peru	Aug. 4, 1953
Marlin (Blue)	845	0	Elliot J. Fishman	St. Thomas, Virgin Is.	July 4, 1968
Marlin (Pacific Blue)	1,153	0	Greg D. Perez	Ritidian Point, Guam	Aug. 21, 1969
Marlin (Striped)	415	0	B. C. Bain	Cape Brett, New Zealand	Mar. 31, 1964
Marlin (White)	159	8	W. E. Johnson	Pompano Beach, Florida	Apr. 25, 1953
*Pike (Northern)	46	2	Peter Dubuc	Sacandaga Reservoir, New York	Sept. 15, 1940
Sailfish (Atlantic)	141	1	Tony Burnand	Ivory Coast, Africa	Jan. 26, 1961
Sailfish (Pacific)	221	0	C. W. Stewart	Santa Cruz I., Galapagos Is.	Feb. 12, 1947
Salmon (Chinook)§	92	0	H. Wichmann	Skeena River, B.C. Canada	July 19, 1959
Sawfish	890	8	Jack Wagner	Fort Amador, Canal Zone	May 26, 1960
Shark (Blue)	410	0	Richard C. Webster	Rockport, Massachusetts	Sept. 1, 1960
	410	0	Martha C. Webster	Rockport, Massachusetts	Aug. 17, 1967
**Shark (Mako)	1061	0	James B. Penwarden	Mayor Island, New Zealand	Feb. 17, 1970
Shark (White or Man-Eating)	2,664	0	Alfred Dean (See photo)	Aduna, South Australia	Apr. 21, 1959
Shark (Porbeagle)	430	0	Desmond Bougourd	South of Jersey, England	June 29, 1969
Shark (Thresher)	729	0	Mrs. V. Brown	Mayor Island, New Zealand	June 3, 1959
Shark (Tiger)	1,780	0	Walter Maxwell	Cherry Grove, South Carolina	June 14, 1964
*Sturgeon (White)	360	0	Willard Cravens	Snake River, Idaho	Apr. 24, 1956
Swordfish	1,182	0	L. E. Marron	Iquique, Chile	May 7, 1953
Tarpon	283	0	M. Salazar	Lago de Maracaibo, Venezuela	Mar. 19, 1956
*Trout (Lake)‖			Record being reviewed		
Tuna (Allison or Yellowfin)	296	0	Edward C. Malnar	San Benedicts Is., Mexico	Mar. 7, 1971
Tuna (Atlantic Big-eyed)	321	12	Vito Locaputo	Hudson Canyon, New York	Aug. 19, 1972
Tuna (Pacific Big-eyed)	435	0	Dr. Russel V. A. Lee	Cabo Blanco, Peru	Apr. 17, 1957
Tuna (Bluefin)	1,065	0	Robert Glen Gibson	Cape Breton, Nova Scotia	Nov. 19, 1970
Wahoo	149	0	John Pirovano	Cat Cay, Bahamas	June 15, 1962

† A carp weighing 83 lbs, 8 oz. was taken (not by rod) near Pretoria, South Africa. A 60 lb. specimen was taken by bow and arrow by Ben A. Topham in Wythe Co., Virginia, on July 5, 1970. § A salmon weighing 126 lbs. 8 oz. was taken (not by rod) near Petersburg, Alaska. ‖ A 102-lb. trout was taken from Lake Athabasca, northern Saskatchewan, Canada, on August 8, 1961. ** A 1,295-lb. specimen was taken by two anglers off Natal, South Africa, on March 17, 1939, and a 1,500-lb. specimen harpooned inside Durban Harbour, South Africa, in 1933.

THE ULTIMATE IN ANGLING: Alf Dean (Australia) with his record 2,664-lb. white shark.

Marathon. Lynda Hamilton of Kelvedon and District Angling Club, England, fished for 137 hours at Rivenhall Sand Pit, near Silver End, Essex, between August 4 and 10, 1972. Approximately 5 minutes per hour were used as rest breaks.

Football

Origins. The origin of modern football stems from the "Boston Game" as played at Harvard. Harvard declined to participate in the inaugural meeting of the Intercollegiate Football Association in New York City in October, 1873, on the grounds that the proposed rules were based on the non-handling "Association" code of English football. Instead, Harvard accepted a proposal from McGill University of Montreal, Canada, who played the more closely akin

English Rugby Football. The first football match under the Harvard Rules was thus played against McGill at Cambridge, Mass., in May, 1874. In November, 1876, a New Intercollegiate Football Association, based on modern football, was inaugurated at Springfield, Mass., with a pioneer membership of five colleges.

Professional football dates from the Latrobe, Pa. *vs.* Jeannette, Pa., match at Latrobe, in August, 1895. The National Football League was founded in Canton, Ohio, in 1920, although it did not adopt its present name until 1922. The year 1969 was the final year in which professional football was divided into separate National and American Leagues, for record purposes.

All-America Selections

The earliest All-America selections were made in 1889 by Caspar Whitney of *The Week's Sport* and later of *Harper's Weekly*.

College Series Records

The oldest collegiate series is that between Princeton and Rutgers dating from 1869, or 7 years before the passing of the Springfield rules. The most regularly contested series is between Lafayette and Lehigh, who have met 109 times between 1884 and the end of 1973.

Longest Streaks

The longest winning streak is 47 straight by Oklahoma. The longest unbeaten streak is 63 games (59 won, 4 tied) by Washington from 1907 to 1917.

MODERN MAJOR-COLLEGE INDIVIDUAL RECORDS

Points

Most in a Game	43	Jim Brown (Syracuse)	1956
Most in a Season	174	Lydell Mitchell (Penn State)	1971
Most in a Career	354	Glenn Davis (Army)	1943–46

Touchdowns

Most in a Game	7	Arnold Boykin (Mississippi)	1951
Most in a Season	29	Lydell Mitchell (Penn State)	1971

Field Goals

Most in a Game	6	Frank Nester (West Virginia)	1972
	6	Charley Gogolak (Princeton)	1965
Most in a Season	18	Bob Jacobs (Wyoming)	1969
	18	Rod Garcia (Stanford)	1973
Most in a Career	42	Rod Garcia (Stanford)	1971–73

SEASON RECORDS

Total Offense	3,343 yds.	Bill Anderson (Tulsa)	1965
Most Rushing and Passing Plays	580	Bill Anderson (Tulsa)	1965
Most Times Carried	358	Steve Owens (Oklahoma)	1969
Yards Gained Rushing	1,881 yds.	Ed Marinaro (Cornell)	1971
Highest Average Gain per Rush	9.35 yds.	Greg Pruitt (Oklahoma)	1971
Most Passes Completed	296	Bill Anderson (Tulsa)	1965
Most Touchdown Passes	39	Dennis Shaw (San Diego St.)	1969
Highest Completion Percentage	68.7%	Jerry Rhome (Tulsa)	1964
Most Yards Gained Passing	3,464 yds.	Bill Anderson (Tulsa)	1965
Most Passes Caught	134	Howard Twilley (Tulsa)	1965
Most Yards Gained on Catches	1,779 yds.	Howard Twilley (Tulsa)	1965
Most Touchdown Passes Caught	18	Tom Reynolds (San Diego St.)	1969
Most Passes Intercepted by	14	Al Worley (Washington)	1968

Longest Service Coach

The longest service head coach was Amos Alonzo Stagg, who served Springfield in 1890–91, Chicago from 1892 to 1932 and College of Pacific from 1933 to 1946, making a total of 57 years.

All-Star Games

The reigning N.F.L. Champions first met an All-Star College selection in the annual August series in Chicago in 1934. The highest scoring match was that of 1940 in which Green Bay beat the All-Stars 45–28. The biggest professional win was in 1949 when Philadelphia won 38–0, and the biggest All-Stars win was in 1943 when Washington was defeated 27–7.

ALL-TIME PROFESSIONAL INDIVIDUAL RECORDS

Service

Most Seasons, Active Player
24 George Blanda, Chi. Bears 1949–58; Balt. 1950; AFL: Hou. 1960–66; Oak. 1967–73

Most Games Played, Lifetime
312 George Blanda, Chi. Bears 1949–58; Balt. 1950; AFL: Hou. 1960–66; Oak. 1967–73

Most Consecutive Games Played, Lifetime
196 George Blanda, Hou. 1960–66; Oak. 1960–73
Jim Otto, Oak. 1960–73

Most Seasons, Head Coach
40 George Halas, Chi. Bears 1920–29, 33–42, 46–55, 58–67

Scoring

Most Seasons Leading League
5 Don Hutson, Green Bay 1940–44
Gino Cappelletti, Bos. 1961, 63–66 (AFL)

Most Points, Lifetime
1842 George Blanda, Chi. Bears 1949–58; Balt. 1950; AFL: Hou. 1960–66; Oak. 1967–73 (9-td, 855-pat, 311-fg)

Most Points, Season
176 Paul Hornung, Green Bay 1960 (15-td, 41-pat, 15-fg)

Most Points, Rookie, Season
132 Gale Sayers, Chi. 1965 (22-td)

Most Points, Game
40 Ernie Nevers, Chi. Cards vs Chi. Bears, Nov. 28, 1929 (6-td, 4-pat)

Most Points, One Quarter
29 Don Hutson, Green Bay vs Det., Oct. 7, 1945 (4-td, 5-pat) 2nd Quarter

Touchdowns

Most Seasons Leading League
8 Don Hutson, Green Bay, 1935–38, 41–44

Most Touchdowns, Lifetime
126 Jim Brown, Cleve. 1957–65 (106-r, 20-p)

Most Touchdowns, Season
22 Gale Sayers, Chi. 1965 (14-r, 6-p, 1-prb, 1-krb)

Most Touchdowns, Rookie Season
22 Gale Sayers, Chi. 1965 (14-r, 6-p, 1-prb, 1-krb)

ENDURANCE RECORDS as well as passing and field goal records were set in 1973 by George Blanda (Oakland) who was still starring as a quarterback at the age of 46.

MOST EFFICIENT PASSER:
Sammy Baugh (Wash.) had a 70.3
percentage for the season in 1945.
Baugh also holds punting records.

N.F.L. Records (continued)

Most Touchdowns, Game
  6 Ernie Nevers, Chi. Cards vs Chi.
     Bears, Nov. 28, 1929 (6-r)
     William (Dub) Jones, Cleve. vs
     Chi. Bears, Nov. 25, 1951 (4-r,
     2-p)
     Gale Sayers, Chi. vs S. F., Dec.
     12, 1965 (4-r, 1-p, 1-prb)
Most Consecutive Games Scoring
     Touchdowns
 18 Lenny Moore, Balt. 1963–65

Points after Touchdown

Most Seasons Leading League
  7 George Blanda, Chi. Bears 1956;
     AFL: Hou. 1961–62; Oak. 1967–
     69, 72
Most Points After Touchdown, Lifetime
855 George Blanda, Chi. Bears 1949–
     58; Balt. 1950; AFL: Hou.
     1960–66; Oak. 1967–73
Most Points After Touchdown, Season
 64 George Blanda, Hou. 1961 (AFL)
Most Points After Touchdown, Game
  9 Marlin (Pat) Harder, Chi. Cards
     vs N. Y., Oct. 17, 1948
     Bob Waterfield, L. A. vs Balt.,
     Oct. 22, 1950
     Charlie Gogolak, Wash. vs N. Y.,
     Nov. 27, 1966

Most Consecutive Points After Touch-
     down
234 Tommy Davis, S. F. 1959–65
Most Points After Touchdown (no
     misses), Season
 56 Danny Villanueva, Dall. 1966
Most Points After Touchdown (no
     misses), Game
  9 Marlin (Pat) Harder, Chi. Cards
     vs N. Y., Oct. 17, 1948
     Bob Waterfield, L. A. vs Balt.,
     Oct. 22, 1950

Field Goals

Most Seasons Leading League
  5 Lou Groza, Cleve., 1950, 52–54,
     57
Most Field Goals, Lifetime
311 George Blanda, Chi. Bears 1949–
     58; Balt. 1950; AFL: Hou.
     1960–66; Oak. 1967–73
Most Field Goals, Season
 34 Jim Turner, N.Y. 1968 (AFL)
Most Field Goals, Game
  7 Jim Bakken, St. L. vs Pitt., Sept.
     24, 1967
Most Consecutive Games, Field Goals
 31 Fred Cox, Minn. 1968–70
Most Consecutive Field Goals
 16 Jan Stenerud, K.C. 1969 (AFL)

**THREW MOST TOUCHDOWN
PASSES** (one game): Sid Luckman
(Chi.) shares record of 7 with
George Blanda and others.

GAINS MOST YARDS RUSHING IN GAME: O. J. Simpson (Buffalo) is seen here in the first game of the 1973 season carrying the ball against New England for a record 250 yards on the ground. He also set a season's rushing mark with 2,003 total yards.

Longest Field Goal
63 yds. Tom Dempsey, New Orl. vs Det.
  Nov. 8, 1970

Rushing

Most Seasons Leading League
  8   Jim Brown, Cleve. 1957–61, 63–65

Most Yards Gained, Lifetime
12,312 Jim Brown, Cleve., 1957–65

Most Yards Gained, Season
2,003 O. J. Simpson, Buff., 1973

Most Yards Gained, Game
  250 O. J. Simpson, Buff. vs N.E.,
        Sept. 16, 1973

GREATEST ALL-TIME RUSHER: Jim Brown (Cleve.) holds the record for 12,312 yards gained in a lifetime and has the highest lifetime rushing average per carry. Here he is vaulting over a few Baltimore Colts in the 1964 championship game.

N.F.L. Records (continued)

Longest Run from Scrimmage
  97 yards Andy Uram, Green Bay vs Chi. Cards, Oct. 8, 1939 (td)
  Bob Gage, Pitt. vs Chi. Bears, Dec. 4, 1949 (td)

Highest Average Gain, Lifetime (700 att.)
  5.22 Jim Brown, Cleve. 1957–65 (2,359–12,312)

Highest Average Gain, Season (100 att.)
  9.9 Beattie Feathers, Chi. Bears, 1934 (101–1004)

Highest Average Gain, Game (10 att.)
  17.1 Marion Morley, Cleve. vs Pitt., Oct. 29, 1950 (11–188)

Most Touchdowns Rushing, Lifetime
  106 Jim Brown, Cleve., 1957–65

Most Touchdowns Rushing, Season
  19 Jim Taylor, Green Bay, 1962

Most Touchdowns Rushing, Game
  6 Ernie Nevers, Chi. Cards vs Chi. Bears, Nov. 28, 1929

Passing

Most Seasons Leading League
  6 Sammy Baugh, Wash., 1937, 40, 43, 45, 47, 49

Most Passes Attempted, Lifetime
5,186 John Unitas, Balt. 1956–72; S.D. 1973 (2,830 completions)

Most Passes Attempted, Season
  508 C. A. (Sonny) Jurgensen, Wash., 1967 (288 completions)

Most Passes Attempted, Game
  68 George Blanda, Hou. vs Buff., Nov. 1, 1964 (AFL) (37 completions)

Most Passes Completed, Lifetime
2,830 John Unitas, Balt. 1956–72; S.D. 1973 (5,186 attempts)

Most Passes Completed, Season
  288 C. A. (Sonny) Jurgensen, Wash., 1967 (508 attempts)

Most Passes Completed, Game
  37 George Blanda, Hou. vs Buff., Nov. 1, 1964 (AFL) (68 attempts)

Most Consecutive Passes Completed
  15 Len Dawson, K.C. vs Hou., Sept. 9, 1967 (AFL)
  Joe Namath, N.Y. Jets vs Mia. (12) Oct. 22; vs Bos. (3) Oct. 29, 1967

Passing Efficiency, Lifetime (1,000 att.)
57.4 Bart Starr, Green Bay, 1956–71 (3,149–1,808)

Passing Efficiency, Season (100 att.)
70.3 Sammy Baugh, Wash., 1945
(182–128)

Passing Efficiency, Game (20 att. or
more)
86.2 Ken Stabler, Oak. vs Balt., Oct.
28, 1973 (25–29)

Most Yards Gained Passing, Lifetime
40,239 John Unitas, Balt. 1956–72;
S.D. 1973

Most Yards Gained Passing, Season
4,007 Joe Namath, N. Y. 1967 (AFL)

Most Yards Gained Passing, Game
554 Norm Van Brocklin, L. A. vs
N. Y. Yanks, Sept. 28, 1951
(41–27)

Longest Pass Completion (all TDs)
99 Frank Filchock (to Farkas),
Wash. vs Pitt., Oct. 15, 1939
George Izo (to Mitchell), Wash.
vs Cleve., Sept. 15, 1963
Karl Sweetan (to Studstill), Det.
vs Balt., Oct. 16, 1966
C. A. Jurgensen (to Allen), Wash.
vs Chi., Sept. 15, 1968

Shortest Pass Completion for Touchdown
2″ Eddie LeBaron (to Bielski), Dall.
vs Wash., Oct. 9, 1960

Most Touchdown Passes, Lifetime
290 John Unitas, Balt. 1956–72;
S.D. 1973

Most Touchdown Passes, Season
36 George Blanda, Hou. 1961 (AFL)
Y. A. Tittle, N. Y. 1963

Most Touchdown Passes, Game
7 Sid Luckman, Chi. Bears vs N. Y.
Nov. 14, 1943
Adrian Burk, Phil. vs Wash.,
Oct. 17, 1954
George Blanda, Hou. vs N. Y.,
Nov. 19, 1961 (AFL)
Y. A. Tittle, N. Y. vs Wash.,
Oct. 28, 1962
Joe Kapp, Minn. vs Balt., Sept.
28, 1969

Most Consecutive Games, Touchdown
Passes
47 John Unitas, Balt., 1956–60

Passes Had Intercepted

Fewest Passes Intercepted, Season (100
att.)
1 Bill Nelsen, Pitt., 1966 (112
attempts)

Most Consecutive Passes Attempted,
None Intercepted
294 Bryan (Bart) Starr, Green Bay,
1964–65

RECORD PASSER: Joe Namath of the N.Y. Jets passed for gains of 4,007 yards
in 1967, including 15 consecutive completed passes—12 in one game and the first 3 in
the next.

MOST SUCCESSFUL FORWARD PASSER: Len Dawson of the Kansas City Chiefs (AFL) completed 15 consecutive passes to set a world record in a game against Houston in September, 1967. This record was tied by Joe Namath of the Jets in the same season.

N.F.L. Records (continued)

Most Passes Intercepted, Game
8 Jim Hardy, Chi. Cards vs Phil., Sept. 24, 1950 (39 attempts)

Lowest Percentage Passes Intercepted, Lifetime (1,000 att.)
3.29 Roman Gabriel, L. A., 1962–72; Phil. 1973

Lowest Percentage Passes Intercepted, Season (100 att.)
0.89 Bill Nelsen, Pitt., 1966 (1–112)

Pass Receptions

Most Seasons Leading League
8 Don Hutson, Green Bay, 1936–37, 39, 41–45

Most Pass Receptions, Lifetime
633 Don Maynard, N.Y. Giants 1958; N.Y. Jets 1960–72; St. L. 1973

Most Pass Receptions, Season
101 Charley Hennigan, Hou. 1964 (AFL)

Most Pass Receptions, Game
18 Tom Fears, L. A. vs Green Bay, Dec. 3, 1950 (189 yds.)

Most Consecutive Games, Pass Receptions
96 Lance Alworth, San Diego 1962–69 (AFL)

Longest Pass Reception (all TDs)
99 Andy Farkas (Filchock), Wash. vs Pitt., Oct. 15, 1939
     Bobby Mitchell (Izo), Wash. vs Cleve., Sept. 15, 1963
     Pat Studstill (Sweetan), Det. vs Balt., Oct. 16, 1966
     Gerry Allen (Jurgensen), Wash. vs Chi., Sept. 15, 1968

Shortest Pass Reception for Touchdown
2" Dick Bielski (LeBaron), Dall. vs
Wash., Oct. 9, 1960

Touchdowns Receiving

Most Touchdown Passes, Lifetime
99 Don Hutson, Green Bay, 1935–45

Most Touchdown Passes, Season
17 Don Hutson, Green Bay, 1942
Elroy (Crazy Legs) Hirsch, L. A.,
1951
Bill Groman, Hou. 1961 (AFL)

Most Touchdown Passes, Game
5 Bob Shaw, Chi. Cards vs Balt.,
Oct. 2, 1950

Most Consecutive Games, Touchdown
Passes
11 Elroy (Crazy Legs) Hirsch, L.A.,
1950–51
Gilbert (Buddy) Dial, Pitt., 1959–
60

Pass Interceptions

Most Interceptions by, Lifetime
79 Emlen Tunnell, N. Y. (74), 1948–
58; Green Bay (5), 1959–61

Most Interceptions by, Season
14 Richard (Night Train) Lane,
L. A., 1952

Most Interceptions by, Game
4 By many players

Interception Yardage

Most Yards Gained, Lifetime
1,282 Emlen Tunnell, N. Y., 1948–58;
Green Bay, 1959–61

Most Yards Gained, Season
349 Charley McNeil, San Diego 1961
(AFL)

Most Yards Gained, Game
177 Charley McNeil, San Diego vs
Hou., Sept. 24, 1961 (AFL)

Longest Gain (all TDs)
102 Bob Smith, Det. vs Chi. Bears,
Nov. 24, 1949
Erich Barnes, N. Y. vs Dall., Oct.
22, 1961

Touchdowns on Interceptions

Most Touchdowns, Lifetime
9 Ken Houston, Hou. 1967–71

Most Touchdowns, Season
4 Ken Houston, Hou. 1971
Jim Kearney, K.C. 1972

Punting

Most Seasons Leading League
4 Sammy Baugh, Wash., 1940–43
Jerrel Wilson, K.C., 1965, 68,
72–73

Most Punts, Lifetime
970 Bobby Joe Green, Pitt. 1960–61;
Chi. 62–73

MOST CONSECUTIVE GAMES (96) WITH PASS RECEPTIONS was the record set in 1969 in the AFL by Lance Alworth of the San Diego Chargers.

Most Punts, Season
105 Bob Scarpitto, Den. 1967 (AFL)

Most Punts, Game
14 Sammy Baugh, Wash. vs Phil.,
Nov. 5, 1939
John Kinscherf, N. Y. vs Det.,
Nov. 7, 1943
George Taliaferro, N. Y. Yanks
vs L. A., Sept. 28, 1951

Longest Punt
98 yards Steve O'Neal, N. Y. vs
Den., Sept. 21, 1969 (AFL)

LONGEST PUNTER: Steve O'Neal (N.Y. Jets) kicked 98 yards in the AFL in 1969.

Average Yardage Punting

Highest Punting Average, Lifetime (300 punts)
45.1 yards Sammy Baugh, Wash., 1937–52 (338)

Highest Punting Average, Season (20 punts)
51.4 yards Sammy Baugh, Wash., 1940 (35)

Highest Punting Average, Game (4 punts)
59.4 yards Sammy Baugh, Wash. vs Det., Oct. 27, 1940 (5)

Kickoffs

Yardage Returning Kickoffs

Most Yards Gained, Lifetime
6,502 Ron Smith, Chi. 1965, 70–72; Atl. 1966–67; L.A. 1968–69; S.D. 1973

Most Yards Gained, Season
1,317 Bobby Jancik, Hou. 1963 (AFL)

Most Yards Gained, Game
294 Wally Triplett, Det. vs L. A., Oct. 29, 1950 (4)

Longest Kickoff Return for Touchdown
106 Al Carmichael, Green Bay vs. Chi. Bears, Oct. 7, 1956
Noland Smith, K.C. vs Den., Dec. 17, 1967 (AFL)

Average Yardage Returning Kickoffs

Highest Average, Lifetime (75 returns)
30.6 Gale Sayers, Chi. 1965–71

SNATCHED 4 OF HIS OWN FUMBLES (one game in 1969): **Roman Gabriel (L.A.).**

Highest Average, Season (15 returns)
41.1 Travis Williams, Green Bay, 1967 (18)

Highest Average, Game (3 returns)
73 Wally Triplett, Det. vs L. A., Oct. 29, 1950 (4–294)

Touchdowns Returning Kickoffs

Most Touchdowns, Lifetime
6 Ollie Matson, Chi. Cards, 1952 (2), 54, 56, 58 (2)
Gale Sayers, Chi., 1965, 66 (2), 67 (3)
Travis Williams, G.B., 1967 (4), 69, 71

Most Touchdowns, Season
4 Travis Williams, Green Bay, 1967
Cecil Turner, Chi. 1970

Most Touchdowns, Game
2 Thomas (Tim) Brown, Phil. vs Dall., Nov. 6, 1966
Travis Williams, Green Bay vs Cleve., Nov. 12, 1967

Fumbles

Most Fumbles, Lifetime
95 John Unitas, Balt. 1956–72; S.D. 1973

Most Fumbles, Season
16 Don Meredith, Dall., 1964

Most Fumbles, Game
7 Len Dawson, K.C. vs San Diego, Nov. 15, 1964 (AFL)

Most Own Fumbles Recovered, Lifetime
38 Jack Kemp, Pitt. 1957; AFL: L. A./San Diego 1960–62; Buff. 1962–67, 69

Most Own Fumbles Recovered, Season
8 Paul Christman, Chi. Cards, 1945
Bill Butler, Minn., 1963

Most Own Fumbles Recovered, Game
4 Otto Graham, Cleve. vs N. Y., Oct. 25, 1953
Sam Etcheverry, St. L. vs N. Y., Sept. 17, 1961
Roman Gabriel, L. A. vs S. F., Oct. 12, 1969

Most Opponents' Fumbles Recovered, Lifetime
25 Dick Butkus, Chi. 1965–73

Most Opponents' Fumbles Recovered, Season
9 Don Hultz, Minn., 1963

Most Opponents' Fumbles Recovered, Game
3 Corwin Clatt, Chi. Cards vs Det., Nov. 6, 1949
Vic Sears, Phil. vs Green Bay, Nov. 2, 1952
Ed Beatty, S. F. vs L. A., Oct. 7, 1956

Longest Fumble Run
104 Jack Tatum, Oak. vs G.B., Sept. 24, 1972

DEFENSIVE STAR: Dick Butkus of the Chicago Bears recovered 25 fumbles by his opponents in 8 seasons.

Miscellaneous

Most Drop Kick Field Goals, Game
4 John (Paddy) Driscoll, Chi. Cards vs Columbus, Oct. 11, 1925 (23, 18, 50, 35 yards)
Elbert Bloodgood, Kansas City vs Duluth, Dec. 12, 1926 (35, 32, 20, 25 yards)

Longest Drop Kick Field Goal
50 Wilbur (Pete) Henry, Canton vs Toledo, Nov. 13, 1922
John (Paddy) Driscoll, Chi. Cards vs Milwaukee, Sept. 28, 1924; vs Columbus, Oct. 11, 1925

Most Yards Returned Missed Field Goal
101 Al Nelson, Phil. vs Dall., Sept. 26, 1971 (TD)

SEASON RECORDS—OFFENSE

Most Seasons League Champion
11 Green Bay, 1929–31, 36, 39, 44, 61–62, 65–67

Most Consecutive Games Without Defeat (Regular Season)
24 Canton, 1922–23 (Won–21, Tied–3)
Chicago Bears, 1941–43 (Won–23, Tied–1)

Most Consecutive Victories (All Games)
18 Chicago Bears (1933–34; 1941–42)
Miami (1972–73)

Most Consecutive Victories (Regular Season)
17 Chicago Bears, 1933–34

Most Consecutive Victories, One Season (All Games)
17 Miami, 1972

Most Consecutive Shutout Games Won
7 Detroit, 1934

Scoring

Most Seasons Leading League
9 Chicago Bears, 1934–35, 39, 41–43, 46–47, 56

Most Points, Season
513 Houston, 1961 (AFL)

Most Points, Game
72 Washington vs N. Y., Nov. 27, 1966

Most Touchdowns, Season
66 Houston, 1961 (AFL)

Most Touchdowns, Game
10 Philadelphia vs Cin., Nov. 6, 1934
Los Angeles vs Balt., Oct. 22, 1950
Washington vs N. Y., Nov. 27, 1966

Most Touchdowns, Both Teams, Game
16 Washington (10) vs N. Y. (6), Nov. 27, 1966

Most Points After Touchdown, Season
65 Houston, 1961 (AFL)
59 Los Angeles, 1950

Most Points After Touchdown, Game
10 Los Angeles vs Balt., Oct. 22, 1950

Most Points After Touchdown, Both Teams, Game
14 Chicago Cards (9) vs N. Y. (5), Oct. 17, 1948
Houston (7) vs Oakland (7), Dec. 22, 1963 (AFL)
Washington (9) vs N. Y. (5), Nov. 27, 1966

Most Field Goals Attempted, Season
49 Los Angeles, 1966
Washington, 1971

Most Field Goals Attempted, Game
9 St. Louis vs Pitt., Sept. 24, 1967

Most Field Goals Attempted, Both Teams, Game
11 St. Louis (6) vs Pitt. (5), Nov. 13, 1966
Washington (6) vs Chi. (5), Nov. 14, 1971

Most Field Goals, Season
34 New York, 1968 (AFL)

Most Field Goals, Game
7 St. Louis vs Pitt., Sept. 24, 1967

Most Field Goals, Both Teams, Game
8   Cleveland (4) vs St. L. (4), Sept. 20, 1964
    Chicago (5) vs Phil. (3), Oct. 20, 1968
    Washington (5) vs Chi. (3), Nov. 14, 1971
    Kansas City (5) vs. Buff. (3), Dec. 19, 1971

Most Consecutive Games Scoring Field Goals
31   Minnesota, 1968–70

First Downs

Most Seasons Leading League
8   Chicago Bears, 1935, 41, 43, 45, 47–49, 55

Most First Downs, Season
297   Dallas, 1968
      Oakland, 1972

Most First Downs, Game
38   Los Angeles vs N. Y., Nov. 13, 1966

Most First Downs, Both Teams, Game
58   Los Angeles (30) vs Chi. Bears (28), Oct. 24, 1954

Most First Downs, Rushing, Season
177   Los Angeles, 1973

Most First Downs, Rushing, Game
25   Philadelphia vs Wash., Dec. 2, 1951

Most First Downs, Passing, Season
186   Houston, 1964 (AFL)
      Oakland, 1964 (AFL)

Most First Downs, Passing, Game
24   Houston vs Buffalo, Nov. 1, 1964 (AFL)
     Minnesota vs Baltimore, Sept. 28, 1969

LONGEST FIELD GOAL in NFL competition (63 yards) was kicked by a man with only half a foot—Tom Dempsey of the New Orleans Saints, who wears a special shoe over his wooden foot, and has only a stump of a right arm. His record kick beat the Detroit Lions, 19-17, on the last play of the game on November 8, 1970.

Net Yards Gained (Rushes and Passes)

Most Seasons Leading League
12 Chicago Bears, 1932, 34–35, 39,
    41–44, 47, 49, 55–56

Most Yards Gained, Season
6,288 Houston, 1961 (AFL)

Most Yards Gained, Game
735 Los Angeles vs N. Y. Yanks,
     Sept. 28, 1951 (181-r, 554-p)

Most Yards Gained, Both Teams, Game
1,133 Los Angeles (636) vs N. Y.
      Yanks (497), Nov. 19, 1950

Rushing

Most Seasons Leading League
11 Chicago Bears, 1932, 34–35, 39–
    42, 51, 55–56, 68

Most Rushing Attempts, Season
659 Los Angeles, 1973

Most Rushing Attempts, Game
72 Chicago Bears vs Brk., Oct. 20,
    1935

Most Rushing Attempts, Both Teams,
Game
108 Chicago Cards (70) vs Green Bay
     (38), Dec. 5, 1948

Most Yards Gained Rushing, Season
3,088 Buffalo 1973

Most Yards Gained Rushing, Game
426 Detroit vs Pitt., Nov. 4, 1934

Most Yards Gained Rushing, Both
Teams, Game
595 L. A. (371) vs N. Y. Yanks (224),
     Nov. 18, 1951

Highest Average Gain Rushing, Season
5.7 Cleveland, 1963

Most Touchdowns Rushing, Season
36 Green Bay, 1962

Most Touchdowns Rushing, Game
6 By many teams. Last: N. Y. vs
   Boston, Oct. 27, 1968 (AFL)

Most Touchdowns Rushing, Both
Teams, Game
8 Los Angeles (6) vs N. Y. Yanks
   (2), Nov. 18, 1951
   Cleveland (6) vs L. A. (2), Nov.
   24, 1957

Passing

Most Seasons Leading League
9 Washington, 1937, 39–40, 42–45,
   47, 67

Most Passes Attempted, Season
592 Houston, 1964 (AFL)

Most Passes Attempted, Game
68 Houston vs Buffalo, Nov. 1, 1964
    (AFL) (37 comp.)

Most Passes Attempted, Both Teams,
Game
98 Minn. (56) vs Balt. (42), Sept. 28,
    1969

Most Passes Completed, Season
301 Washington, 1967 (527-att.)

Most Passes Completed, Game
37 Houston vs Buffalo, Nov. 1, 1964
    (AFL) (68 att.)

Most Passes Completed, Both Teams,
Game
56 Minn. (36) vs Balt. (20), Sept. 28,
    1969

Most Yards Gained Passing, Season
4,392 Houston, 1961 (AFL)

Most Yards Gained Passing, Game
554 Los Angeles vs N. Y. Yanks,
     Sept. 28, 1951

Most Yards Gained Passing, Both
Teams, Game
834 Philadelphia (419) vs St. L. (415),
     Dec. 16, 1962

Most Seasons Leading League (Completion Pct.)
11 Washington, 1937, 39–40, 42–45,
    47–48, 69-70

Most Touchdowns Passing, Season
48 Houston, 1961 (AFL)

Most Touchdowns Passing, Game
7 Chicago Bears vs N. Y., Nov. 14,
   1943
   Philadelphia vs. Wash., Oct. 17,
   1954
   Houston vs N. Y., Nov. 19, 1961
   and Oct. 14, 1962 (AFL)
   New York vs Wash., Oct. 28,
   1962
   Minnesota vs Balt., Sept. 28, 1969

Most Touchdowns Passing, Both Teams,
Game
12 New Orleans (6) vs St. Louis (6),
    Nov. 2, 1969

Most Passes Had Intercepted, Season
48 Houston, 1962 (AFL)

Fewest Passes Had Intercepted, Season
5 Cleveland, 1960 (264-att.)
   Green Bay, 1966 (318-att.)

Most Passes Had Intercepted, Game
9 Detroit vs Green Bay, Oct. 24,
   1943
   Pittsburgh vs Phil., Dec. 12, 1965

Punting

Most Seasons, Leading League (Avg.
Distance)
6 Washington, 1940–43, 45, 58

Highest Punting Average, Season
47.6 Detroit, 1961

Punt Returns

Most Seasons; Leading League
8 Detroit, 1943–45, 51–52, 62, 66, 69

Most Yards Gained Punt Returns, Season
781 Chicago Bears, 1948

Most Yards Gained Punt Returns, Game
231 Detroit vs S. F., Oct. 6, 1963

Highest Average Punt Returns, Season
20.2 Chicago Bears, 1941

Most Touchdowns Punt Returns, Season
5 Chicago Cards, 1959

Most Touchdowns Punt Returns, Game
2 Detroit vs L. A., Oct. 14; vs Green Bay, Nov. 22, 1951
Chicago Cards vs Pitt., Nov. 1; vs N. Y., Nov. 22, 1959
New York vs Den., Sept. 24, 1961 (AFL)

Kickoff Returns

Most Seasons Leading League
5 New York, 1944, 46, 49, 51, 53
Chicago Bears, 1943, 48, 58, 66, 72

Most Yards Gained Kickoff Returns, Season
1,824 Houston, 1963 (AFL)

Most Yards Gained Kickoff Returns, Game
362 Detroit vs L. A., Oct. 29, 1950

Most Yards Gained Kickoff Returns, Both Teams, Game
560 Detroit (362) vs L. A. (198), Oct. 29, 1950

Highest Average Kickoff Returns, Season
29.4 Chicago, 1972

Most Touchdowns Kickoff Returns, Season
4 Green Bay, 1967
Chicago, 1970

Most Touchdowns Kickoff Returns, Game
2 Chicago Bears vs Green Bay, Nov. 9, 1952
Philadelphia vs Dall., Nov. 6, 1966
Green Bay vs Cleve., Nov. 12, 1967

Fumbles

Most Fumbles, Season
56 Chicago Bears, 1938

Fewest Fumbles, Season
8 Cleveland, 1959

Most Fumbles, Game
10 Phil/Pitts vs N. Y., Oct. 9, 1943
Detroit vs Minn., Nov. 12, 1967
Kansas City vs Hou., Oct. 12, 1969 (AFL)

Most Fumbles, Both Teams, Game
14 Chicago Bears (7) vs Cleve. (7), Nov. 24, 1940
St. Louis (8) vs N. Y. (6), Sept. 17, 1961
Kansas City (10) vs Hou. (4), Oct. 12, 1969 (AFL)

Most Opponents' Fumbles Recovered, Season
31 Minnesota, 1963 (50 fumbles)

Most Opponents' Fumbles Recovered, Game
7 Buffalo vs Cinci., Nov. 30, 1969 (AFL)

Most Own Fumbles Recovered, Season
27 Philadelphia, 1946 (54 fumbles)
Minnesota, 1963 (45 fumbles)

Most Fumbles (Opponents' and Own) Recovered, Season
58 Minnesota, 1963 (95 fumbles)

Most Fumbles (Opponents' and Own), Recovered, Game
10 Denver vs Buff., Dec. 13, 1964 (AFL)
Pittsburgh vs Hou., Dec. 9, 1973

Penalties

Most Seasons Leading League, Fewest Penalties
9 Pittsburgh, 1946–47, 50–52, 54, 63, 65, 68

Fewest Penalties, Season
19 Detroit, 1937 (139 yards)

Most Penalties, Game
22 Brooklyn vs Green Bay, Sept. 17, 1944 (170 yards)
Chicago Bears vs Phil., Nov. 26, 1944 (170 yards)

Fewest Penalties, Game
0 By many teams.

Fewest Penalties, Both Teams, Game
0 Brooklyn vs Pitt., Oct. 28, 1934; vs Bos., Sept. 28, 1936
Cleveland Rams vs Chi. Bears, Oct. 9, 1938
Pittsburgh vs Phil., Nov. 10, 1940

Most Yards Penalized, Season
1,274 Oakland, 1969 (AFL)

Fewest Yards Penalized, Season
139 Detroit, 1937 (19 pen.)

Most Yards Penalized, Game
209 Cleveland vs Chi. Bears, Nov. 25, 1951 (21 pen.)

DEFENSE

Fewest Points Allowed, Season (since 1932)
44 Chicago Bears, 1932

Fewest Touchdowns Allowed, Season (since 1932)
7 Detroit, 1934

Fewest First Downs Allowed, Season
86 Philadelphia, 1944

Fewest First Downs Allowed, Rushing, Season
35 Chicago Bears, 1942

Fewest First Downs Allowed, Passing, Season
33 Chicago Bears, 1943

Fewest Yards Allowed, Season
1,578 Chicago Cards, 1934

Fewest Yards Allowed Rushing, Season
519 Chicago Bears, 1942

Fewest Touchdowns Allowed, Rushing, Season
1 New York Giants, 1927

Fewest Yards Allowed Passing, Season
625 Chicago Cards, 1934

Most Opponents Tackled Attempting Passes, Season
67 Oakland, 1967 (AFL)

Fewest Touchdowns Allowed, Passing, Season
2 New York Giants, 1927

Most Seasons Leading League, Interceptions Made
8 New York, 1937–39, 44, 48, 51, 54, 61
Green Bay, 1940, 42–43, 47, 55, 57, 62, 65

Most Pass Interceptions Made, Season
49 San Diego, 1961 (AFL)

Most Yards Gained, Interceptions, Season
929 San Diego, 1961 (AFL)

Most Yards Gained, Interceptions, Game
314 Los Angeles vs S. F., Oct. 18, 1964

Most Touchdowns, Interception Returns, Season
9 San Diego, 1961 (AFL)

Fewest Yards Allowed Punt Returns, Season
22 Green Bay, 1967

Fewest Yards Allowed Kickoff Returns, Season
225 Brooklyn, 1943

Most Touchdowns, Interception Returns, Game
3 Baltimore vs Green Bay, Nov. 5, 1950
Cleveland vs Chi., Dec. 11, 1960
Philadelphia vs Pitt., Dec. 12, 1965
Baltimore vs Pitt., Sept. 29, 1968
Buffalo vs N. Y., Sept. 29, 1968 (AFL)
Houston vs S.D., Dec. 19, 1971
Cincinnati vs Hou., Dec. 17, 1972

Gliding

The earliest man-carrying glider was designed by Sir George Cayley (1773–1857) and carried his coachman (possibly John Appleby) about 500 yards across a valley near Brompton Hall, Yorkshire, England, in the summer of 1853. Gliders now attain speeds of 145 m.p.h. and the Jastrzab acrobatic sailplane is designed to withstand vertical dives at up to 280 m.p.h.

Kite Descents. The greatest altitude from which a manned kite descent has been made is 10,500 feet by Bill Moyes near Sydney, Australia, on April 7, 1973. He launched himself from a balloon and glided 12 miles. The record drop from land is 10,023 feet by Robert L. and Chris Wills from Haleakala on Maui, Hawaii, to sea level on August 28, 1973. The longest reported flight duration for hang-gliding is 8 hours 24 minutes by Robert L. Wills (U.S.) at Waimanalo, Hawaii, on September 15, 1973.

HIGHEST SPEED: Walter Neubert (W. Germany) stands beside his glider which set a 94.16 m.p.h. mark over a 300-km. triangular course in 1972.

WORLD RECORDS

DISTANCE

Single seaters 907.7 miles Hans-Werner Grosse (W. Germany) in an ASW-12 on April 25, 1972.

DECLARED GOAL FLIGHT

653.1 miles Klaus Tesch (W. Germany) in an LS-1, on April 25, 1972, from Hamburg to Nantes, France.

ABSOLUTE ALTITUDE

46,266 feet Paul F. Bikle, Jr. (U.S.) in a Schweizer SGS-1-23E over Mojave, Calif. (released at 3,963 feet) on Feb. 25, 1961 (also record altitude gain—42,303 feet).

GOAL AND RETURN

782 miles W. C. Holbrook (U.S.) in a Libelle 301 on May 5, 1973.

SPEED OVER TRIANGULAR COURSE

100 km. 98.30 m.p.h. Klaus Holighaus (W. Germany) in a Nimbus 2 over Samaden, Switzerland, on August 14, 1973.

300 km. 94.16 m.p.h. Walter Neubert (W. Germany) in a Kestrel 604 over Kenya on March 3, 1972.

500 km. 85.25 m.p.h. M. Jackson (South Africa) in a BJ-3 in South Africa on December 28, 1967

Most World Titles

World individual championships (instituted 1948) have been 4 times won by West Germans, including two Standard titles by Heinz Huth (1960, 1963).

Golf

Origins. The earliest mention of golf occurs in a prohibiting law passed by the Scottish Parliament in March, 1457, under which "golfe be utterly cryed downe." The Romans had a cognate game called *paganica*, which may have been carried to Britain before 400 A.D. In February, 1962, the Soviet newspaper *Izvestiya* claimed that the game was of 15th-century Danish origin. Gutta percha balls succeeded feather balls in 1848, and were in turn succeeded in 1902 by rubber-cored balls, invented in 1899 by Haskell (U.S.). Steel shafts were authorized in 1929.

Clubs

Oldest. The oldest club of which there is written evidence is the Gentleman Golfers (now the Honourable Company of Edinburgh Golfers) formed in March, 1744—10 years prior to the institution of the Royal and Ancient Club at St. Andrews, Fife, Scotland. The oldest existing club in North America is the Royal Montreal Club (1873) and the oldest in the U.S. is St. Andrews, Westchester County, New York (1888). An older claim is by the Foxbury Country Club, Clarion County, Pennsylvania (1887).

Largest. The only club in the world with 15 courses is the Eldorado Golf Club in California. The club with the highest membership in the world is the Wanderer's Club, Johannesburg, South Africa, with 9,120 members, of whom 850 are golfers. The Royal and Ancient Golf Club at St. Andrews, Fife, Scotland, the club with the largest membership in the British Isles, has 1,750.

Courses

Highest. The highest golf course in the world is the Tuctu Golf Club in Morococha, Peru, which is 14,335 feet above sea level at its lowest point. Golf has, however, been played in Tibet at an altitude of over 16,000 feet.

Lowest. The lowest golf course in the world was that of the Sodom and Gomorrah Golfing Society at Kallia, on the northeastern shores of the Dead Sea, 1,250 feet below sea level. The clubhouse was burnt down in 1948 but the game is now played on the nearby Kallia Hotel course.

Longest Hole. The longest hole in the world is the 17th hole (par 6) of 745 yards at the Black Mountain Golf Club, North Carolina. It was opened in 1964. In August, 1927, the 6th hole at Prescott Country Club in Arkansas, measured 838 yards.

Largest Green. Probably the largest green in the world is the 5th green at Runaway Brook G.C., Bolton, Massachusetts, with an area greater than 28,000 square feet.

Biggest Bunker. The world's biggest trap is Hell's Half Acre on the 7th hole of the Pine Valley course, New Jersey, built in 1912 and generally regarded as the world's most trying course.

Longest "Course." Floyd Satterlee Rood used the whole United States as a course when he played from the Pacific surf to the Atlantic surf from September 14, 1963 to October 3, 1964, in 114,737 strokes. He lost 3,511 balls on the 3,397.7-mile trip.

Lowest Scores

9 holes and 18 holes—Men. The lowest recorded score on any 18-hole course with a par of 70 or more is 55 first achieved by A. E. Smith, the English professional, at Woolacombe on January 1, 1936. The course measured 4,248 yards. The detail was 4, 2, 3, 4, 2, 4, 3, 4, 3=29 out, and 2, 3, 3, 3, 3, 2, 5, 4, 1=26 in.

Homero Blancas (b. March 7, 1938) of Houston, Texas, also scored 55 (27+28) on a course of 5,022 yards (par 70) at the Premier Golf Course, Longview, Texas, on August 19, 1962.

Nine holes in 25 (4, 3, 3, 2, 3, 3, 1, 4, 2) was recorded by A. J. "Bill" Burke in a round of 57 (32+25) on the 6,389-yard par 71 Normandie course in St. Louis on May 20, 1970.

The United States P.G.A. tournament record for 18 holes is 60 by Al Brosch (30+30) in the Texas Open on February 10, 1951; William Nary in the El Paso Open, Texas, on February 9, 1952; Ted Kroll (born August, 1919) in the Texas Open on February 20, 1954; Wally Ulrich in the Virginia Beach Open on June 11, 1954; Tommy Bolt (b. March 31, 1918) in the Insurance City Open on June 25, 1954; Mike Souchak (see below) in the Texas Open on February 17, 1955; and Samuel Jackson Snead (born May 27, 1912) in the Dallas Open, in September, 1957. Snead had 59 in the Greenbrier Open (now called the Sam Snead Festival), a non-P.G.A. tournament, at White Sulphur Springs, West Virginia, on May 16, 1959.

36 holes. The record for 36 holes is 122 (59 + 63) by Sam Snead in the 1959 Greenbrier Open (now called the Sam Snead Festival) (non-P.G.A.) (see above) May 16–17, 1959. Horton Smith (see below) scored 121 (63+58) on a short course on December 21, 1928.

72 holes. The lowest recorded score on a first-class course is 257 (27 under par) by Mike Souchak (born May, 1927) in the Texas Open at San Antonio in February, 1955, made up of 60 (33 out and 27 in), 68, 64, 65 (average 64.25 per round), exhibiting, as one critic said, his "up and down form." The late Horton Smith (1908–63), a U.S. Masters Champion, scored 245 (63, 58, 61 and 63) for 72 holes on the 4,700-yard course (par 64) at Catalina Country Club, California, to win the Catalina Open on December 21–23, 1928.

The lowest 72 holes in a national championship is 262 by Percy Alliss (born January 8, 1897) of Britain, with 67, 66, 66 and 63 in the Italian Open Championship at San Remo in 1932, and by Liang Huan Lu (b. 1936) (Taiwan) in the 1971 French open at Biarritz.

Women. The lowest recorded score on an 18-hole course for a woman is 62 (30+32) by Mary (Mickey) Kathryn Wright (born February 14, 1935), of Dallas, on the Hogan Park Course (6,286 yards) at Midland, Texas, in November, 1964.

LOWEST SCORERS: Mickey Wright (left) holds the women's record for 18 holes with a 62 scored in 1964. Arnold Palmer (right) scored 276 for the 72-hole British Open to set the record in 1962 only since equalled by Tom Weiskopf in 1973.

Highest Round Score. It is recorded that Chevalier von Cittern went round 18 holes at Biarritz, France, in 1888 in 316 strokes—an average of more than 17 shots per hole.

Highest Single-Hole Scores. The highest score for a single hole in a tournament (the British Open) is 21 by a player in the inaugural meeting at Prestwick in 1860. Double figures have been recorded on the card of the winner only once, when Willie Fernie (1851–1924) scored a 10 at Musselburgh, Midlothian, Scotland, in 1883. Ray Ainsley of Ojai, California, took 19 strokes for the par-4 16th hole during the second round of the U.S. Open at Cherry Hills Country Club, Denver, Colorado, on June 10, 1938. Most of the strokes were used in trying to extricate the ball from a brook. Hans Merrell of Mogadore, Ohio, took 19 strokes on the par-3 16th (222 yards) during the third round of the Bing Crosby National Tournament at the Cypress Point course, Del Monte, California, on January 17, 1959.

Most Shots—Women. A woman player in the qualifying round of the Shawnee Invitational for Ladies at Shawnee-on-Delaware, Pennsylvania, in *c.* 1912, took 166 strokes for the 130-yard 16th hole. Her tee shot went into the Binniekill River and the ball floated. She put out in a boat with her exemplary, but statistically minded, husband at the oars. She eventually beached the ball 1½ miles downstream, but was not yet out of the woods. She had to play through a forest on the home stretch.

Most Rounds in a Day

The greatest number of rounds played in 24 hours is 22 rounds plus 5 holes (401 holes) by Ian Colston, 35 at Bendigo G.C., Victoria, Australia (6,061 yards) on November 27–28, 1971. He covered more than 100 miles.

GOLF CHAMPIONS: Jack Nicklaus (left) in winning his third P.G.A. Championship on August 12, 1973 set a record with 14 major titles. The late Bobby Jones (right) won the U.S. Open 4 times and the U.S. Amateur title 5 times. He never turned professional.

Edward A. Ferguson of Detroit played 828 holes (46 rounds) in 158 hours August 25 to September 1, 1930. He walked 327½ miles.

Fastest and Slowest Rounds

With such variations in the lengths of courses, speed records, even for rounds under par, are of little comparative value.

Bob Williams at Eugene, Oregon, completed 18 holes (6,010 yds.) in 27 minutes 48.2 seconds in 1971, but this test permitted him to stroke the ball while it was still moving. The record for a still ball is 31 minutes 22 seconds by Len Richardson, the South African Olympic athlete, at Mowbray, Cape Town, over a 6,248-yard course in November, 1931.

At the Doon Valley Golf Club, Kitchener, Ontario, Canada, 48 members completed the 18-hole 6,358-yard course in 10 minutes 58.4 seconds on July 16, 1972.

The slowest major-tournament round was one of 5 hours 15 minutes by Sam Snead and Ben W. Hogan (born August 13, 1912) of the U.S. *vs.* Stan Leonard and Al Balding (born April, 1924) of Canada in the Canada Cup contest on the West Course, at Wentworth, Surrey, England, in 1956. This was a 4-ball medal round, everything holed out.

The final round of the women's Panaga Open at Seria, State of Brunei, took 5 hours 25 minutes for a 3-ball stroke play round on July 16, 1973.

Longest Drive

In long-driving contests 330 yards is rarely surpassed at sea level. The United States P.G.A. record is 341 yards by Jack William Nicklaus (born Columbus, Ohio, January 21, 1940), then weighing 206 lbs., in July, 1963.

The world record is 392 yards by an amateur member of the Irish P.G.A., Tommie Campbell, made at Dun Laoghaire, Co. Dublin, in July, 1964.

However, under freak conditions of wind, slope, parched or frozen surfaces, or ricochet from a stone or wall, much greater distances are achieved. The greatest recorded drive is one of 445 yards by E. C. Bliss (1863–1917), a 12-handicap player, at the 9th hole of the Old Course, Herne Bay, Kent, England, in August, 1913. Bliss, 6 feet tall and more than 182 lbs., drove to the back of the green on the left-handed dog-leg. The drive was measured by a government surveyor, Capt. Lloyd, who also measured the decline from tee to resting place as 57 feet.

Other freak drives include the driving of the 483-yard 13th hole at Westward Ho!, Devon, England, by F. Lemarchand, backed by a gale; and to the edge of the 465-yard downhill 9th on the East Devon Course, Budleigh, Salterton, Devon, England, by T. H. V. Haydon in September, 1934. Neither drive was accurately measured.

RECORD DRIVE: The longest drive in any long-drive competition was 392 yards hit by Tommie Campbell, the Irish golfer, in 1964.

LONG DRIVE: In an exhibition, Tony Jacklin (b. July 7, 1944) British Open and U.S. Open champion in 1969 and 1970 respectively, in an attempt to drive a golf ball across the River Thames from the roof of the Savoy Hotel, London, 125 feet above street level, drove it 353 yards, but it fell short of the opposite bank.

Perhaps the longest recorded drive on level ground was one of an estimated 430 yards by Craig Ralph Wood (1901–68) (U.S.) on the 530-yard 5th hole at the Old Course, St. Andrews, Fife, Scotland, in the Open Championship in June, 1933. The ground was parched and there was a strong following wind.

Arthur Lynskey claimed a drive of 200 yards out and 2 miles down off Pike's Peak, Colorado, on June 28, 1968.

A drive of 2,640 yards (1½ miles) across ice was achieved by an Australian meteorologist named Nils Lied at Mawson Base, Antarctica, in 1962. On the moon, the energy expended on a mundane 300-yard drive would achieve, craters permitting, a distance of a mile.

Longest Hitter. The golfer regarded as the longest consistent hitter the game has ever known is the 6-foot-5-inch tall, 230-lb. George Bayer (U.S.), the 1957 Canadian Open Champion. His longest measured drive was one of 420 yards at the fourth in the Las Vegas Invitational in 1953. It was measured as a precaution against litigation since the ball struck a spectator. Bayer also drove a ball pin high on a 426-yard hole in Tucson, Arizona. Radar measurements show that an 87-m.p.h. impact velocity for a golf ball falls to 46 m.p.h. in 3.0 seconds.

Longest Putt

The longest recorded holed putt in a major tournament was one of 86 feet on the vast 13th green at the Augusta National, Georgia, by Cary Middlecoff (b. January, 1921) in the 1955 Masters Tournament.

Most Tournament Wins

The record for winning tournaments in a single season is 19 (out of 31) by Byron Nelson (born February 4, 1912), of Fort Worth, Texas, in 1945. Of these 11 were consecutive, including the U.S. Open, P.G.A., Canadian P.G.A. and Canadian Open, from March 16 to August 15. He was a money prize winner in 113 consecutive tournaments.

Most Titles

U.S. Open	W. Anderson	4	1901–03–04–05
	Robert Tyre Jones, Jr.	4	1923–26–29–30
	Ben W. Hogan	4	1948–50–51–53
U.S. Amateur	R. T. Jones, Jr. (1902–71)	5	1924–25–27–28–30
British Open	Harry Vardon (1870–1937)	6	1896–98–99, 1903, 1911–14
British Amateur	John Ball (1861–1940)	8	1888–90–92–94–99, 1907–10, 1912
P.G.A. Championship (U.S.)	Walter C. Hagen	5	1921–24–25–26–27
Masters Championship (U.S.)	Arnold D. Palmer	4	1958–60–62–64
U.S. Women's Open	Miss Elizabeth (Betsy) Earle Rawls	4	1951–53–57–60
	Miss "Mickey" Wright	4	1958–59–61–64
U.S. Women's Amateur	Mrs. Glenna Vare (née Collett)	6	1922–25–28–29–30–35

Jack Nicklaus (U.S.) is the only golfer who has won the British and U.S. Opens, the Masters and the P.G.A. crowns at least twice, and 14 major tournaments in all.

The Open (British)

The Open Championship was inaugurated in 1860 at Prestwick, Ayrshire, Scotland. The lowest score for 9 holes is 29 by Tom Haliburton (Wentworth) and Peter W. Thomson (Australia), in the first round at the Open on the Royal Lytham and St. Anne's course at Lytham St. Anne's, Lancashire, England, on July 10, 1963.

The lowest scoring round is 63 (all in qualifying rounds) by Frank Jowle (born May 14, 1912) at the New Course, St. Andrews, Scotland (6,526 yards), on July 4, 1955, by Peter W. Thomson (born August 23, 1929), of Australia at Royal Lytham and St. Anne's, England (6,635 yards) on June 30, 1958, and Maurice Bembridge (Little Aston) at Delamere Forest, Cheshire, England, on July 7, 1967. The lowest 72-hole aggregate is 276 (71, 69, 67, 69) by Arnold Daniel Palmer (born September 10, 1929) of Latrobe, Pennsylvania, at Troon, Ayrshire, Scotland, ending on July 13, 1962 and by Tom

Weiskopf (b. November 9, 1942) also at Troon on July 11–14, 1973 with 68–67–71–70.

U.S. Open

This championship was inaugurated in 1894. The lowest 72-hole aggregate is 275 (71, 67, 72 and 65) by Jack Nicklaus on the Lower Course (7,015 yards) at Baltusrol Golf Club, Springfield, New Jersey, on June 15–18, 1967, and by Lee Trevino (b. Horizon City, Texas, December 1, 1939) at Oak Hill Country Club, Rochester, New York, on June 13–16, 1968. The lowest score for 18 holes is 63 by John Miller (b. April 29, 1947) of California on the 6,921-yard, par-71 Oakmont (Pennsylvania) course on June 17, 1973.

U.S. Masters

The lowest score in the U.S. Masters (instituted at 6,980-yard Augusta National Golf Course, Georgia, in 1934) was 271 by Jack Nicklaus in 1965. The lowest rounds have been 64 by Lloyd Mangrum (b. August 1, 1914) (1st round, 1940) and Jack Nicklaus (3rd round, 1965).

U.S. Amateur

This championship was inaugurated in 1893. The lowest score for 9 holes is 30 by Francis D. Ouimet (1893–1967) in 1932.

British Amateur

The lowest score for nine holes in the British Amateur Championship (inaugurated in 1885) is 29 by Richard Davol Chapman (born March 23, 1911) of the U.S. at Sandwich in 1948. Michael Francis Bonallack (b. 1924) shot a 61 (32–29) on the 6,905-yard par-71 course at Ganton, Yorkshire, on July 27, 1968, on the 1st 18 of the 36 holes in the final round.

Richest Prize

The greatest first place prize money was $100,000 (total purse $500,000) in the 144-hole "World Open" played at Pinehurst, North Carolina, on November 8–17, 1973, won by Miller Barber, 42, of Texas.

Highest Earnings

The greatest amount ever won in official golf prizes is $2,009,168 by Jack Nicklaus to December 31, 1973. His record for official tournaments in a calendar year is $320,542 in 1972.

The highest career earnings by a woman is $488,319 by Kathy Whitworth (b. September 27, 1938) through January 1, 1974. Miss Whitworth won 54 tournaments of the Ladies' P.G.A. to the end of 1971. The season record for women (all tournaments) is $82,864.25 (official earnings) by Miss Whitworth in 1973.

Youngest and Oldest Champions. The youngest winner of the British Open was Tom Morris, Jr. (b. 1850, d. December 25, 1875) at Prestwick, Ayrshire, Scotland, in 1868, aged 18. The youngest winner of the British Amateur title was John Charles Beharrel (born May 2, 1938) at Troon, Ayrshire, Scotland, on June 2, 1956,

SCORES HIS AGE:
C. Arthur Thompson of Victoria, B.C., Canada, is the oldest golfer to do this— he shot 103 at age 103 in 1973, and at age 104 still plays regularly.

aged 18 years 1 month. The oldest winner of the British Amateur was the Hon. Michael Scott at Hoylake, Cheshire, England, in 1933, when 54. The oldest British Open Champion was "Old Tom" Morris (b. 1821) who was aged 46 when he won in 1867. The oldest U.S. Amateur Champion was Jack Westland (born 1905) at Seattle, Washington, in 1952, aged 47.

Holes-in-One

Longest. The longest hole ever holed in one shot is the 10th hole (444 yards) at Miracle Hills Golf Club, Omaha, Nebraska. Robert Mitera achieved a hole-in-one there on October 7, 1965. Mitera, aged 21 and 5 feet 6 inches tall, weighed 165 lbs. A two-handicap player, he normally drove 245 yards. A 50-m.p.h. gust carried his shot over a 290-yard drop-off. The group in front testified to the remaining 154 yards.

The 453-yard, dogleg 8th hole at the Crescent Country Club, Burlington, North Carolina, was reportedly aced by Dickie Hogan on July 5, 1973. The straight line of his drive measured an estimated 330 yards from tee to pin.

The women's record is 393 yards by Marie Robie of Wollaston, Massachusetts, on the first hole at the Furnace Brook Golf Club, Wollaston, Massachusetts, on September 4, 1949.

Most. The greatest number of holes-in-one in a career is 38 by Art Wall, Jr. (born November, 1923), between 1936 and 1970. The record total number of "aces" recorded in the U.S. in a year was 18,319 (indicating more than 100 on some days) in 1969. The late Dr. Joseph O. Boydstone was reputed to have scored holes-in-one at the 3rd, 4th and 9th holes on the Bakersfield Public Golf Course, California, on October 10, 1962. The holes measured 210, 132 and 135 yards. Full investigation by the *Bakersfield Californian* did not, however, impress its editor with the validity of this claim.

Consecutive. There is no recorded instance of a golfer performing three consecutive holes-in-one, but there are at least 13 cases of "aces" being achieved in two consecutive holes of which the greatest was Norman L. Manley's unique "double albatross" on two par 4 holes (330-yard 7th and 290-yard 8th) on the Del Valle Country Club course, Saugus, California, on September 2, 1964.

Two consecutive aces were scored back-to-back on the same hole by a father and son playing together in a unique performance on June 16, 1972, at Glen Eagles White Course in Lemont, Illinois. The hole was the 165-yard seventh, and the father, Charles Calozzo, teed off first, using a 5-wood. Then his son, Phil, using a 4-iron duplicated the feat.

Youngest and Oldest. The youngest golfer recorded to have shot a hole-in-one was Tommy Moore (6 years 36 days) of Hagerstown, Maryland, on the 145-yard 4th at the Woodbrier Golf Course, Martinsville, West Virginia, on March 8, 1968. The oldest golfer to have performed the feat was Walter Fast, aged 92 years 199 days, at Madison Golf Club, Peoria, Illinois, on the 13th hole on June 25, 1971. A Canadian, Charles Youngman of the Tam O'Shanter Club, Toronto, is reputed to have been 93 years old when he scored a hole-in-one.

Shooting Your Age

The record for scoring one's age in years over an 18-hole round is held by Weller Noble, who between 1955 (scoring 64 when aged 64) and December 31, 1971, has amassed 644 "age scores" on the Claremont Country Club, Oakland, California (par 68) of 5,735 yards. The course is provenly harder than many of 6,000 yards or more on which to produce low scores.

The oldest player to score his age is C. Arthur Thompson (born 1869) of Victoria, British Columbia, Canada, who scored 103 on the Uplands course of 6,215 yards when aged 103 in 1973. He was still regularly playing, aged 104, 2 or 3 days a week.

World Cup (formerly Canada Cup)

The Canada Cup (instituted 1953) has been won most often by the U.S. with eleven victories in 1955–56, 1960–61–62–63–64–66–67–69–71. The only man to have been on six winning teams has been Arnold Palmer (1960 to 1967). The only man to take the individual title three times is Jack Nicklaus (U.S.) in 1963–64–71. The lowest aggregate score for 144 holes is 545 by Australia (Bruce Devlin and

David Graham) at San Isidro, Buenos Aires, Argentina, on November 12–15, 1970, and the lowest score by an individual winner was 269 by Roberto de Vicenzo, 47, on the same occasion.

Walker Cup

The biennial Walker Cup (instituted 1921) amateur match between the U.S. and Great Britain-Ireland has been won by the U.S. $21\frac{1}{2}$–$2\frac{1}{2}$ to date (July, 1973). Joe Carr (G.B.-I.) played in 10 contests (1947–67).

Ryder Trophy

The biennial Ryder Cup (instituted 1927) professional match between the U.S. and G.B., has been won by the U.S. $14\frac{1}{2}$–$4\frac{1}{2}$ to date (July, 1973). Billy Casper has the record of winning most singles, with 11 won (1961–69).

Throwing the Golf Ball

The lowest recorded score for throwing a golf ball around 18 holes (over 6,000 yards) is 84 by Douglas V. Shipe at the 6,220-yard University of Missouri course, Columbia, Missouri, on November 16, 1971.

Greyhound Racing

Earliest Meeting. In September, 1876, a greyhound meeting was staged at Hendon, North London, England, with a railed hare operated by a windlass. Modern greyhound racing originated with the perfecting of the mechanical hare by Oliver P. Smith at Emeryville, California, in 1919.

Fastest Dog. The highest speed at which any greyhound has been timed is 41.72 m.p.h. (410 yards in 20.1 secs.) by *The Shoe* for a track record at Richmond, New South Wales, Australia. It is estimated that he covered the last 100 yards in 4.5 seconds or at 45.45 m.p.h. The fastest *photo*-timing is 28.17 seconds over 525 yards or 38.12 m.p.h. by *Easy Investment* on June 30, 1973. The fastest photo-timing over 525-yard hurdles is 29.10 seconds (36.90 m.p.h.) by *Sherry's Prince* on May 8, 1971.

Gymnastics

Earliest References. Gymnastics were widely practiced in Greece during the period of the ancient Olympic Games (776 B.C. to 393 A.D.), but they were not revived until *c.* 1780.

World Championships. The greatest number of individual titles won by a man in the World Championships is 10 by Boris Shakhlin (U.S.S.R.) between 1954 and 1964. He was also on three winning teams. The women's record is 10 individual wins and 5 team titles by Larissa Semyonovna Latynina (born September 27, 1934, retired 1966) of the U.S.S.R., between 1956 and 1964.

WORLD CHAMPION TEN TIMES: Larissa Latynina (U.S.S.R.), who retired
in 1966, also shared in 5 team titles, and won a record 18 Olympic medals.

Olympic Games. Italy has won most Olympic team titles with
four victories in 1912, 1920, 1924 and 1932.

The only man to win six gold medals is Boris Shakhlin (U.S.S.R.),
with one in 1956, four (two shared) in 1960 and one in 1964.

GYMNASTIC TITLE HOLDERS: Vera Caslavska-Odlozil (left), Czech gymnast, has been the most successful woman in Olympic Games competition with seven individual gold medals and a share of team silver medals. The late Lillian Leitzel (U.S.) (right) set the women's record for one-handed chin-ups with 27 in 1918.

The most successful woman has been Vera Caslavska-Odlozil (Czechoslovakia), with seven individual gold medals, three in 1964 and four (one shared) in 1968. Larissa Latynina of the U.S.S.R. won six individual and three team gold medals, five silver, and four bronze for an all-time record total of 18 Olympic medals.

Chinning the Bar. The record for 2-arm chins from a dead hang position is 106 by William D. Reed (University of Pennsylvania) on June 23, 1969. The women's record for one-handed chin-ups is 27 in Hermann's Gym, Philadelphia, in 1918, by Lillian Leitzel (Mrs. Alfredo Codona) (U.S.), who was killed in Copenhagen, Denmark, on February 12, 1931. Her total would be unmatched by any male, but it is doubtful if they were achieved from a "dead hang" position. It is believed that only one person in 100,000 can chin a bar one-handed. Francis Lewis (born 1896) of Beatrice, Nebraska, in May, 1914, achieved 7 consecutive chins using only the middle finger of his left hand. His bodyweight was 158 lbs.

Rope Climbing. The U.S. Amateur Athletic Union records are tantamount to world records: 20 feet (hands alone) 2.8 secs., Don Perry, at Champaign, Illinois, on April 3, 1954; 25 feet (hands alone), 4.7 secs., Garvin S. Smith at Los Angeles, on April 19, 1947.

Push-ups. The greatest recorded number of consecutive push-ups is 6,006 in 3 hours 54 minutes by Chick Linster, aged 16, of Wilmette,

Illinois, on October 5, 1965. Masura Noma of Mihara, Japan, did 1,227 push-ups in 37 minutes in January, 1968. James Ullrich at Yutan High School, Nebraska, on March 10, 1973, achieved 115 one-arm push-ups on his right arm in 70 secs., followed by 80 on his left arm in 51 secs. Noel Berry Mason performed 101 push-ups on his fingertips at Abbots Bromley, Staffordshire, England, on February 2, 1973.

Sit-ups. The greatest recorded number of consecutive sit-ups on a hard surface without feet pinned is 25,222 in 11 hours 14 minutes by Richard John Knecht, aged 8, at the Idaho Falls High School Gymnasium on December 23, 1972.

Jumping Jacks. The greatest number of side-straddle hops is 14,053, performed in 3 hours 53 minutes (better than 1 per sec.) by Dale D. Cummings, Jr., in Atlanta, Georgia, on December 6, 1966.

Greatest Tumbler. The greatest tumbler of all time is Dick Browning (U.S.) who made a backward somersault over a 7-foot-3-inch bar at Santa Barbara, California, in April, 1954. In his unique repertoire was a "round-off," backward handspring, backward somersault with half-twist, walk-out, tinsica tigna round-off, backward handspring, double backward somersault.

Hand-to-Hand Balancing. The longest horizontal dive achieved in any hand-to-hand balancing act is 22 feet by Harry Berry (top mounter) and the late Nelson Soule (understander) of the Bell-Thazer Brothers from Kentucky, who played at state fairs and in vaudeville from 1912 to 1918. Berry used a 10-foot tower and trampoline for impetus.

Largest Gymnasium. The world's largest gymnasium is Yale University's Payne Whitney Gymnasium at New Haven, Connecticut, completed in 1932 and valued at $18,000,000. The building, known as the "Cathedral of Muscle," has nine stories with wings of five stories each. It is equipped with 4 basketball courts, 3 rowing tanks, 28 squash courts, 12 handball courts, a roof jogging track and a 25-yard by 42-foot swimming pool on the first floor and a 55-yard long pool on the third floor.

Handball (Court)

Origin. Handball is a game of ancient Celtic origin. In the early 19th century only a front wall was used, but later side and back walls were added. The court is now standardized 60 feet by 30 feet in Ireland and Australia, and 40 feet by 20 feet in Canada, Mexico and the U.S. The game is played with both a hard and soft ball in Ireland, and a soft ball only elsewhere.

The earliest international contest was in New York City in 1887, between the champions of the U.S. and Ireland.

Championship. World championships were inaugurated in New York in October, 1964, with competitors from Australia, Canada, Ireland, Mexico and the U.S. The U.S. beat Canada for the team title.

In November, 1967, Canada and the U.S. shared the team title and in October, 1970, it was won by Ireland.

Most Titles. The most successful player in the U.S.H.A. National Four-Wall Championships has been James Jacobs (U.S.), who won 6 singles titles (1955–56–57–60–64–65) and shared in 6 doubles titles (1960–62–63–65–67–68).

Handball (Field)

Origins. Field handball was first played *c.* 1895. The earliest international match was when Sweden beat Denmark on March 8, 1935. It was introduced into the Olympic Games at Berlin in 1936 as an 11-a-side outdoor game. The standard size of team for the indoor version has been 7 since 1952. Field handball is played somewhat like soccer but with hands instead of feet.

By 1972 there were 41 countries affiliated with the International Handball Federation, a World Cup competition, and an estimated 5,000,000 participants.

Harness Racing

Origins. The trotting gait (the simultaneous use of the diagonally opposite legs) was first recorded in England in *c.* 1750. The sulky first appeared in harness racing in 1829. Pacers thrust out their fore and hind legs simultaneously on one side.

RECORDS AGAINST TIME
TROTTING

World (mile track)	1:54.8	Nevele Pride (U.S.), Indianapolis	Aug. 31, 1969
Australia	2:01.8	Gramel, Harold Park, Sydney	1964
New Zealand	2:02.4	Control, Addington, Christchurch	1964

PACING

World (mile track)	1:52.0	Steady Star, Lexington, Ky.	Oct. 1, 1971
Australia	1:57.3	Halwes, Harold Park, Sydney	1968
New Zealand	1:56.2	Cardigan Bay, Wellington	1963

RECORDS SET IN RACES

Trotting	1:55.6	Noble Victory (U.S.) at Du Quoin, Illinois	Aug. 31, 1966
Pacing	1:54.6	Albatross (U.S.) at Sportsman's Park, Cicero, Illinois	July 1, 1972

Highest Price. The highest price paid for a trotter is $3,000,000 for *Nevele Pride* by the Stoner Creek Stud of Lexington, Kentucky, from Louis Resnick and Nevele Acres in 1969. The highest for a pacer is $2,500,000 for *Albatross* in 1972.

Greatest Winnings. The greatest amount won by a trotting horse is $1,764,802 by *Une de Mai* to April 15, 1973. The record for a pacing horse is $1,201,470 by *Albatross*, who was retired to stud in December, 1972.

Most Successful Driver

The most successful sulky driver has been Herve Filion (Canada) (b. Quebec, February 1, 1940) who reached a record of 4,065 wins at Roosevelt Raceway, Long Island, New York, after a record 605 victories in the 1972 season.

HOCKEY originated in Holland in the 17th century, as this picture proves.

Hockey

Origins. There is pictorial evidence of hockey being played on ice in the Netherlands in the 17th century. The game probably was first played in 1860 at Kingston, Ontario, Canada, but Montreal and Halifax also lay claim to priority.

Olympic Games. Canada has won the Olympic title six times (1920–24–28–32–48–52) and the world title 19 times, the last being at Geneva in 1961. The longest Olympic career is that of Richard Torriani (Switzerland) from 1928 to 1948. The most gold medals won by any player is three; this was achieved by four U.S.S.R. players in the 1964–68–72 Games—Vitaliy Davidov, Aleksandr Ragulin, Anatoliy Firssov and Viktor Kuzkin. Davidov and Ragulin had played in nine World Championship teams prior to the 1972 Games.

Stanley Cup. This cup presented by the Governor-General Lord Stanley (original cost $48.67), became emblematic of world professional team supremacy several years after the first contest at Montreal in 1893. It has been won most often by the Montreal Canadiens, with 18 wins in 1916, 1924, 1930, 1931, 1944, 1946, 1953, 1956, 1957, 1958, 1959, 1960, 1965, 1966, 1968, 1969, 1971, and 1973. Henri Richard played in his eleventh finals in 1973.

Longest Match. The longest match was 2 hours 56 minutes 30 seconds when the Detroit Red Wings eventually beat the Montreal Maroons 1–0 in the sixth period of overtime at the Forum, Montreal, at 2:25 a.m. on March 25, 1936.

Longest Career. Gordie Howe skated a record 25 years for the Detroit Red Wings from 1946–47 through the 1970–71 season, playing in a record total of 1,687 games. During that time he also set records for most career goals, assists, and scoring points. He also collected 500 stitches in his face.

Most Consecutive Games. Andy Hebenton, playing for both the New York Rangers and the Boston Bruins, skated in 630 consecutive games without a miss—9 complete seasons from 1955–56 through 1963–64. The most consecutive complete games by a goaltender is 502, set by Glenn Hall (Detroit, Chicago), beginning in 1955 and ending when he suffered a back injury in a game against Boston on November 7, 1962.

Longest Season. The only man ever to play 82 games in a 78-game season is Ross Lonsberry. He began the 1971–72 season with the Los Angeles Kings where he played 50 games. Then, in January, he was traded to the Philadelphia Flyers (who had played only 46 games at the time) where he finished out the season (32 more games).

MOST RELIABLE: Andy Hebenton (New York, Boston) skated 9 complete seasons (630 games) without missing a game.

Most Wins and Losses

The Boston Bruins had the winningest season in N.H.L. history in 1970–71. They ended the regular 78-game season with a record 121 points earned, with an all-time record of 57 victories and 7 ties against only 14 losses. They also scored a record 399 goals and 697 assists in that season.

The New York Islanders set the record for seasonal losses with 60 in their maiden season in the league (1972–73). They won only 12 games.

Longest Winning Streak. In the 1929–30 season, the Boston Bruins won 14 straight games. The longest a team has ever gone without a defeat is 23 games, again set by Boston. From December 22, 1940, to February 25, 1941, they won 15 games and tied 8.

Longest Losing Streak. The Philadelphia Quakers went from November 29, 1930 to January 10, 1931 without gaining a point—a total of 15 straight defeats. The longest time a team has gone without a win was when the New York Rangers played 25 games, over two seasons, before scoring a victory—starting January 23, 1944, they lost 21 games and tied 4 games before ending the drought on November 11, 1944.

Team Scoring

Most Goals. The greatest number of goals recorded in a World Championship match has been 31–1 when Hungary beat Belgium in 1971. The N.H.L. record for both teams is 21 goals, scored when the Montreal Canadiens beat Toronto St. Patricks at Montreal 14–7 on January 10, 1920. The most goals ever scored by one team in a single game was set by the Canadiens, when they defeated the Quebec Bulldogs on March 3, 1920 by a score of 16–3.

Individual Scoring

Most Goals. The career record in North America for goals is 786 by Gordie Howe of the Detroit Red Wings. Phil Esposito (Boston Bruins) scored 76 goals in the 1970–71 season.

The most goals ever scored in one game is 7 by Joe Malone of the Quebec Bulldogs against the Toronto St. Patricks on January 31, 1920. Four different men have scored 4 goals in one period—Harvey Jackson (Toronto), Max Bentley (Chicago), Clint Smith (Chicago), and Red Berenson (St. Louis).

In 1921–22, Harry (Punch) Broadbent of the Ottawa Senators scored 25 goals in 16 consecutive games to set an all-time "consecutive game goal-scoring streak" record.

Most Points and Assists. The most points ever scored in a career is 1,809 by Gordie Howe of Detroit. Howe also had the most career assists with 1,023. Phil Esposito (Boston) scored a record 152 points in the 1970–71 season (76 goals and 76 assists). Bobby Orr, also of Boston, assisted on 102 goals in the same year for a record. His average of 1.31 assists per game is a league record.

HIGH SCORING CENTER: Phil Esposito (left) (Boston Bruins) put in a record 76 goals in the 1970-71 season. Added to his 76 assists, he totaled 152 points, also a N.H.L. record.

Phil Esposito has also scored 100 or more points in 4 different seasons, and 50 or more goals in 3 consecutive years. Bobby Orr had 4 consecutive 100-or-more-point seasons from 1969–70 to 1972–73. Bobby Hull (Chicago) had 5 50-or-more-goal years when he left the N.H.L.

The most assists recorded in one game is 7 by Billy Taylor of Detroit on March 16, 1947 against Chicago. Detroit won 10–6.

The most points ever scored in one game is 8, a record set by two Montreal Canadiens—Maurice (Rocket) Richard against Detroit on December 28, 1944, and Bert Olmstead against Chicago on January 9, 1954.

Most 3-Goal Games. In his 15-year N.H.L. career, Bobby Hull of Chicago scored 3 or more goals in 28 games. Four of these were 4-goal efforts. The term "hat-trick" properly applies when 3 goals are scored consecutively by one player in a game without interruption by either an answering score by the other team or a goal by any other player on his own team. In general usage, a "hat-trick" is any 3-goal effort by a player in one game.

Fastest Scoring

The Pittsburgh Penguins scored 5 goals in 2 minutes 7 seconds against the St. Louis Blues on November 22, 1972. The Montreal

Maroons scored 2 goals in 4 seconds against Boston in the third period of a game played in Montreal on January 3, 1931. Both of them were put in the net by Nels Stewart. Bill Mosienko (Chicago) scored three goals in 21 seconds against the New York Rangers on March 23, 1952.

The fastest goal that has ever been scored from the opening whistle came at 6 seconds of the first period by Henry Boucha of the Detroit Red Wings on January 28, 1973, against Montreal. Claude Provost of the Canadiens scored a goal against Boston after 4 seconds of the opening of the second period on November 9, 1957.

Goaltending

The longest any goalie has gone without a defeat is 33 games, a record set by Gerry Cheevers of Boston in 1971–72. The longest a goalie has ever kept successive opponents scoreless is 460 minutes 49 seconds by Alex Connell of the Ottawa Senators in 1927–28. He registered 6 consecutive shutouts in this time.

The most shutouts ever recorded in one season is 22 by George Hainsworth of Montreal in 1928–29 (this is also a team record). This feat is even more remarkable considering that the season was only 44 games long at that time, compared to the 78-game season currently used.

Terry Sawchuk registered a record 103 career shutouts in his 20 seasons in the N.H.L. He played for Detroit, Boston, Toronto, Los Angeles, and the New York Rangers during that time.

MOST ASSISTS:
Bobby Orr, star defenseman of the Boston Bruins, assisted on 102 goals in 1970-71. This was an average of 1.31 assists per game.

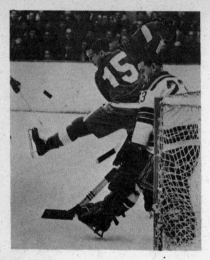

MOST PENALIZED:
During his 17 seasons
with Chicago and
Detroit, Ted Lindsay
(No. 15) was slapped with
1,808 minutes in penalties.

Most Penalties

The most any team has been penalized in one season is the 1,756 minutes accessed against the Philadelphia Flyers in 1972–73.

Ted Lindsay, playing for Detroit and Chicago, set an individual career record for penalties with 1,808 minutes over a period of 17 seasons. Keith Magnuson of Chicago was called for a record 291 minutes in the 1970–71 season.

Jim Dorey of the Toronto Maple Leafs set an all-time record in Toronto on October 16, 1968, in a game against the Pittsburgh Penguins. He was whistled down for a total of 9 penalties in the game, 7 of which came in the second period (also a record). The 4 minor penalties, 2 major penalties, 2 10-minute misconducts, and 1 game misconduct added up to a record total of 48 minutes for one game.

Penalty Shots. "Scotty" Bowman of the old St. Louis Eagles (he is now the coach of the Montreal Canadiens) was the first player in the N.H.L. to attempt a penalty shot on November 13, 1934. He scored. Since 1963, when records on penalty shots were first kept, 35.7 per cent of those awarded have resulted in goals. The most penalty shots called in a single season was 9 in both 1963–64 and 1971–72.

Fastest Player. The highest speed measured for any player is 29.7 m.p.h. for Bobby Hull (Chicago Black Hawks) (b. January 3, 1939). The highest puck speed is also attributed to Hull, whose left-handed slap shot has been measured at 118.3 m.p.h.

Horse Racing

Origins. Horsemanship was an important part of the Hittite culture of Anatolia, Turkey, in the 2nd millenium B.C. The 23rd ancient Olympic Games of 624 B.C. featured horse racing. The earliest horse race recorded in England was one held in *c.* 210 A.D. at Netherby, Yorkshire, among Arabians brought to Britain by Lucius Septimius Severus (146–211 A.D.), Emperor of Rome. The oldest race still being run annually is the Lanark Silver Bell, instituted in Scotland by William Lion (1165–1214). Organized horse racing began in New York State at least as early as March, 1668.

Racecourses. The world's largest racecourse is the Newmarket course in England (founded 1636), on which the Beacon Course, the longest of the 19 courses, is 4 miles 397 yards long and the Rowley Mile is 167 feet wide. The border between Suffolk and Cambridgeshire runs through the Newmarket course. The world's largest racecourse grandstand was opened in 1968 at Belmont Park, Long Island, N.Y., at a cost of $30,700,000. It is 110 feet tall, 440 yards long and contains 908 mutuel windows. The greatest seating capacity at any racetrack is 40,000 at the Atlantic City Audit, New Jersey. The world's smallest is the Lobong racecourse, Darjeeling, West Bengal, India (altitude 7,000 feet), where the complete lap is 481 yards. It was laid out *c.* 1885 and used as a parade ground.

Longest Race

The longest recorded horse race was one of 1,200 miles in Portugal, won by a horse *Emir*, bred from Egyptian-bred Blunt Arab stock. The holder of the world's record for long distance racing and speed is *Champion Crabbet*, who covered 300 miles in 52 hours 33 minutes, carrying 245 lbs., in 1920.

GREATEST MONEY-WINNING HORSE: Kelso, who retired in 1966, won almost $2,000,000 in prizes. In 63 races, he won 39 and placed second in 12 of them.

UNBEATEN HORSE: The Hungarian mare foaled in 1874, "Kincsem," was the only horse to remain unbeaten in all her 54 races.

In 1831, Squire George Osbaldeston (1787–1866), M.P. of East Retford, England, covered 200 miles in 8 hours 42 minutes at Newmarket, using 50 mounts, so averaging 22.99 m.p.h. In 1967, G. Steecher covered 100 miles on a single horse in 11 hours 4 minutes in Victoria, Australia.

Most Valuable Horse

The highest price ever paid for a horse is $6,080,000 paid by Mrs. Penny Tweedy and 28 other members of a $197,000 per unit syndicate in February, 1973, for the $16.02\frac{1}{2}$-hand-high chestnut *Secretariat*. The price was $345 per ounce, quadruple the price per unit of 22-carat gold. *Secretariat* became the ninth Triple Crown winner, taking the Belmont Stakes by an unprecedented 31 lengths in a world record dirt track time of 2 minutes 24.0 seconds.

Victories. The horse with the best recorded win-loss record was *Kincsem*, a Hungarian mare foaled in 1874, who was unbeaten in 54 races (1877–1880), including the English Goodwood Cup of 1878.

Tallest. The tallest horse ever to race is *Fort d'Or*, owned by Lady Elizabeth (Eliza) Nugent (*née* Guinness) of Berkshire, England, which stands 18 hands 2 inches.

Greatest Winnings. The greatest amount ever won by a horse is $1,977,896 by *Kelso* (foaled in 1957) in the U.S., between 1959 and his retirement on March 10, 1966. In 63 races he won 39, came in second in 12 and third in 2. (See photo, previous page.)

The most successful horse of all time was *Buckpasser*, whose career winnings were $1,462,014 in 1965–66–67. He won 25 races out of 31. The most won by a mare is $783,674 by *Cicada*. In 42 races she won 23, came in second in 8 and third in 6. The most won in a year is $817,941 by *Damascus* in 1967. His total reached $1,176,781.

Horses   Speed Records

Distance	Time	m.p.h.	Name	Course	Date
¼ mile	20.8s.	43.26	Big Racket (U.S.)	Lomas de Sotelo, Mex.	Feb. 5, 1945
⅓ mile (stra.)	45.0s.	40.00	Gloaming (N.Z.)	Wellington, N.Z.	Jan. 12, 1921
½ mile	45.0s.	40.00	Beau Madison (U.S.)	Phoenix, Arizona	Mar. 30, 1957
	45.0s.	40.00	Another Nell (U.S.)	Cicero, Ill.	May 8, 1967
⅝ mile	53.6s.	41.98	Indigenous (G.B.)	Epsom, England	June 2, 1960
¾ mile	1m. 07.4s.	40.06	Zip Pocket (U.S.)	Phoenix, Arizona	Dec. 6, 1966
	1m. 07.4s.	40.06	Vale of Tears (U.S.)	Ab Sar Ben, Omaha, Nebr.	June 7, 1969
	1m. 06.2s.	40.78	Broken Tindril (G.B.)	*Brighton, England	Aug. 6, 1929
Mile	1m. 31.8s.	39.21	Soueida (G.B.)	*Brighton, England	Sept. 19, 1963
	1m. 31.8s.	39.21	Loose Cover (G.B.)	*Brighton, England	June 9, 1966
	1m. 32.2s.	39.04	Dr. Fager (U.S.)	Arlington, Ill.	Aug. 24, 1968
1½ miles	2m. 23.0s.	37.76	Fiddle Isle (U.S.)	Arcadia, Calif.	Mar. 21, 1970
2 miles**	3m. 15.0s.	36.93	Polazel (G.B.)	Salisbury, England	July 8, 1924
3 miles	5m. 15.0s.	34.29	Farragut (Mex.)	Agua Caliente, Mex.	Mar. 9, 1941

* Course downhill for 2/3rd of a mile.

** A more reliable modern record is 3m. 16.75 secs. by *Il Tempo* (N.Z.) at Trentham, Wellington, New Zealand, on January 17, 1970.

TALLEST HORSE: "Fort d'Or" stands 18 hands 2 inches. He is owned by Lady Elizabeth Nugent of England (who was born in Ireland).

Dead Heats

There is no recorded case in turf history of a quintuple dead heat. The nearest approach was in the Astley Stakes, at Lewes, England, in August, 1880, when *Mazurka, Wandering Nun* and *Scobell* triple dead-heated for first place, just ahead of *Cumberland* and *Thora*, who dead-heated for fourth place. Each of the five jockeys thought he had won. The only two known examples of a quadruple dead heat were between *The Defaulter, Squire of Malton, Reindeer* and *Pulcherrima* in the Omnibus Stakes at The Hoo, England, on April 26, 1851, and between *Overreach, Lady Go-Lightly, Gamester* and *The Unexpected* at the Houghton Meeting at Newmarket, England, on October 22, 1855.

Jockeys. The most successful jockey has been Willie Shoemaker (b. weighing 2½ lbs. on August 19, 1931) now weighing 98 lbs. after 23 years in the saddle, beating Johnny Longden's lifetime record of 6,032 winners on September 7, 1970. Shoemaker stands 4 feet 11½ inches. From March 19, 1949, to July 24, 1973, he rode 6,525 winners.

Sandy Hawley (Canada), aged 24, surpassed Shoemaker's record of 485 wins in a season on December 6, 1973, and went on to reach 500 by December 16, 1973.

The greatest amount ever won by any jockey in a year is $3,088,888 by Braulio Baeza (born Panama) in the U.S. in 1967, when he had 256 wins from 1,064 mounts.

The oldest jockey was Levi Barlingame (U.S.), who rode his last race at Stafford, Kansas, in 1932, aged 80. The youngest jockey was Frank Wootton (English Champion jockey 1909–12), who rode his first winner in South Africa aged 9 years 10 months. The lightest recorded jockey was Kitchener (died 1872), who won the Chester Cup in England on *Red Deer* in 1844 at 49 lbs. He was said to have weighed only 40 lbs. in 1840.

The greatest number of winners ridden on one card is 8 by Hubert S. Jones at Caliente, California, on June 11, 1944, of which 5 were photo-finishes.

Trainers. The greatest amount ever won by a trainer in one year is $2,456,250, by Eddie Neloy in 1966, when his horses won 93 races.

Shortest Odds

The shortest odds ever quoted for any racehorse are 10,000 to 1 on for *Dragon Blood*, ridden by Lester Piggott (G.B.) in the Premio Naviglio in Milan, Italy, on June 1, 1967. He won. Odds of 100 to 1 on were quoted for the American horse *Man o' War* (foaled March 29, 1917, died November 1, 1947) on three separate occasions in 1920. In 21 starts in 1919–20 he had 20 wins and one second (on August 13, 1919, in the Sanford Memorial Stakes).

Pari-Mutuel Record

The U.S. pari-mutuel record pay-off is $941.75 to $1 on *Wishing Ring* at Latonia track, Kentucky, in 1912.

Largest Prizes. The richest race ever held was the All-American Futurity, a race for quarter-horses over 400 yards at Ruidoso Downs, New Mexico, on September 3, 1973. The prizes totaled $1,000,000.

Possumjet, the 1972 winner of the All-American Futurity in 20.04 seconds received $336,629.

Biggest Win

The Hon. Raymond Guest (born 1908), U.S. Ambassador to Ireland, won £62,500 ($150,000) from William Hill on May 29, 1968, when his Derby winner *Sir Ivor* won £500 ($1,200) each way at 100–1 in September, 1967. Larger sums have reputedly been won but essential details are lacking.

Horseshoe Pitching

Origin. This sport was derived by military farriers and is of great antiquity. The first formal World Championships were staged at Bronson, Kansas, in 1909.

Most Titles. The record for men's titles is 10 by Ted Allen (Boulder, Colorado) in 1933–34–35–40–46–53–55–56–57–59. The women's record is 8 titles by Vicki Chapelle (Winston, Lamonte, Missouri).

Highest Percentage. The record for percentage of ringers is 88.5 by Elmer Hohl (Wellesey, Ontario, Canada) at Keene, New Hampshire, in 1968. The record for consecutive ringers is 72 by Allen in 1971 for men, and 30 by Sue Gillespie of Portland, Indiana, in 1964 for women.

Ice Skating

Origins. The earliest reference to ice skating is that of a Danish writer dated 1134. The earliest English account of 1180 refers to skates made of bone. Metal blades date from probably *c.* 1600. The earliest skating club was the Edinburgh Skating Club, Scotland, formed in 1742. The earliest artificial ice rink in the world was the "Glaciarium," built in Chelsea, London, in 1876.

Longest Race. The longest race regularly held is the "Elfstedentocht" ("Tour of the Eleven Towns") in the Netherlands. It covers 200 kilometers (124 miles 483 yards) and the fastest time is 7 hours 35 minutes by Jeen van den Berg (born January 8, 1928) on February 3, 1954.

Largest Rink. The world's largest artificial ice rink is the quadruple rink at Burnaby, British Columbia, Canada, completed in December, 1972, which has an ice area of 68,000 sq. ft. The largest artificial outdoor rink is the Fujikyu Highland Promenade Rink, Japan, opened at a cost of $938,000 in 1967 with an area of 165,750 square feet (3.8 acres).

OLYMPIC CHAMPION: Lidia Skoblikova (U.S.S.R.) earned 6 gold medals in speed skating, the most anyone has won.

Longest Marathon. The longest recorded skating marathon is one of 82 hours 30 minutes by Tony Hocking, 19, at the Toombul Ice Rink, Brisbane, Australia, in April, 1973. The fastest time to complete 100 miles is 5 hours 35 minutes by Robert B. Kerns on February 20, 1972, at Glacier Falls Ice Rink, Anaheim, California.

Figure Skating

World. The greatest number of men's figure skating titles (instituted 1896) is ten by Ulrich Salchow (born August 7, 1877), of Sweden, in 1901–05 and 1907–11. The women's record (instituted 1906) is ten titles by Sonja Henie (April 8, 1912–October 12, 1969), of Norway, between 1927 and 1936.

Olympic. The most Olympic gold medals won by a figure skater is three by Gilles Grafström (born June 7, 1893), of Sweden, in 1920, 1924, and 1928 (also silver medal in 1932); and by Sonja Henie (see above) in 1928, 1932 and 1936.

Most Difficult Jump. The triple Lutz has been performed by only 3 skaters—by Don Jackson (Canada) (b. April 2, 1940), in Prague, 1962; by Haig B. Oundjian (G.B.) (b. May 16, 1949) in the Grand Prix de Saint Gervais in August, 1969; and by John Mischa Petkevich, the 1971 U.S. champion.

Most Titles Speed Skating

World. The greatest number of world speed skating titles (instituted 1893) won by any skater is five by Oscar Mathisen (Norway) in 1908–09 and 1912–14, and Clas Thunberg (born April 5, 1893) of Finland, in 1923, 1925, 1928–29 and 1931. The most titles won by a woman is four by Mrs. Inga Voronina, *née* Artomonova (1936–66) of Moscow, U.S.S.R., in 1957, 1958, 1962 and 1965.

Olympic. The most Olympic gold medals won in speed skating is six by Lidia Skoblikova (born March 8, 1939), of Chelyaminsk, U.S.S.R., in 1960 (2) and 1964 (4). The male record is by Ivan Ballangrad (b. March 7, 1904) who won 4 gold, 2 silver and 1 bronze medal.

WORLD SPEED SKATING RECORDS

Distance	mins. secs.	Name and Nationality	Place	Date
Men				
500 meters	38.00*†	Leo Linkovesi (Finland)	Davos, Switz.	Jan. 8, 1972
	38.00*	Hasse Borjes (Sweden)	Inzell, W. Ger.	Mar. 4, 1972
	38.00*	Erhard Keller (W. Ger.)	Inzell, W. Ger.	Mar. 4, 1972
	38.00*	Lasse Efskind (Norway)	Davos, Switz.	Jan. 13, 1973
1,000 meters	1 17.60	Lasse Efskind (Norway)	Davos, Switz.	Jan. 13, 1973
1,500 meters	1 58.70	Ard Schenk (Neth.)	Davos, Switz.	Feb. 15, 1971
3,000 meters	4 08.30	Ard Schenk (Neth.)	Inzell, W. Ger.	Mar. 2, 1972
5,000 meters	7 09.80	Ard Schenk (Neth.)	Inzell, W. Ger.	Mar. 4, 1972
10,000 meters	14 55.96	Ard Schenk (Neth.)	Inzell, W. Ger.	Mar. 14, 1971
Women				
500 meters	41.80	Sheila Young (U.S.)	Davos, Switz.	Jan. 20, 1973
1,000 meters	1 26.10*	Tatiana Averina (U.S.S.R.)	Medeo, U.S.S.R.	Mar. 20, 1973
1,500 meters	2 13.40*	Galina Stepanskaya (U.S.S.R.)	Medeo, U.S.S.R.	Mar. 19, 1973
3,000 meters	4 46.50	Stien Kaiser (Neth.)	Davos, Switz.	Jan. 16, 1971
5,000 meters	9 01.60	Rimma Zhukova (U.S.S.R.)	Medeo, U.S.S.R.	Jan. 24, 1953

* Subject to ratification by the International Skating Union.
† This represents a speed of 29.43 m.p.h.

FASTEST WOMAN SKATER: Rimma Zhukova (U.S.S.R.) (right) set the record for 5,000 meters, and has held it since 1953.

Ice and Sand Yachting

Origin. The sport originated in the Netherlands (earliest patent is dated 1600). The earliest authentic record is Dutch, dating from 1768. The largest ice yacht built was *Icicle*, built for Commodore John E. Roosevelt for racing on the Hudson River, New York, *c.* 1870. It was 68 feet 11 inches long and carried 1,070 square feet of canvas.

Highest Speed. The highest speed officially recorded is 143 m.p.h. by John D. Buckstaff in a Class A stern-steerer on Lake Winnebago, Wisconsin, in 1938. Such a speed is possible in a wind of 72 m.p.h.

Sand Yachting. Land or sand yachts of Dutch construction were first reported on beaches (now in Belgium) in 1595. The earliest international championship was staged in 1914.

The fastest recorded speed for a sand yacht is 59.69 m.p.h. (measured mile in 62.4 secs.) by *Coronation Year Mk. II*, owned by R. Millett Denning and crewed by J. Halliday, Bob Harding, J. Glassbrook and Cliff Martindale at Lytham St. Anne's, England, in 1956.

WORLD'S FASTEST GAME: When the ball is in play in jai-alai, it can reach a speed of 160 m.p.h.

Jai-Alai *(Pelota)*

The game, which originated in Italy as *longue paume* and was introduced into the Basque country between Spain and France in the 13th century, is said to be the fastest of all ball games with speeds of up to 160 m.p.h. Gloves were introduced *c.* 1840 and the *chisterak* (basket-like glove) was invented *c.* 1860 by Gantchiki Dithurbide of Sainte Pée. The long *chistera* was invented by Melchior Curuchage of Buenos Aires, Argentina, in 1888. Games are played in a *fronton* (playing court), with both leather and rubber balls. The sport is governed by the International Federation of Basque Pelote.

The world's largest *fronton* was built for $4,500,000 in Miami, Florida.

Longest Domination. The longest domination as the world's No. 1 player was enjoyed by Chiquito de Cambo (*né* Joseph Apesteguy) (France) (b. May 10, 1881–d. 1955), from the beginning of the century until succeeded in 1938 by Jean Urruty (France) (b. October 19, 1913).

Judo

Origin. Judo is a modern combat sport which developed out of an amalgam of several old Japanese fighting arts, the most popular of which was *ju-jitsu* (*jiu jitsu*), which is thought to be of pre-Christian Chinese origin. Judo has been greatly developed by the Japanese since 1882, when it was first devised by *Shihan* Dr. Jigoro Kano. World Championships were inaugurated in Tokyo on May 5, 1956.

Highest Grade. The efficiency grades in Judo are divided into pupil (*kyu*) and master (*dan*) grades. The highest awarded is the extremely rare red belt *Judan* (10th *dan*), given only to seven men. The Judo protocol provides for a *Juichidan* (11th *dan*), who also would wear a red belt, and even a *Junidan* (12th *dan*), who would wear a white belt twice as wide as an ordinary belt, but these have never been bestowed.

Champions. The only two men to have won 3 world titles have been Antonius (Anton) J. Geesink (born April 6, 1934), of the Netherlands, who won the 1963 (Open), 1964 (Olympic open) and 1965 heavyweight title at a weight of 266 lbs., standing 6 feet 6 inches tall; and Wilhem Ruska of the Netherlands who won the 1971 heavyweight and the 1972 Olympic heavyweight and Open titles.

Marathon. The longest recorded Judo marathon is one of 13 hours by 2 of 8 judoka in 5-minute stints at St. Paul's School, Plumstead, London, on July 3, 1971.

Karate

Origins. Originally *karate* (empty hand) is known to have been developed by the unarmed populace as a method of attack on, and defense against, armed oppressors in Okinawa, in the Ryukyu Islands, based on techniques devised from the 6th century Chinese art of *Chuan-fa* (Kempo). Transmitted to Japan in the 1920's by Funakoshi Gichin, the founder of modern *karate*, this method of combat was further refined and organized into a sport with competitive rules.

The five major schools of *karate* in Japan are *Shotokan, Wado-ryu, Goju-ryu, Shito-ryu,* and *Kyokushinkai. Tae-kwan-do* is a lethal Korean variation on *karate,* which has been used for military purposes.

Most Titles. The only winner of 3 All-Japanese titles has been Takeshi Oishi, who won in 1969–70–71.

The highest *dan* among karetekas is Yamaguchi Gogen (b. 1907), a 10th *dan* of the *Goju-ryu* Karate Do.

Greatest Force. Considerably less emphasis is placed on *Tamashiwara* (wood breaking, etc.) than is generally supposed. Most styles use it only for demonstration purposes. However, the force needed to break a brick with the abductor *digiti quinti* muscle of the hand is normally 130–140 lbs. The highest measured impact is 196 lbs. force.

Brick Breaking. The greatest feat of brick breaking by hand was 3,773 bricks in 2 hours 59 minutes, by Harold Worden (5 ft. 5 in., 132 lbs.) at White Oaks Mall, London, Ontario, Canada, on November 17, 1973. This comes to just less than 21 bricks per minute.

Lacrosse

Origin. The game is of American Indian origin, derived from the inter-tribal game *baggataway*, and was played by Iroquois Indians in lower Ontario, Canada, and upper New York State, before 1492. The game was included in the Olympic Games of 1908.

Longest Throw. The longest recorded throw is 162.86 yards, by Barney Quinn of Ottawa, Canada, on September 10, 1892.

Highest Score. The highest score in any international match was Australia's 19–3 win over England at Manchester in May, 1972.

World Championship. The first World Tournament was held at Toronto, Canada, in 1967 and the U.S. won.

Motorcycling

Earliest Races. The first motorcycle race was one from Paris to Dieppe, France, in 1897. The oldest motorcycle races in the world are the Auto-Cycle Union Tourist Trophy (T.T.) series, first held on the 15.81-mile "Peel" ("St. John's") course on the Isle of Man on May 28, 1907, and still run on the island, on the "Mountain" circuit (37.73 miles).

The first closed-circuit race was held at the Parc des Princes, Paris cycle track, in 1903.

Longest Circuits. The 37.73-mile "Mountain" circuit, over which the two main T.T. races have been run since 1911, has 264 curves and corners and is the longest used for any motorcycle race.

Fastest Circuit. The highest average lap speed attained on any closed circuit is 182 m.p.h. by a Kawasaki racer powered by a 748-c.c. three-cylinder two-stroke engine on a banked circuit in Tokyo, Japan, in December, 1971.

The fastest road circuit is the Francorchamps circuit near Spa, Belgium. It is 14.10 kilometers (8 miles 1,340 yards) in length and was lapped in 4 minutes 0.9 seconds (average speed of 130.929 m.p.h.) by Giacomo Agostini (born Lovere, Italy, June 16, 1942) on a 500-c.c. three-cylinder M.V.-Agusta during the 500-c.c. Belgian Grand Prix on July 1, 1973.

Fastest Race. The fastest race in the world was held at Grenzlandring, West Germany, in 1939. It was won by Georg Meier (b. Germany, 1910) at an average speed of 134 m.p.h. on a supercharged 495-c.c. flat-twin B.M.W.

The fastest road race is the 500-c.c. Belgian Grand Prix held on the Francorchamps circuit (8 miles 1,340 yards) near Spa, Belgium. The record for this 12-lap (105.136 miles) race is 49 minutes 5.3 seconds (average speed 128.506 m.p.h.) by Giacomo Agostini, on a 500-c.c. three-cylinder M.V.-Agusta, on July 1, 1973.

Longest Race. The longest race is the Liège 24 hours. The greatest distance ever covered is 2,456.64 miles (average speed 102.36 m.p.h.) by Charles and John Williams of the United Kingdom, on a 920-c.c. four-cylinder Honda on the Francorchamps circuit (8 miles 1,340 yards) near Spa, Belgium, on Aug. 25–26, 1973.

World Championships. Most world championship titles (instituted by the Fédération Internationale Motorcycliste in 1949) won are 13 by Giacomo Agostini (Italy) in the 350-c.c. class 1968, 69, 70, 71, 72, 73 and in the 500-c.c. class 1966, 67, 68, 69, 70, 71, 72. Giacomo Agostini is the only man to win two world championships in five consecutive years (350- and 500-c.c. titles in 1968–69–70–71–72). Agostini won 108 races in the world championship series between April 24, 1965, and July 30, 1973, including a record 19 in 1970, also achieved by Stanley Michael Bailey "Mike" Hailwood, M.B.E., G.M. (b. Oxford, England, April 2, 1940) in 1966.

Hailwood at 21 was the youngest person to win a world championship (the 250-c.c. title in 1961).

The oldest was Eric Staines Oliver (b. Crowborough, Sussex, England, April 13, 1911) who won the sidecar title in 1953, aged 42.

Most Successful Machines. Italian M.V.-Agusta motorcycles won 37 world championships between 1952 and 1973 and 267 world championship races between 1952 and 1973. Japanese Honda machines won 29 world championship races and five world championships in 1966.

Speed Records. The official world speed record (average speed for two runs over a one-kilometer course) is 224.569 m.p.h. (average time 9.961 seconds) by William A. "Bill" Johnson, 38, of Garden Grove, California, riding a Triumph Bonneville T120 streamliner, with a 667.25-c.c. parallel twin-cylinder engine running on methanol and nitromethane and developing 75 to 80 b.h.p., at Bonneville Salt Flats, Utah, on September 5, 1962. His machine was 17 feet long and weighed 400 lbs. His first run was made in 9.847 seconds (average speed 227.169 m.p.h.).

Calvin G. Rayborn (1940–1973) of the United States recorded higher speeds over the measured mile, without F.I.M. observers, at Bonneville on October 16, 1970, riding his 10-foot 3-inch-long 1,480-c.c. V-twin Harley Davidson streamliner running on methanol and nitromethane. On the first run he covered the mile in 13.494 seconds (266.785 m.p.h.). On the second run his time was 13.626 seconds (264.201 m.p.h.). The average time for the two runs was 13.560 seconds (average speed 265.487 m.p.h.).

Jon S. McKibben, 33, of Costa Mesa, California, covered a measured mile one-way at Bonneville in 12.5625 seconds (286.567 m.p.h.) in November, 1971, riding his 21-foot 6-inch-long Reaction Dynamics *Honda Hawk* streamliner, powered by two turbocharged 736-c.c. in-line four-cylinder Honda engines developing 140 b.h.p. each, running on methanol.

The world record average speed for two runs over one kilometer (1,093.6 yards) from a standing start is 122.77 m.p.h. (18.22 seconds) by David John Hobbs (b. Woodford, Essex, England, June 3, 1947) on his supercharged Triumph *Olympus II* powered by two twin-cylinder 500-c.c. engines, each developing 100 b.h.p., using methanol and nitromethane, at Elvington Airfield, Yorkshire, England, on September 30, 1972.

The world record for two runs over 440 yards from a standing start is 92.879 m.p.h. (9.69 seconds) by Dave Lecoq (b. Tunbridge Wells, Kent, England, April 24, 1940) on the supercharged 1,287-c.c. *Drag-Waye* powered by a flat-four Volkswagen engine, developing 150 b.h.p. using methanol, at Elvington Airfield, Yorkshire, England, on September 27, 1970. The faster run was made in 9.60 seconds. He equaled this record on the same machine at R.A.F. Fairford, Gloucestershire, England, on September 23, 1972.

The fastest time for a single run over 440 yards from a standing start is 8.44 seconds (terminal velocity 169.81 m.p.h.) by Jim Preisler of Minneapolis, Minnesota, riding his 2,600-c.c. twin-engined Harley Davidson, during the National Hot Rod Association's U.S. Nationals at Indianapolis Raceway Park, Indiana, on September 3, 1973.

The highest terminal velocity recorded at the end of a 440-yard run from a standing start is 180.13 m.p.h. (elapsed time 9.35 seconds) by Tom C. Christenson of Kenosha, Wisconsin, riding his 1,490-c.c. *Hogslayer*, powered by two Norton Commando engines developing 150 b.h.p. each using nitromethane, at U.S. 30 drag strip, Gary, Indiana, in August, 1972.

Mountaineering

Origins. Although bronze-age artifacts have been found on the summit (9,605 feet) of the Riffelhorn, Switzerland, mountaineering, as a sport, has a continuous history dating back only to 1854. Isolated instances of climbing for its own sake exist back to the 14th century. The Atacamenans built sacrificial platforms near the summit of

Llullaillaco in South America (22,058 feet) in late pre-Columbian times, *c.* 1490.

Mount Everest. Mount Everest (29,028 feet) was first climbed at 11:30 a.m. on May 29, 1953, when the summit was reached by Edmund Percival Hillary (born July 20, 1919), of New Zealand, and the Sherpa, Tenzing Norkhay (born, as Namgyal Wangdi, in Nepal in 1914, formerly called Tenzing Khumjung Bhutia). The successful expedition was led by Col. (later Brigadier Lord) Henry Cecil John Hunt (born June 22, 1910).

Subsequent ascents of Mount Everest are as follows:

Climbers	Date
Ernst Schmidt, Jurg Marmet (Switz.)	May 23, 1956
Hans Rudolf von Gunten, Adolf Reist (Switz.)	May 24, 1956
*Wang Fu-chou, Chu Yin-hua (China), Konbu	May 25, 1960
James Warren Whittaker, Sherpa Nawang Gombu	May 1, 1963
Barry C. Bishop Luther G. Jerstad (U.S.)	May 22, 1963
Dr. William F. Unsoeld, Dr. Thomas F. Hornbein (U.S.)	May 22, 1963
Capt. A. S. Cheema (India), Sherpa Nawang Gombu	May 20, 1965
Sonam Gyaltso, Sonam Wangyal	May 22, 1965
C. P. Vohra (India), Sherpa Ang Kami	May 24, 1965
Capt. H. P. S. Ahluwalia, H. C. S. Rawat (India), Phu Dorji	May 29, 1965
Nomi Uemura, Tero Matsuura (Japan)	May 11, 1970
Katsutoshi Harabayashi (Japan) and Sherpa Chotari	May 12, 1970
Sgt. Mirko Minuzzo, Sgt. Rinaldo Carrel (Italy) with Lapka Tenzing and Samba Tamang	May 5, 1973
Capt. Fabrizio Innamorati, W. O. Virginio Epis and Sgt. Maj. Claudio Benedetti (Italy) with Sonam Gallien	May 7, 1973

* Not internationally accepted.

Greatest Wall. The highest final stage in any wall climb is that on the south face of Annapurna I (26,545 feet). It was climbed by the British expedition led by Christian Bonnington when on May 27, 1970, Donald Whillans, 36, and Dougal Haston, 27, scaled to the summit.

The longest wall climb is on the Rupal-Flanke from the base camp at 11,680 feet to the South Point 26,384 feet of Nanga Parbat—a vertical ascent of 14,704 feet. This was scaled by the Austro-Germano-Italian Expedition led by Dr. Herrlig Koffer in April, 1970.

Greatest Alpine Wall. Europe's greatest wall is the 6,600 foot (2,000 m.) North face of the Eigerwand (Ogre wall) first climbed on August 20, 1932, by Hans Lauper, Alfred Zurcher, Alexander Graven and Josef Knubel. The first direct ascent was by Heinrich Harrar and Fritz Kasparek of Austria and Andreas Heckmair and Ludvig Vörg of Germany on July 21–24, 1938. The greatest alpine solo climb was that of Walter Bonatti (Italy) of the South West Pillar of the Dru, Montenvers, now called the Bonatti Pillar in 126 hrs. 7 min. on August 17–22, 1955.

Rock Climbing. The world's most demanding XS (extremely severe) rock climb is regarded as the sheer almost totally holdless 3,000 foot Muir Wall of El Capitan (7,564 feet) Yosemite, California, first climbed in November, 1958. In 1968, Royal Robbins (U.S.) climbed this solo with *pitons*.

Olympic Games

Note: These records now include the un-numbered Games held at Athens in 1906, which some authorities ignore. Although inserted between the regular IIIrd Games in 1904 and the IVth Games in 1908, the 1906 Games were both official and were of a higher standard than all three of those that preceded them.

OLYMPIC GOLD MEDAL: Highest award given in the Games. Only once has it been awarded ten times to an individual—Ray Ewry (U.S.) track star, 1900–08.

Origins. The earliest celebration of the ancient Olympic Games of which there is a certain record is that of July, 776 B.C. (when Koroibos, a cook from Elis, won a foot race), though their origin probably dates from *c.* 1370 B.C. The ancient Games were terminated by an order issued in Milan in 393 A.D. by Theodosius I, "the Great" (*c.* 346–395), Emperor of Rome. At the instigation of Pierre de Fredi, Baron de Coubertin (1863–1937), the Olympic Games of the modern era were inaugurated in Athens on April 6, 1896.

Most Olympic Titles. The greatest number of victories resulting in Olympic gold medals is nine by Mark Spitz (U.S.) who won 2 relay golds at Mexico in 1968 and 7 more (4 individual and 3 relay) at Munich in 1972. The latter figure is an absolute Olympic record for one celebration at any sport. Spitz's equals the runner Paavo Nurmi's (Finland) absolute Olympic career record of 9 golds.

Most Medals

In the ancient Olympic Games, victors were given a chaplet (head garland) of olive leaves. Milo (Milon of Kroton) won 6 titles at *palaisma* (wrestling), 540–516 B.C.

Individual. The most individual gold medals won by a male competitor in the modern Games is 10 by Ray Ewry (U.S.) (b. October 14, 1873, d. September 27, 1937). The female record is seven by Vera Caslavska-Odlozil (b. May 3, 1942) of Czechoslovakia (see *Gymnastics*).

National. The total figures for most medals and most gold medals for all Olympic events (including those now discontinued) for the Summer (1896–1972) and Winter Games (1924–1972) and for the Art Competitions (1912–1948) are:—

	Gold	Silver	Bronze	Total
1. U.S.A.	621	473½	408½	1,503
2. U.S.S.R. (formerly Russia)	249	208	201	658
3. G.B. (including Ireland to 1920)	161½	197½	173	532

Oldest and Youngest Competitors. The oldest recorded competitor was Oscar G. Swahn (Sweden), who won a silver medal for shooting running deer in 1920, when aged 73. The youngest woman to win gold medals is Marjorie Gestring (U.S.) (b. November 18, 1922, now Mrs. Bowman) aged 13 years 9 months, in the 1936 women's springboard event. The youngest winner ever was a French boy (whose name is not recorded) who coxed the Netherlands coxed pair in 1900. He was not more than 10 and may have been as young as 7. He substituted for Dr. Hermanus Brockmann, who coxed in the heats but proved too heavy.

Longest Span. The longest competitive span of any Olympic competitor is 40 years by Dr. Ivan Osiier (Denmark), who competed as a fencer in 1908, 1912 (silver medal), 1920, 1924, 1928, 1932 and 1948, totaling seven celebrations. He refused to compete in the 1936 Games on the grounds that they were Nazi-dominated. The longest span for a woman is 24 years (1932–56) by the Austrian fencer Ellen Müller-Preiss. The only Olympian to win 4 consecutive individual titles has been Alfred A. Oerter (b. September 19, 1936, New York City) who won the discus title in 1956–60–64–68.

Largest Crowd. The largest crowd at any Olympic site was 150,000 at the 1952 ski-jumping at the Holmenkollen, outside Oslo, Norway. Estimates of the number of spectators of the marathon race through Tokyo, Japan, on October 21, 1964, have ranged from 500,000 to 1,500,000.

Most Participations. Five countries have never failed to be represented at the 21 Celebrations of the Games: Australia, Greece, Great Britain, Switzerland and the United States of America.

Pentathlon, Modern

The Modern Pentathlon (Riding, Fencing, Shooting, Swimming and Running) was inaugurated into the Olympic Games at Stockholm in 1912.

Point scores in riding, fencing, cross country and hence overall scores have no comparative value between one competition and another. In shooting and swimming (300 meters), where measurements are absolute, the point scores are of record significance.

Most World Titles. The record number of world titles won is 5 by András Balczó (Hungary) in 1963, 1965, 1966, 1967 and 1969.

Olympic Titles. The greatest number of Olympic gold medals won is three by Balczó, a member of Hungary's winning team in 1960 and 1968, and the 1972 individual champion. Lars Hall (Sweden) uniquely has won two individual Championships (1952 and 1956). Balczó has won a record number of five medals (3 gold and 2 silver).

	Points			
Shooting	1,066	P. Macken (Australia) and R. Phelps (U.K.)	Leipzig, E. Germ.	Sept. 20, 1965
	1,066	I. Mona (Hungary)	Jönköping, Sweden	Sept. 11, 1967
Swimming	1,260	Robert Vonk (Neth.)	San Antonio, Tex.	Oct. 13, 1971

Pigeon Racing

Earliest References. Pigeon racing was the natural development of the use of homing pigeons for the carrying of messages—a quality utilized in the ancient Olympic Games (776 B.C.–393 A.D.). The sport originated in Belgium. The earliest major long-distance race was from Crystal Palace, South London, England, in 1871.

Longest Flights. The greatest recorded homing flight by a pigeon was made by one owned by the 1st Duke of Wellington (1769–1852). Released from a sailing ship off the Ichabo Islands, West Africa, on April 8, it dropped dead a mile from its loft at Nine Elms, London, England, on June 1, 1845, 55 days later, having flown an airline route of 5,400 miles, but an actual distance of possibly 7,000 miles to avoid the Sahara Desert. It was reported on November 27, 1971, that an exhausted pigeon bearing a Hanover (Germany) label was found 10,000 miles away at Cunnamulla, Queensland, Australia.

Highest Speeds. In level flight in windless conditions it is very doubtful if any pigeon can exceed 60 m.p.h. The highest race speed recorded is 3,229 yards in 1 minute (110.07 m.p.h.) in East Anglia, England, on May 8, 1965, when 1,428 birds were backed by a powerful southwest wind. The winner was A. Vidgeon & Son.

The highest speed race recorded over a distance of more than 1,000 kilometers is 82.93 m.p.h. by a hen pigeon in the Central Cumberland Combine Race over 683 miles 147 yards from Murray Bridge, South Australia, to North Ryde, Sydney, on October 2, 1971.

The world's longest reputed distance in 24 hours is 803 miles (velocity 1,525 yards per minute) by E. S. Peterson's winner of the 1941 San Antonio (Texas) Racing Club event.

Polo

Earliest Games. Polo is usually regarded as being of Persian origin, having been played as *Pula c.* 525 B.C. Other claims have come from Tibet and the Tang dynasty of China 250 A.D.

Stone goalposts (probably 12th century), 8 yards wide and 300 yards apart, still stand at Isfahan, Iran. The earliest club of modern times was the Kachar Club (founded in 1859) in Assam, India. The game was introduced into England from India in 1869 by the 10th Hussars at Aldershot, Hampshire, and the earliest match was one between the 9th Lancers and the 10th Hussars on Hounslow Heath, west of London, in July, 1871. The earliest international match between England and the U.S. was in 1886.

Playing Field. The game is played on the largest field of any ball game in the world. The ground measures 300 yards long by 160 yards wide with side boards or, as in India, 200 yards wide without boards.

Highest Handicap. The highest handicap based on eight 7½-minute "chukkas" is 10 goals, introduced in the U.S. in 1891 and in the United Kingdom and in Argentina in 1910. The most recent addition to the select ranks of the 33 players ever to have received 10-goal handicaps are H. Heguy, F. Dorignac, G. Dorignac, and G. Tanoira, all of Argentina.

Highest Score. The highest aggregate number of goals scored in an international match is 30, when Argentina beat the U.S. 21–9 at Meadow Brook, Long Island, New York, in September, 1936.

Most Olympic Medals. Polo has been part of the Olympic program on five occasions: 1900, 1908, 1920, 1924 and 1936. Of the 21 gold medalists, a 1920 winner, John Wodehouse, the 3rd Earl of Kimberly (b. 1883–d. 1941) uniquely also won a silver medal (1908).

Most Internationals. Thomas Hitchcock, Jr. (1900–44) played five times for the U.S. vs. England (1921–24–27–30–39) and twice vs. Argentina (1928–36).

Most Expensive Pony. The highest price ever paid for a polo pony was $22,000, paid by Stephen Sanford for Lewis Lacey's *Jupiter* after the 1928 U.S. vs. Argentina international.

Largest Trophy. Polo claims the world's largest sporting trophy —the Bangalore Limited Handicap Polo Tournament Trophy. This massive cup standing on its plinth is 6 feet tall and was presented in 1936 by the Indian Raja of Kolanke.

Largest Crowd. Crowds of more than 50,000 have watched floodlit matches at the Sydney, Australia, Agricultural shows.

Powerboat Racing

Origins. The earliest application of the gasoline engine to a boat was Gottlieb Daimler's experimental powerboat on the Seine River, Paris, in 1887. The sport was given impetus by the presentation of a championship cup by Sir Alfred Harmsworth of England in 1903, which was also the year of the first offshore race from Calais to Dover.

Harmsworth Cup. Of the 25 contests from 1903 to 1961, the U.S. has won 16, the United Kingdom 5, Canada 3 and France 1.

The greatest number of wins has been achieved by Garfield A. Wood (U.S.) with 8 (1920–21, 1926, 1928–29–30, 1932–33). The only boat to win three times is *Miss Supertest III*, owned by James G. Thompson (Canada), in 1959–60–61. This boat also achieved the record speed of 115.972 m.p.h. at Picton, Ontario, Canada, in 1960.

Gold Cup. The Gold Cup (instituted 1903) has been four times won by Garfield A. Wood (U.S.) (1917, 1919–20–21) and by Bill Muncey (1956–57, 1961–62). The record speed attained is 120.356 m.p.h. by the Rolls-Royce engined *Miss Exide*, owned by Milo Stoen, and driven by Bill Brow at Seattle, Washington, on August 4, 1965.

Highest Offshore Speed. The highest speed attained is 93.1 m.p.h. by L. Sonny Kay (U.S.) in his 36-foot *Aeromarine II*, powered by two 7,669-c.c. 600-h.p. Kiekhaefer Aeromarine engines. This average speed was recorded over the 63 statute miles of the Cleveland Yachting Club's Firecracker 50 race on Lake Erie, Cleveland, Ohio, on June 30, 1973.

Longest Race. The longest race has been the Port Richborough (London) to Monte Carlo Marathon Offshore International Event. The race extended over 2,947 miles in 14 stages on June 10–25, 1972. It was won by HTS (G.B.), driven by Mike Bellamy, Eddie Chater and Jim Brooks in 71 hours 35 minutes 56 seconds (average 41.15 m.p.h.).

Propeller Driven. Larry Hill drove the supercharged propeller-driven hydroplane *Mr. Ed* at 202.42 m.p.h. at Long Beach, California, in August, 1971. *Climax* recorded 205.19 m.p.h. in a one-way run.

Longest Jump. The longest jump achieved by a powerboat has been 110 feet by Jerry Comeaux, 29, in a Glustron GT-150 with a 135-h.p. Evinrude Starflite on an isolated waterway in Louisiana, in mid-October, 1972. The take-off speed was 56 m.p.h. The jump was required for a sequence in the eighth James Bond film *Live and Let Die*.

Rodeo

Origins. Rodeo came into being with the early days of the North American cattle industry. The earliest references to the sport are from Sante Fe, New Mexico, in 1847. Steer wrestling began with Bill Pickett (Oklahoma) in 1903. The other events are calf roping, bull riding, saddle and bareback bronc riding.

The largest rodeo in the world is the Calgary Exhibition and Stampede at Calgary, Alberta, Canada. The record attendance has been 993,777 on July 5–14, 1973. The record for one day is 133,506 on July 14, 1973.

LARGEST RODEO: This is the stampede event at the Calgary Exhibition in Canada, which broke all rodeo attendance records in 1973.

Champion Bull. The top bucking bull is No. 17, a 1,700-lb. cross-bred, owned by Beutler Bros. and Cervi, of Sterling, Colorado. When cowboys do manage to ride this seldom-ridden beast they win first place.

Champion Bronc. Currently the greatest bronc is *Descent*, a 16-year-old Palomino gelding, owned by Beutler Bros. and Cervi, which has been voted "Bucking Horse of the Year" for a record sixth year. Traditionally a bronc called *Midnight* owned by Jim McNab of Alberta, Canada, was never ridden in 12 appearances at the Calgary Stampede.

CHAMPION COWBOY:
Larry Mahan (U.S.) won the all-round world title five consecutive years, to share this record with Jim Shoulders (U.S.).

Most World Titles. The record number of all-round titles is five by Jim Shoulders (U.S.), in 1949 and 1956–57–58–59 and Larry Mahan (b. November 21, 1943) (1966–67–68–69–70). The record figure for prize money in a single season is $60,852 by Phil Lyne (U.S.) (b. January 18, 1947) of George West, Texas.

Time Records. Records for timed events, such as calf roping and steer wrestling, are meaningless, because of the widely varying conditions due to the size of arenas and amount of start given the stock. The fastest time recently recorded for roping a calf is 7.5 seconds by Junior Garrison of Marlow, Oklahoma, at Evergreen, Colorado, in 1967, and the fastest time for overcoming a steer is 2.4 seconds by James Bynum of Waxahachie, Texas, at Marietta, Oklahoma, in 1955.

The standard required time to stay on in bareback, saddle bronc and bull riding events is 8 seconds. In the now obsolete ride-to-a-finish events, rodeo riders have been recorded to have survived 90 minutes or more, until the mount had not a buck left in it.

Roller Skating

Origin. The first roller skate was devised by Joseph Merlin of Huy, Belgium, in 1760. Several "improved" versions appeared during the next century, but a really satisfactory roller skate did not materialize before 1866, when James L. Plimpton of New York City produced the present four-wheeled type, patented it, and opened the first public rink in the world at Newport, Rhode Island, that year. The great boom periods were 1870–75, 1908–12 and 1948–54, each originating in the U.S.

Largest Rink. The largest indoor rink ever to operate was located in the Grand Hall, Olympia, London, England. It had an actual skating area of 68,000 square feet. It first opened in 1890, for one season, then again from 1909 to 1912.

Roller Hockey. Roller hockey was first introduced in England as Rink Polo, at the old Lava rink, Denmark Hill, London, in the late 1870's. The Amateur Rink Hockey Association was formed in 1905, and in 1913 became the National Rink Hockey (now Roller Hockey) Association. Britain was undefeated in all international championships from 1925 to 1939. Portugal won 11 titles from 1947 to 1972.

Most Titles. Most world speed titles have been won by Miss A. Vianello (Italy) with 16 between 1953 and 1965. Most world pair titles have been taken by Dieter Fingerle (W. Germany) with four in 1959–65–66–67. The records for figure titles are 5 by Karl Heinz Losch in 1958–59–61–62–66 and 4 by Astrid Bader, also of West Germany, in 1965 to 1968.

Speed Records. The fastest speed (official world's record) is 25.78 m.p.h. by Giuseppe Cantarella (Italy) who recorded 34.9 seconds for 440 yards on a road at Catania, Italy, on September 28, 1963. The mile record on a rink is 2 minutes 25.1 seconds by Gianni Ferretti (Italy). The greatest distance skated in one hour on a rink by a woman is 20 miles 1,355 yards by C. Patricia Barnett (U.K.) at Brixton, London, on June 24, 1962. The men's record on a closed road circuit is 22 miles 465 yards by Alberto Civolani (Italy) at Bologna, Italy, on October 15, 1967.

Marathon Record. The longest recorded continuous roller skating marathon was one of 147 hours performed by Walter Miller at the White City rink, Boise, Idaho, in June, 1935. The longest reported skate was by Clinton Shaw from Victoria, British Columbia, to St. John's, Newfoundland (4,900 miles) on the Trans-Canadian Highway *via* Montreal from April 1 to November 11, 1967.

Rowing

Oldest Race. The earliest established sculling race is the Doggett's Coat and Badge, first rowed on August 1, 1716, on a 5-mile course from London Bridge to Chelsea. It is still being rowed every year over the same course, under the administration of the Fishmongers' Company. The first English regatta probably took place on the Thames by the Ranelagh Gardens, near Putney, London, in 1775. Boating began at Eton, England, in 1793. The oldest club, the Leander Club, was formed in *c.* 1818.

Henley Royal Regatta. The annual regatta at Henley-on-Thames, Oxfordshire, England, was inaugurated on March 26, 1839.

Since 1839 the course, except in 1923, has been about 1 mile 550 yards, varying slightly according to the length of boat. In 1967, the shorter craft were "drawn up" so all bows start level. Prior to 1922, there were two slight angles. Classic Records (year in brackets indicates the date instituted):

				mins. secs.	
Grand Challenge Cup (1839)	8 oars	Ratzeburger Ruderclub (W. Germany)		6:16	July 3, 1965
Ladies' Challenge Plate (1845)	8 oars	University of Wisconsin (U.S.)		6:32	July 6, 1973
Thames Challenge Cup (1868)	8 oars	Princeton University (U.S.)		6:33	July 5, 1973
		University of Wisconsin (U.S.)		6:33	July 6, 1973
Princess Elizabeth Challenge (1946)	8 oars	Ridley College (Canada)		6:38	July 6, 1973
Stewards' Challenge (1841)	4 oars	Quintin B.C. (U.K.)		6:55	July 3, 1965
Prince Philip Cup (1963)	4 oars	Northeastern University Rowing Association (U.S.)		7:00	July 6, 1973
Visitors' Challenge (1847)	4 oars	Univ. of London		7:09	July 5, 1973
Wyfold Challenge (1855)	4 oars	Thames Tradesmen's R.C.		7:02	July 7, 1973
Britannia Challenge (1969)	4 oars	Isis B.C. (U.K.)		7:15	July 5, 1973
Silver Goblets and Nickalls' Challenge Cup (1895)	Pair oar	Peter Gorny and Gunther Bergau (ASK Vorwaerts Rostock, East Germany)		7:35	July 1, 1965
Double Sculls (1939)	Sculls	M. J. Hart and C. L. Baillieu (Leander Club and Cambridge Univ., U.K.)		6:59	July 6, 1973
Diamond Challenge (1844)	Sculls	Donald M. Spero (New York A.C., U.S.)		7:42	July 3, 1965

Olympic Games. Since 1900 there have been 105 Olympic finals of which the U.S. has won 26, Germany (now West Germany) 15 and Great Britain 14. Four oarsmen have won 3 gold medals: John B. Kelly (U.S.) (1889–1960), father of Princess Grace of Monaco, in the sculls (1920) and double sculls (1920 and 1924); his cousin Paul V. Costello (U.S.) (b. December 27, 1899) in the double sculls (1920, 1924 and 1928); Jack Beresford, Jr. (G.B.) (b. January 1, 1899) in the sculls (1924), coxless fours (1932) and double sculls (1936) and Vyacheslav Ivanov (U.S.S.R.) (b. July 30, 1938) in the sculls (1956, 1960 and 1964).

Sculling. The record number of wins in the Wingfield Sculls (instituted 1830) is seven by Jack Beresford, Jr., from 1920 to 1926. The record number of world professional sculling titles (instituted 1831) won is seven by W. Beach (Australia) between 1884 and 1887. Stuart A. Mackenzie (Great Britain and Australia) performed the unique feat of winning the Diamond Sculls at Henley for the sixth consecutive occasion on July 7, 1962. In 1960 and 1962 he was in Leander colors.

Highest Rate. The highest rate of stroking recorded in international competition is 56 by the Japanese Olympic eight at Henley, England, in 1936.

Highest Speed. Speeds in tidal or flowing water are of no comparative value. The highest recorded speed for 2,000 meters by

TRIPLE WINNER OF OLYMPIC GOLD MEDAL: Jack Beresford of Great Britain is one of only four men who have won three rowing events—in 1924, 1932, and 1936.

an eight in the World Championships is 5 mins. 32.54 secs. (13.45 m.p.h.) by East Germany in the European Championships at Copenhagen, Denmark, on August 21, 1971.

Marathon. An eight from the Adelaide High School Rowing Club of South Australia covered 101¾ miles on the Murray River in 15 hours 1 minute on August 29, 1973.

Scrabble

Origins. This word game was invented in 1949 by Jim Brunot (U.S.). The National Scrabble Championships were instituted in 1971. The rules were codified by the periodical *Games and Puzzles* in their November, 1972, issue.

Record. The highest single move score so far discovered that is theoretically possible is 1,961 points, published in October, 1973, by Ronald E. Jerome of Bracknell, Berkshire, England.

Marathon. The longest scrabble game on record is one of 100 hours set by Mike Borrello, Pat Edmond, Rick Varyas and Mike Wilson at Lakewood, California, on April 14–18, 1973.

Shooting

Olympic Games. The record number of gold medals won is five by seven marksmen: Carl Osburn (U.S.) (1912–1924); Konrad Stäheli (Switz.) (1900 and 1906); Willis Lee (U.S.) (1920); Louis Richardet (Switz.) (1900 and 1906); Ole Andreas Lilloe-Olsen (Norway) (1920–1924); Alfred Lane (U.S.) (1912 and 1920) and Morris Fisher (U.S.) (1920 and 1924). Osburn also won 4 silver and 2 bronze medals to total 11. The only marksman to win 3 individual gold medals has been Gulbrandsen Skatteboe (Norway) (b. July 18, 1875) in 1906–1908–1912.

Record Heads. The world's finest head is the 23-pointer stag head in the Maritzburg collection, Germany. The outside span is $75\frac{1}{2}$ inches, the length $47\frac{1}{2}$ inches and the weight $41\frac{1}{2}$ lbs. The greatest number of points is probably 33 (plus 29) on the stag shot in 1696 by Frederick III (1657–1713), the Elector of Brandenburg, later King Frederick I of Prussia.

BLOCK SHOT CHAMPION: Tom Frye (left) missed only 6 blocks out of 100,010 in 1959. SKEET SHOOTING CHAMPION: Nikolai Durnev (right) (U.S.S.R.) hit 200 in 200 shots.

Largest Shoulder Guns. The largest bore shoulder guns made were 2 bores. Less than a dozen of these were made by two English wildfowl gunmakers in *c.* 1885. Normally the largest guns made are double-barrelled 4 bore weighing up to 26 lbs. which can be handled only by men of exceptional physique. Larger smooth-bore guns have been made, but these are for use as punt-guns.

Highest Muzzle Velocity. The highest muzzle velocity of any rifle bullet is 7,100 feet per second (4,840 m.p.h.) by a 1937 .30 caliber M 1903 Standard U.S. Army Ordnance Department rifle.

Bench Rest Shooting. The smallest group on record at 1,000 yards is 7.68 inches by Mary Louise De Vito with a 7 m.m.-300 Wetherby at the Pennsylvania 1,000-yard Benchrest Club, Inc., on October 11, 1970.

Block Tossing. Using a pair of auto-loading Remington Nylon 66 .22 caliber guns, Tom Frye (U.S.) tossed 100,010 blocks (2½-inch pine cubes) and hit 100,004—his longest run was 32,860—on October 5–17, 1959. (See photo, opposite page.)

Clay Pigeon Shooting. The record number of clay birds shot in an hour is 1,572 by Dave Berlet, 29, of New Knoxville, Ohio, at Camp Troy on September 4, 1971. Using 5 guns and 5 loaders, he shot 1,000 birds in 38 minutes 30 seconds.

Most world titles have been won by S. De Lumniczer (Hungary) in 1929, 1933 and 1939. The only woman to win two world titles has been Gräfin von Soden (West Germany) in 1966–67.

WORLD RECORDS
Possible Score

Free Pistol	50 m. 6 × 10 shot series	600— 572	G. J. Kosych (U.S.S.R.) Pilsen, 1969
Free Rifle	300 m. 3 × 40 shot series	1,200—1,157	G. L. Anderson (U.S.) Mexico City, 1968
Small Bore Rifle	50 m. 3 × 40 shot series	1,200—1,164	L. W. Wigger, Jr. (U.S.) Tokyo, 1964
		1,200—1,164	G. L. Anderson (U.S.) Johannesburg, 1969
Small Bore Rifle	50 m. 60 shots prone	600— 599	N. Rotaru (Rumania) Moscow, 1972
Center-Fire Pistol	25 m. 60 shots	600— 597	T. D. Smith (U.S.) Sao Paulo, 1963
Rapid-Fire Pistol	25 m. silhouettes 60 shots	600— 598	G. Liverzani (Italy) Phoenix, Ariz., 1970
Running Target	50 m. 40 shots	171	M. Nordfors (Sweden) Pistoia, Italy, 1967
Trap	300 birds	300— 297	K. Jones (U.S.) Wiesbaden, 1966
Skeet	200 birds	200— 200	N. Durnev (U.S.S.R.) (see photo) Cairo, 1962
		200— 200	E. Petrov (U.S.S.R.) Phoenix, Ariz., 1970

Biggest Bag. The largest animal ever shot by any big game hunter was a bull African elephant (*Loxodonta africana*) shot by J. J. Fénykövi (Hungary), 48 miles north-northwest of Macusso, Angola, on

November 13, 1955. It required 16 heavy caliber bullets from a 0.416 Rigby and weighed an estimated 24,000 lbs., standing 13 feet 2 inches at the shoulders. In November, 1965, Simon Fletcher, 28, a Kenyan farmer, claims to have killed two elephants with one 0.458 bullet.

The greatest recorded lifetime bag is 556,000 birds, including 241,000 pheasants, by the 2nd Marquess of Ripon (1867–1923) of England. He himself dropped dead on a grouse moor after shooting his 52nd bird on the morning of September 22, 1923.

Revolver Shooting. The greatest rapid fire feat was that of Ed McGivern (U.S.), who twice fired from 15 feet 5 shots which could be covered by a silver half dollar piece in 0.45 of a second at the Lead Club Range, South Dakota, on August 20, 1932.

Quickest Draw. The super-star of fast drawing and described as The Fastest Gun Ever Alive is Bob Munden (b. Kansas City, Missouri, February 8, 1942). His single-shot records include Walk and Draw Level Blanks in 15/100ths sec. at Areadia, California, on June 4, 1972, and Standing Reaction Blanks (4-inch balloons at 8 feet) in 16/100ths sec. at Norwalk, California, on January 21, 1973, and Self Start Blanks in 2/100ths sec. at Baldwin Park, California on August 17, 1968. His fastest shot with live ammunition is 21/100ths sec. at 21 feet, hitting a man-sized silhouette, in 1963. Munden also holds the 5 shot at balloons at 8 feet record at 1.06 seconds.

Trick Shooting. The most renowned trick shot of all time was Annie Oakley (*née* Moses) (1860–1926). She demonstrated the ability to shoot 100 ex 100 in trap shooting for 35 years, aged between 27 and 62. At 30 paces she could split a playing card end-on, hit a dime in mid-air or shoot a cigarette from the lips of her husband—one Frank Butler.

Skiing

Origins. The earliest dated skis found in Fenno-Scandian bogs have been dated to *c.* 2500 B.C. A rock carving of a skier at Rodoy, northern Norway, dates from 2000 B.C. The earliest recorded isolated military competition was in Oslo, Norway, in 1767, though it did not grow into a sport until 1843 at Tromsø. Skiing was known in California by 1856, having been introduced by "Snowshoe" Thompson from Norway. The Trysil Shooting and Ski-ing Club (founded 1861), in Australia, claims to be world's oldest. Skiing was not introduced into the Alps until 1883, though there is some evidence of earlier use in the Carniola district. The first Slalom event was run at Mürren, Switzerland, on January 6, 1921. The International Ski Federation (F.I.S.) was founded on February 2, 1924. The Winter Olympics were inaugurated on January 25, 1924.

Highest Speed. The highest speed ever recorded for any skier is 114.479 m.p.h. by Alessandro Casse (Italy) on the Kilometro Lanciato (Flying Kilometer) at Cervinia, Italy, in July, 1973.

BROUGHT SKIING TO AMERICA FROM NORWAY: "Snowshoe" Thompson introduced the sport to California in 1856.

The average race speeds by the 1968 Olympic Downhill champion on the Chamrousse course, Grenoble, France, were Jean-Claude Killy (France) (b. August 30, 1943) (53.93 m.p.h.) and Olga Pall (Austria) (47.90 m.p.h.).

Duration. The longest non-stop overland skiing marathon was one that lasted 48˙ hours by Onni Savi, aged 35, of Padasjoki, Finland, who covered 305.9 kilometers (190.1 miles) between noon on April 19 and noon on April 21, 1966.

Most World Titles. The World Alpine Championships were inaugurated at Mürren, Switzerland, in 1931. The greatest number of titles won is 12 by Christel Cranz (born July 1, 1914), of Germany, with four Slalom (1934–37–38–39), three Downhill (1935–37–39) and five Combined (1934–35–37–38–39). She also won the gold medal for the Combined in the 1936 Olympics. The most titles won by a man is seven by Anton ("Toni") Sailer (born November 17, 1935), of Austria, who won all four in 1956 (Giant Slalom, Slalom, Downhill and the non-Olympic Alpine Combination) and the Downhill, Giant Slalom and Combined in 1958.

In the Nordic events Sixten Jernberg (Sweden) won eight titles, 4 at 50 km., one at 30 km., and 3 in relays, in 1956–64. Johan Gröttumsbraaten (born February 24, 1899), of Norway, won six individual titles (two at 18 kilometers and four Combined) in 1926–

32. The record for a jumper is five by **Birger Ruud** (born August 23, 1911), of Norway, in 1931–32 and 1935–36–37.

The World Cup, instituted in 1967, has been won three times by Gustav Thorni (Italy) (b. February 28, 1921) in 1971–73. The women's cup has been won three times by Annemarie Moser (*née* Proel) (Austria) in 1971–72–73. In the 1972–73 season she won a unique 8 out of 8 downhill races and a record 28 World Cup events.

Most Olympic Victories. The most Olympic gold medals won by an individual for skiing is four (including one for a relay) by Sixten Jernberg (born February 6, 1929), of Sweden, in 1956–60–64. In addition, Jernberg has won three silver and two bronze medals. The only women to win three gold medals are Klavdiya Boyarskikh (b. November 11, 1939) and Galina Koulakova, 30, both of U.S.S.R., who each won the 5 kilometers and 10 kilometers, and were members of the winning 3×5 kilometers relay team, at Innsbruck, Austria, and Sapporo, Japan in 1964 and 1972 respectively.

The most Olympic gold medals won in men's alpine skiing is three, by Anton ("Toni") Sailer in 1956 and Jean-Claude Killy in 1968.

Longest Jump. The longest ski jump ever recorded is one of 169 meters ($554\frac{1}{2}$ feet) by Heinz Wosipiwo (East Germany) at Obersdorf, East Germany, on March 9, 1973. The record for a 20-meter hill is $280\frac{1}{2}$ feet by Tauno Käyhkö at Falun, Sweden, on February 19, 1973, when scoring 247.8 points for distance and style.

Heaviest Heavyweight Champion. The greatest winner of the "World Heavyweight Ski Championship" at Sugarloaf Mountain, Maine, was John Truden (U.S.) who weighed in at 401 lbs. in 1972. It has been said that, apart from avalanches, his best event is giant slalom.

Greatest Race. The world's greatest Nordic ski race is the "Vasa Lopp," which commemorates an event of 1521 when Gustavus Vasa (1496–1560), later King of Sweden, skied 85 kilometers (52.8 miles) from Mora to Sälen, Sweden. The re-enactment of this journey in reverse direction is now an annual event, with 9,397 starters on March 4, 1970. The record time is 4 hours 39 minutes 49 seconds by Janne Stefansson on March 3, 1968.

Longest Run. The longest all-downhill ski run in the world is the Weissfluhjoch-Küblis Parsenn course (9 miles long), near Davos, Switzerland. The run from the Aiguille du Midi top of the Chamonix lift (vertical lift 8,176 feet) across the Vallée Blanche is 13 miles.

Longest Lift. The longest chair lift in the world is the Alpine Way to Kosciusko Châlet lift above Thredbo, near the Snowy Mountains, New South Wales, Australia. It takes from 45 to 75 minutes to ascend the 3.5 miles, according to the weather. The highest is at Chactaltaya, Bolivia, rising to 16,500 feet.

MOST TITLED SKIER: (Left) Toni Sailer (Austria) has won 7 world alpine titles, including all four in 1956, more than any other man. **WOMEN'S OLYMPIC CHAMPION:** (Right) Klavdiya Boyarskikh (U.S.S.R.) is one of only two women to win 3 gold medals for skiing.

LEADING RACER: Jean-Claude Killy (France), before turning professional, won the Olympic Downhill at 53.93 m.p.h. in 1968 and the World Cup twice.

Greatest Descent. The greatest reported descent in a 7 hour day is 104,000 feet by Jean Mayer at Taos Ski Valley, New Mexico, in 1964. He made 61 runs using a Poma lift for ascents.

Highest Altitude. Yuichiro Miura (Japan) skied 1.6 miles down Mt. Everest starting from 26,200 feet. In a run from a height of 24,418 feet he reached speeds of 93.6 m.p.h. on May 6, 1970. Sylvian Saudan (Switzerland) became the first man to ski down Mount McKinley (20,320 feet) on June 10, 1972. He took 7 hours to reach the 7,000 foot level and made 2,700 jump turns on the 50-55° top slopes.

Skijoring. The record speed reached in aircraft skijoring (being towed by an aircraft) is 109.23 m.p.h. by Reto Pitsch on the Silsersee, St. Moritz, Switzerland, in 1956.

Ski Parachuting. The greatest recorded vertical descent in parachute ski-jumping is 2,300 feet by Rick Sylvester, 29 (U.S.), who on January 31, 1972 skied off the 3,200-foot sheer face of El Capitan, Yosemite Valley, California. His parachute opened at 1,500 feet.

Ski-bob. The ski-bob was invented by a Mr. Stevens of Hartford, Connecticut, and patented (No. 47334) on April 19, 1892, as a "bicycle with ski-runners." The Fédération Internationale de Skibob was founded on January 14, 1961, in Innsbruck, Austria. The highest speed attained is 103.4 m.p.h. by Erick Brenter (Austria) at Cervina, Italy, in 1964. The only ski-bobbers to retain world championships are Gerhilde Schiffkorn (Austria) who won the women's title in 1967 and 1969, and Gertrude Geberth, who won in 1971 and 1973.

Snowmobiling

The record speed for a snowmobile stood at 127.3 m.p.h. by a Ski Doo XR-2 on February 10, 1973.

Soccer

Origins. A game with some similarities termed *Tsu-chin* was played in China in the 3rd and 4th centuries B.C. The earliest clear representation of the game is in a print from Edinburgh, Scotland, dated 1672–73. The game became standardized with the formation of the Football Association in England on October 26, 1863. A 26-a-side game, however, existed in Florence, Italy, as early as 1530, for which rules were codified in *Discorsa Calcio* in 1580. The world's oldest club was Sheffield F.C. of England, formed on October 24, 1857. Eleven for a side was standardized in 1870.

BIGGEST SCORER: Geoffrey Hurst (left, above) scored 3 goals for England in a World Cup final in 1966. HIGHEST CAREER SCORE: Pelé (right) of Brazil scored his 1,000th goal for his club, Santos, in 1969 in his 909th first-class match. His career total is 1,026.

Highest Scores

Teams. The highest score recorded in any first-class match is 36. This occurred in the Scottish Cup match between Arbroath and Bon Accord on September 5, 1885, when Arbroath won 36–0 on their home ground. But for the lack of nets, the playing time might have been longer and the score possibly even higher.

The highest goal margin recorded in any international match is 17. This occurred in the England vs. Australia match at Sydney on June 30, 1951, when England won 17–0. This match is not listed by England as a *full* international.

Individuals. The most goals scored by one player in a first-class match is 16 by Stains for Racing Club de Lens vs. Aubry-Asturies, in Lens, France, on December 13, 1942.

Artur Friedenreich (b. 1892) is believed to have scored an undocumented 1,329 goals in Brazilian football, but the greatest total of goals scored in a specified period is 1,026 by Edson Arantes do Nascimento (b. Baurú, Brazil, June 28, 1940), known as Pelé, the Brazilian inside left from 1957 to the World Cup final on June 21, 1970. His best year was 1958 with 139, as well as his *milesimo* (1,000th) which came in a penalty for his club, Santos, in the Maracaña Stadium, Rio de Janeiro, when he was playing in his 909th first-class match. He passed 1,000 goals for Santos in club matches during 1972. Franz ("Bimbo") Binder (b. 1911) scored 1,006 goals in 756 games in Austria and Germany between 1930 and 1950.

Fastest Goals

The fastest goal on record is 6 seconds jointly held by Albert Mundy of Aldershot in a Fourth Division match against Hartlepools United at Victoria Ground, Hartlepool, England on October 25, 1958 and Keith Smith of Crystal Palace in a Second Division match against Derby County at Baseball Ground, Derby, England, on December 12, 1964. A goal 4 seconds after the kick-off is claimed by Jim Fryatt of Bradford in a Fourth Division match against Tranmere Rovers at Park Avenue, Bradford, England, on April 25, 1964.

The record for an international match is 3 goals in 3½ minutes by Willie Hall (Tottenham Hotspur) for England against Ireland on November 16, 1938, at Old Trafford, Manchester, England.

Most Appearances

Robert ("Bobby") Moore of West Ham United set a new record of full international appearances by playing in his 107th game for England vs. Italy on June 14, 1973 in Turin. His first appearance was vs. Peru on May 20, 1962.

Longest Match

The world duration record for a first-class match was set in the Copa Libertadores championship in Santos, Brazil, on August 2–3, 1962, when Santos drew 3–3 with Penarol F.C. of Montevideo, Uruguay. The game lasted 3½ hours (with interruptions), from 9:30 p.m. to 1 a.m.

Heaviest Goalkeeper

The biggest goalie on record was Willie J. Foulke of England (1874–1916) who stood 6 feet 3 inches and weighed 311 lbs. By the time he died, he tipped the scales at 364 lbs.

Transfer Fees

The world's highest reported transfer fee is £922,300 ($2,305,750) for the Amsterdam Ajax striker Johann Cruyft, signed by F.C. Barcelona of Spain, on August 18, 1973.

Signing Fee. On May 26, 1961, Luis Suarez, the Barcelona inside-forward was transferred to Internazionale (Milan) for $405,200, of which Suarez himself received a record $165,200.

Crowds and Gates

The greatest recorded crowd at any football match was 205,000 (199,854 paid) for the Brazil vs. Uruguay World Cup final in Rio de Janeiro, Brazil, on July 16, 1950. The receipts were 6,000,000 cruzeiros (then $350,000).

Receipts

The greatest receipts at a World Cup final were £204,805 ($573,454) from an attendance of 96,924 for the match between England and West Germany at the Empire Stadium, Wembley, Greater London, on July 30, 1966.

World Cup

The *Fédération Internationale de Football* (F.I.F.A.) was founded in Paris on May 21, 1904, and instituted the World Cup Competition in 1930, two years after the four British Isles' associations had resigned. The record attendance was for the 1966 competition, which totaled 5,549,521.

The only country to win three times has been Brazil (1958–1962–1970). Brazil was also third in 1938 and second in 1950, and is the only one of the 40 participating countries to have played in all 9 competitions.

The record goal scorer has been Just Fontaine (France) with 13 goals in 6 games in the final stages of the 1958 competition. The most goals scored in a final is 3 by Geoffrey Hurst (West Ham United) for England vs. West Germany on July 30, 1966.

Antonian Carbajal (b. 1923) played for Mexico in goal in the competitions of 1950–54–58–62 and 1966.

Soccer (Amateur)

Most Olympic Wins. The only country to have won the Olympic football title three times is Hungary in 1952, 1964 and 1968. The United Kingdom won in 1908 and 1912 and also the unofficial tournament of 1900. These contests have now virtually ceased to be amateur. The highest Olympic score is Denmark 17 vs. France "A" 1 in 1908.

LARGEST GOALKEEPER: Willie Foulke (England) covered a large part of the goal at 6 feet 3 inches and 311 lbs.

Marathons. The longest recorded 11-a-side soccer marathon played without substitutes is 28 hours by the Brentwood Soccer Club and Village Lanterns Tavern S.C. in the Long Island Soccer Football League on June 21–22, 1973.

The longest recorded authenticated 5-a-side games have been (outdoors) 38 hours 5 minutes by two teams (no substitutes) from Portishead Youth Centre, Bristol, England, ending at 10:15 a.m. on November 15, 1970, and (indoors) 52 hours 20 minutes by two teams (no substitutes) from the Knutton Centre, Newcastle, Staffordshire, England, on March 24–26, 1972.

Largest Crowd. The highest attendance at any amateur match is 100,000 at the English Football Association Amateur Cup Final between Pegasus and Bishop Auckland at Wembley, London, on April 21, 1951.

Heading. The highest recorded number of repetitions for heading a ball is 6,375 in 44 minutes by Tony Marshall, age 17, of St. Austell, Cornwall, England, in November, 1972.

Table Football. The most protracted game of 2-a-side table football on record was one of 170 hours maintained by 8 students from Hatfield Polytechnic, Hertfordshire, England, on February 19–26, 1971.

Squash

(Note: "1971," for example, refers to the 1971–72 season.)

Earliest Champion. Although racquets with a soft ball was evolved in *c.* 1850 at Harrow School (England), there was no recognized champion of any country until J. A. Miskey of Philadelphia won the American Amateur Singles Championship in 1906.

World Title. The inaugural international (world) championships were staged in Australia in August, 1967, when Australia won the team title in Sydney, and Geoffrey B. Hunt (Victoria) took the individual title, both titles being retained in 1969 and 1971.

Most Victories

Open Championship. The most wins in the Open Championship (amateur or professional), held annually in Britain, is seven by Hashim Khan (Pakistan) in 1950–51–52–53–54–55 and 1957.

Amateur Championship. The most wins in the Amateur Championship is six by Abdel Fattah Amr Bey (Egypt), later appointed Ambassador in London, who won in 1931–32–33 and 1935–36–37.

Professional Championship. The most wins in the Professional Championship is five, a record shared by J. St. G. Dear

(Great Britain) in 1935–36–37–38 and 1949, and Hashim Khan (Pakistan) in 1950–51–52–53–54.

Longest Championship Match. The longest recorded championship match was one of 2 hours 13 minutes in the final of the Open Championship of the British Isles in Birmingham in December, 1969, when Jonah P. Barrington (Ireland) beat Geoffrey B. Hunt (Australia) 9–7, 3–9, 3–9, 9–4, 9–4, with the last game lasting 37 minutes.

Most Victories in the Women's Championship. The most wins in the Women's Squash Rackets Championship is 12 by Mrs. Heather McKay (*née* Blundell) of Australia, 1961 to 1972.

Marathon Record. In squash marathons a rest interval of 1 minute is allowed between games and 2 minutes between the 4th and 5th games with 5 minutes additional rest per hour. The rate of play must not exceed 11 games per hour.

The longest recorded squash marathon (under these competition conditions) has been one of 60 hours 10 minutes by Dennis Glennon at Ndola Squash Club, Zambia, on December 1–4, 1972. He played 925 games of which he won 610 against various opponents. The longest single marathon by a pair is 54 hours 45 minutes by Nick Chapman and Derek Thorpe at the New University of Ulster, Coleraine, Northern Ireland, on March 28–31, 1973.

Surfing

Origins. The traditional Polynesian sport of surfing in a canoe (*ehorooe*) was first recorded by the British explorer, Captain James Cook (1728–79) on his third voyage to Tahiti in December, 1771. Surfing on a board (*Amo Amo iluna ka lau oka nalu*) was first described ("most perilous and extraordinary . . . altogether astonishing, and is scarcely to be credited") by Lt. (later Capt.) James King of the Royal Navy in March, 1779, at Kealakekua Bay, Hawaii Island. A surfer was first depicted by this voyage's official artist John Webber. The sport was revived at Waikiki by 1900. Australia's first club, the Bondi Surf Bathers Lifesaving Club, was formed in February, 1906. Hollow boards came in in 1929 and the plastic foam type in 1956.

Highest Waves Ridden. Makaha Beach, Hawaii, provides reputedly the best consistently high waves for surfing, often reaching the rideable limit of 30–35 feet. The highest wave ever ridden was the *tsunami* of "perhaps 50 feet," which struck Minole, Hawaii, on April 3, 1868, and was ridden to save his life by a Hawaiian named Holua.

Longest Ride. About 4 to 6 times each year rideable surfing waves break in Matanchen Bay near San Blas, Nayarit, Mexico, which make rides of *c.* 5,700 feet possible.

WORLD'S LARGEST SWIMMING POOL: The Orthlieb Pool in Casablanca, Morocco, is 1,575 feet long and 246 feet wide.

Swimming

Earliest References. It is recorded that inter-school swimming contests in Japan were ordered by Imperial edict of Emperor Go-Yoozei as early as 1603. Competitive swimming originated in London c. 1837, at which time there were five or more pools, the earliest of which had been opened at St. George's Pier Head, Liverpool, in 1828.

Largest Pools. The largest swimming pool in the world is the salt-water Orthlieb Pool in Casablanca, Morocco. It is 480 meters (1,574.8 feet) long and 75 meters (246 feet) wide, an area of 8.9 acres.

The largest land-locked swimming pool with heated water is the Fleishhacker Pool on Sloat Boulevard, near Great Highway, San Francisco. It measures 1,000 feet by 150 feet (3.44 acres), is up to 14 feet deep, and contains 7,500,000 gallons of heated water. The world's largest competition pool is at Osaka, Japan. It accommodates 25,000 spectators.

Fastest Swimmer. Excluding relay stages with their anticipatory starts, the highest speed reached by a swimmer is 5.05 m.p.h. by David Holmes Edgar (U.S.), who recorded 20.23 seconds for 50 yards in a 25-yard pool at Tuscaloosa, Alabama, on March 4, 1971. Mark Spitz (U.S.), in setting the 100-meter record of 51.22 secs. in 1972, required an average of 4.367 m.p.h.

Most Difficult Dives. Those with the highest tariff (degree of difficulty 3.0) are the "$3\frac{1}{2}$ forward somersault in tuck position, the $1\frac{1}{2}$ forward with triple twist and the backward $2\frac{1}{2}$ somersault piked from the 1-meter board; the reversed $2\frac{1}{2}$ piked and the forward $3\frac{1}{2}$ piked from the 10-meter board." Joaquín Capilla of Mexico has performed a $4\frac{1}{2}$-somersault dive from a 10-meter board, but this is not on the international tariff.

Olympic Swimming Records

Most Olympic Gold Medals. The greatest number of Olympic gold medals won is 9 by Mark Andrew Spitz (U.S.) (b. February 10, 1950), as follows:

100 meter free-style	1972
200 meter free-style	1972
100 meter butterfly	1972
200 meter butterfly	1972
4 × 100 meter free-style relay	1968 and 1972
4 × 200 meter free-style relay	1968 and 1972
4 × 100 meter medley relay	1972

All but one of these performances (the 4 × 200 meter relay of 1968) were also world records at the time.

The record number of gold medals won by a woman is 4 shared by Mrs. Patricia McCormick (*née* Keller) (U.S.) (b. May 12, 1930) with the High and Springboard Diving double in 1952 and 1956 (also the women's record for individual golds) and by Dawn Fraser (now Mrs. Gary Ware) (Australia) (b. September 4, 1937) with the 100 meter free-style (1956–60–64) and the 4 × 100 meter free-style relay (1956).

WOMEN'S CHAMPS: Dawn Fraser (Australia) (above), sprinter, and Mrs. Pat McCormick (U.S.) (right), diver, share the record for Olympic gold medals with 4 each.

MOST OLYMPIC GOLD MEDALS: Mark Spitz (left) won 9 in two Olympics, all but one taken in setting world records. **SUPER-STAR Shane Gould (Australia),** before she was 16 years old, broke every free-style record from 100 to 1,500 meters.

Most Olympic Medals. The most medals won is 11 by Spitz, who in addition to his 9 golds (see above), won a silver (100 m. butterfly) and a bronze (100 m. free-style) both in 1968.

The most medals won by a woman is 8 by Dawn Fraser, who in addition to her 4 golds (see above) won 4 silvers (400 m. free-style 1956, 4 × 100 m. free-style relay 1960 and 1964ᵈ, 4 × 100 m. medley relay 1960).

Most Individual Gold Medals. The record number of individual gold medals won is 4 shared by three swimmers: Charles M. Daniels (U.S.) (b. July 12, 1884) (100 m. free-style 1906 and 1908, 220 yard free-style 1904, 440 yard free-style 1904); Roland Matthes (E. Germany) (b. November 17, 1950) with 100 m. and 200 m. backstroke 1968 and 1972 and Spitz (see above).

Most World Records. Men: 32, Arne Borg (Sweden) (b. 1901), 1921–29. Women: 42, Ragnhild Hveger (Denmark) (b. December 10, 1920), 1936–42.

Long Distance Swimming

A unique achievement in long distance swimming was established in 1966 by the cross-channel swimmer Mihir Sen of Calcutta, India. These were the Palk Strait from India to Ceylon (in 25 hours 36 minutes on April 5–6); the Strait of Gibraltar (Europe to Africa in 8 hours 1 minute on August 24); the Dardanelles (Gallipoli, Europe, to Sedulbahir, Asia Minor, in 13 hours 55 minutes on September 12) and the entire length of the Panama Canal in 34 hours 15 minutes on October 29–31. He had earlier swum the English Channel in 14 hours 45 minutes on September 27, 1958.

Longest Distance Ocean Swim

The longest recorded ocean swim is one of 90¾ miles by Walter Poenisch (U.S.) in the Florida Straits (in a shark cage) in 21 hours 18 minutes on June 27–28, 1972.

Treading Water

The duration record for treading water (vertical posture in an 8-foot square without touching the lane markers) is 25½ hours nonstop by M. C. "Monnie" Lewis at Winter Park, Florida, on September 2–3, 1973. At Brigham Young University, Utah, on November 15–17, 1973, Mark Aikele, Kris Haeger, Carolyn Royce Snapp and Sue Troub logged 32 hours with 5 min. rest breaks each completed hour.

Ice Swimming

Jenny Kammersgård, 53, swam 200 meters in 7 minutes 13 seconds in Denmark on February 19, 1972 in water at a temperature of 34.7° F.

Most Dangerous Swim

One of the most dangerous swims on record was the unique crossing of the Potoro River in Guyana, South America, just above the 741-foot high Kaieteur Falls by Private Robert Howatt (U.K.) (the Black Watch) on April 17, 1955. The river is 464 feet wide at the lip of the falls.

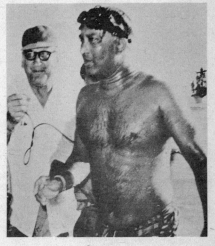

LONG DISTANCE SWIMMING RECORD HOLDER: Mihir Sen (India) has swum from India to Ceylon, and across the Dardanelles, Strait of Gibraltar, and the length of the Panama Canal.

SWIMMING—WORLD RECORDS—MEN

At distances recognized by the Fédération Internationale de Natation Amateur as of February 1, 1974. F.I.N.A. no longer recognizes any records made for non-metric distances. (A performance marked with † is the best improvement awaiting ratification.) Only performances set up in 50-meter pools are recognized as World Records.

Distance	min. sec.	Name and Nationality	Place	Date
		FREE-STYLE		
100 meters	51.22	Mark Spitz (U.S.)	Munich, West Germany	Sept. 3, 1972
200 meters	1:52.78	Mark Spitz (U.S.)	Munich, West Germany	Aug. 29, 1972
400 meters	3:58.18	Rick De Mont (U.S.)	Belgrade, Yugoslavia	Sept. 6, 1973
800 meters	8:15.88†	Stephen Holland (Australia)	Christchurch, New Zealand	Feb. 1, 1974
1,500 meters	15:31.85	Stephen Holland (Australia)	Belgrade, Yugoslavia	Sept. 8, 1973
4 × 100 Relay	3:26.42	U.S. National Team	Munich, West Germany	Aug. 28, 1972
		(David H. Edgar, John Murphy, Jerry Heidenreich, Mark Spitz)		
4 × 200 Relay	7:33.22	U.S. National Team	Belgrade, Yugoslavia	Sept. 7, 1973
		(Kurt Krumpleholz, Robin Backhaus, Richard Klatt, John Montgomery)		
		BREAST STROKE		
100 meters	1:04.02	John Hencken (U.S.)	Belgrade, Yugoslavia	Sept. 4, 1973
200 meters	2:19.28	David Andrew Wilkie (U.K.)	Belgrade, Yugoslavia	Sept. 6, 1973
		BUTTERFLY STROKE		
100 meters	54.37	Mark Spitz (U.S.)	Munich, West Germany	Aug. 31, 1972
200 meters	2:00.70	Mark Spitz (U.S.)	Munich, West Germany	Aug. 28, 1972
		BACK STROKE		
100 meters	*56.3*	Roland Matthes (East Germany)	Leipzig, East Germany	Apr. 9, 1972
100 meters	56.30	Roland Matthes (East Germany)	Munich, West Germany	Sept. 4, 1972
200 meters	2:01.87	Roland Matthes (East Germany)	Belgrade, Yugoslavia	Sept. 6, 1973
		INDIVIDUAL MEDLEY		
200 meters	2:07.17	Gunnar Larsson (Sweden)	Munich, West Germany	Sept. 3, 1972
400 meters	4:30.81	Gary Hall (U.S.)	Chicago, Illinois	Aug. 3, 1972
		MEDLEY RELAY		
		(Back Stroke, Breast Stroke, Butterfly Stroke, Free Style)		
4 × 100 meters	3:48.16	U.S. National Team	Munich, West Germany	Sept. 4, 1972
		(Michael E. Stamm, Thomas E. Bruce, Mark Spitz, Jerry Heidenreich)		

* Record accepted timed to 1/10th second.

Channel Swimming

Earliest Man. The first man to swim across the English Channel (without a life jacket) was the merchant navy captain Matthew Webb (1848–83) (G.B.), who swam breaststroke from Dover, England, to Cap Gris Nez, France, in 21 hours 45 minutes on August 24–25, 1875. Webb swam an estimated 38 miles to make the 21-mile crossing. Paul Boyton (U.S.) had swum from Cap Gris Nez to the South Foreland in his patent lifesaving suit in 23 hours 30 minutes on May 28–29, 1875. There is good evidence that Jean-Marie Saletti, a French soldier, escaped from a British prison hulk off Dover by swimming to Boulogne in July or August, 1815. The first crossing from France to England was made by Enrique Tiraboschi, a wealthy Italian living in Argentina, who crossed in 16 hours 33 minutes on August 11, 1923, to win a $5,000 prize.

Woman. The first woman to succeed was Gertrude Ederle (U.S.) who swam from Cap Gris Nez, France, to Dover, England, on August 6, 1926, in the then record time of 14 hours 39 minutes. The first woman to swim from England to France was Florence Chadwick of California, in 16 hours 19 minutes on September 11, 1951. She repeated this on September 4, 1953, and October 12, 1955.

Youngest. The youngest conqueror is Leonore Modell of Sacramento, California, who swam from Cap Gris Nez to near Dover in 15 hours 33 minutes on September 3, 1964, when aged 14 years 5 months.

Oldest. The oldest conqueror of the 21-mile crossing has been William E. (Ned) Barnie, who was 55 when he swam from France to England in 15 hours 1 minute on August 16, 1951.

Fastest. The official Channel Swimming Association record is 9 hours 35 minutes by Barry Watson, 25, of Yorkshire, England, who swam from France to England on August 16, 1964. The fastest

CHANNEL SWIMMING WOMAN RECORD HOLDER: Lynne Cox (U.S.) at age 16 on August 10, 1973, made the 21-mile crossing in 9 hours 36 minutes.

SWIMMING—WORLD RECORDS—WOMEN

Distance	Min. sec.	Name and Nationality	Place	Date
		FREE-STYLE		
100 meters	57.54	Kornelia Ender (E. Germany)	Belgrade, Yugoslavia	Sept. 9, 1973
200 meters	2:03.56	Shane Elizabeth Gould (Australia)	Munich, West Germany	Sept. 1, 1972
400 meters	4:18.07	Keena Rothhammer (U.S.)	Louisville, Kentucky	Aug. 22, 1973
800 meters	8:50.1*	Jenny Turrell (Australia)	Sidney, Australia	Jan. 1, 1974
1,500 meters	16:49.9*	Jenny Turrell (Australia)	Sidney, Australia	Dec. 7, 1973
		FREE-STYLE RELAY		
4 × 100 meters	3:52.45	East German National Team	Belgrade, Yugoslavia	Sept. 8, 1973
		(Kornelia Ender, Andrea Eife, Andrea Hübner, Sylvia Eichner)		
		BREAST STROKE		
100 meters	1:13.58	Catherine Carr (U.S.)	Munich, West Germany	Sept. 2, 1972
200 meters	2:38.5*	Catie Ball (U.S.)	Los Angeles, California	Aug. 26, 1972
		BUTTERFLY STROKE		
100 meters	1:03.05	Kornelia Ender (E. Germany)	East Berlin, E. Germany	Apr. 14, 1973
200 meters	2:13.76	Rosemarie Kother (E. Germany)	Belgrade, Yugoslavia	Sept. 8, 1973
		BACK STROKE		
100 meters	1:04.78**	Wendy Cook (Canada)	Christchurch, New Zealand	Jan. 31, 1974
200 meters	2:19.19	Melissa Belote (U.S.)	Munich, West Germany	Sept. 4, 1972
		INDIVIDUAL MEDLEY		
200 meters	2:20.51	Andrea Hübner (E. Germany)	Belgrade, Yugoslavia	Sept. 4, 1973
400 meters	4:57.51	Gudrun Wegner (E. Germany)	Belgrade, Yugoslavia	Sept. 6, 1973
		MEDLEY RELAY		
4 × 100 meters	4:16.84	East German National Team	Belgrade, Yugoslavia	Sept. 4, 1973
		(Back Stroke, Breast Stroke, Butterfly Stroke, Free Style)		
		(Ulriche Richter, Renate Vogel, Rosemarie Kother, Kornelia Ender)		

* Record accepted timed to 1/10th second.
** Set in medley relay.

time ever by a woman is 9 hours 36 minutes by Lynne Cox (U.S.), 16, who swam from England to France on August 10, 1973.

First Double Crossing. Antonio Abertondo (Argentina), aged 42, swam from England to France in 18 hours 50 minutes (8:35 a.m. on September 20 to 3:25 a.m. on September 21, 1961) and after about 4 minutes rest returned to England in 24 hours 16 minutes, landing at St. Margaret's Bay at 3:45 a.m. on September 22, 1961, to complete the first "double crossing" in 43 hours 10 minutes.

Fastest Double Crossing. The fastest double crossing, and only the second ever achieved, was one of 30 hours 3 minutes by Edward (Ted) Erikson, aged 37, a physiochemist from Chicago. He left St. Margaret's Bay, near Dover, at 8:20 p.m. on September 19, 1965, and landed at a beach about a mile west of Calais, after a swim of 14 hours 15 minutes. After a rest of about 10 minutes, he returned and landed at South Foreland Point, east of Dover, at 2:23 a.m. on September 21, 1965.

Most Conquests. Three swimmers have swum the Channel six times: Brojan Das (Pakistan), 1958–61; Thomas J. Hetzel (U.S.), 1967–73; Mervyn Sharp (U.K.), 1967–73. Greta Andersen-Sonnichsen (U.S.) has swum the Channel five times (1957–65).

Underwater. The first underwater cross-Channel swim was achieved by Fred Baldasare (U.S.), aged 38, who completed the distance from France to England with scuba in 18 hours 1 minute on July 11, 1962. Simon Paterson, aged 20, a frogman from Egham, Surrey, England, traveled underwater from France to England with an airhose attached to his pilot boat in 14 hours 50 minutes on July 28, 1962.

In other underwater swimming, Vladimir Kon covered 100 meters underwater with flippers in 40.6 seconds at Chelyabinsk, U.S.S.R., on March 10, 1972.

Table Tennis

Earliest Reference. The earliest evidence relating to a game resembling table tennis has been found in the catalogues of London sporting goods manufacturers in the 1880's. The old Ping Pong Association was formed there in 1902, but the game proved only a temporary craze until resuscitated in 1921.

Marathon Records. In the Swaythling Cup final match between Austria and Rumania in Prague, Czechoslovakia, in 1936, the play lasted for 25 or 26 hours, spread over three nights. In this same 1936 tournament, Alex Ehrlich (Poland) and Paneth Farcas (Rumania) had an opening rally that lasted 2 hours 12 minutes. On April 14,

FASTEST SMASH IN TABLE TENNIS: The ball flies at more than 60 m.p.h. when smashed by Chuang Tse-tung of China.

Most Wins in Table Tennis World Championships
(Instituted 1926–27)

Event	Name and Nationality	Times	Date
Men's Singles (St. Bride's Vase)	G. Viktor Barna (Hungary)	5	1930, 32, 33, 34, 35
Women's Singles (G. Geist Prize)	Angelica Rozeanu (Rumania)	6	1950, 51, 52, 53, 54, 55
Men's Doubles	G. Viktor Barna (Hungary) with two different partners	8	1929, 30, 31, 32, 33, 34, 35, 39
Women's Doubles	Maria Mednyanszky (Hungary) with three different partners	7	1928, 30, 31, 32, 33, 34, 35
Mixed Doubles (Men)	Ferenc Sido (Hungary) with two different partners	4	1949, 50, 52, 53
(Women)	M. Mednyanszky (Hungary) with three different partners	6	1927, 28, 30, 31, 33, 34

G. Viktor Barna gained a personal total of 15 world titles, while 18 have been won by Miss Mednyanszky

Note: With the staging of championships biennially, the breaking of the above records would now be virtually impossible.

Men's Team (Swaythling Cup)	Hungary	11	1927, 28, 29, 30, 31, 33, 34, 35, 38, 49, 52
Women's Team (Marcel Corbillon Cup)	Japan	8	1952, 1954, 1957, 1959, 1961, 1963, 1967, 1971

1973, Nick Krajancie and Graham Lassen *staged* a 2 hour 31 minute rally in Auckland, New Zealand.

The longest recorded time for a marathon singles match by two players is 73 hours 10 minutes by Peter Broad and Gary Stevenson of Maranui S.L.S.C. at Lyall Bay, New Zealand, on June 2–5, 1973. Craig Harris, 16, played 77 hours 7 minutes on December 20–23, 1971, against a series of opponents in Davis, California.

The longest doubles marathon by 4 players is 42 hours 1 minute by 4 members of the Chatham Technical High School for Boys, Kent, England, on June 27–29, 1973.

Marathons as long as 650 hours have been achieved by 5 players maintaining a continuous game with substitutions, notably a group in Binghamton, New York, in July, 1973.

Highest Speed. No conclusive measurements have been published, but Chuang Tse-tung (China) the world champion of 1961–63–65, has probably smashed at a speed of more than 60 m.p.h. The ball weighs $2\frac{1}{2}$ grams.

Youngest International. The youngest international (probably in any sport) was Joy Foster, aged 8, the 1958 Jamaican singles and mixed doubles champion.

Tennis

Origins. The modern game of lawn tennis is generally agreed to have evolved as an outdoor form of Royal Tennis, and to have first become organized with the court and equipment devised, and patented in February, 1874, by Major Walter Clopton Wingfield, of England (1833–1912). This was introduced as "sphairistike," but the game soon became known as lawn tennis.

Amateurs were permitted to play with and against professionals in Open tournaments starting in 1965.

Oldest Courts. The oldest court for Royal Tennis is one built in Paris in 1496. The oldest of 16 surviving tennis courts in the British Isles is the Royal Tennis Court at Hampton Court Palace, which was built by order of King Henry VIII in 1529–30, and rebuilt by order of Charles II in 1660.

Greatest Domination. The earliest occasion upon which any player secured all four of the world's major titles was in 1935 when Frederick John Perry (U.K.) (b. 1909) won the French title, having won Wimbledon (1934), the U.S. title (1933–34) and the Australian title (1934).

The first player to hold all four titles simultaneously was J. Donald Budge (U.S.) (b. 1915), who won the championships of Wimbledon (1937), the U.S. (1937), Australia (1938), and France (1938). He subsequently retained Wimbledon (1938) and the U.S. (1938). Rodney George Laver (Australia) (b. August 9, 1938) repeated this grand slam in 1962 and in 1969 became the first to take all four of these now Open titles.

MOST GAMES AND LONGEST MATCHES

Note: The increasing option since 1970 by tournament organisers to use various "tie break" systems, which are precisely designed to stop long sets, is reducing the likelihood of these records being broken and they may shortly become of mere historic interest.

	No. of Games	Players and Score	Place and Date
Any match	147	Dick Leach–Dick Dell (U. of Mich.) bt. Tommy Mozur–Lenny Schloss 3–6, 49–47, 22–20	Newport, R.I., August 18–19, 1967
Any singles	126	Roger Taylor (G.B.) bt. Wieslaw Gasiorek (Poland) 27–29, 31–29, 6–4 (4 hrs. 35 mins.)	King's Cup, Warsaw, Poland, November 5, 1966
Any women's singles	62	Kathy Blake (U.S.) bt. Elena Subirats (Mexico) 12–10, 6–8, 14–12	Piping Rock, Locust Valley, N.Y., 1966
Any women's match	81	Nancy Richey–Carole Graebner (née Caldwell) bt. Justina Bricka–Carol Hanks (all U.S.) 31–33, 6–1, 6–4	South Orange, N.J., 1964
Any mixed doubles	71	William F. Talbot–Margaret du Pont (née Osborne) bt. Robert Falkenburg–Gertrude Moran (all U.S.) 27–25, 5–7, 6–1	Forest Hills, N.Y., 1948
Any set	96	See middle set of any match above	
Longest time for Any match	6 hrs. 23 mins.	Mark Cox–Robert K. Wilson (U.K.) bt. Charles M. Pasarell, R. A. (Pancho) Gonzales (U.S.) 26–24, 17–19, 30–28	U.S. Indoor Championships, Salisbury, Md., August 18–19, 1967
Any Wimbledon match	112	R. A. (Pancho) Gonzales (U.S.) bt. Charles M. Pasarell (U.S.) 22–24, 1–6, 16–14, 6–3, 11–9	First round, June 24–25, 1969
Any Wimbledon doubles	98	Eugene L. Scott (U.S.)–Nicola Pilic (Yugoslavia) bt. G. Cliff Richey (U.S.)–Torben Ulrich (Denmark) 19–21, 12–10, 6–4, 4–6, 9–7	First round, June 22, 1966
Any Wimbledon set	62	Pancho Segura (Ecuador)–Alex Olmedo (Peru) bt. Abe A. Segal–Gordon L. Forbes (S. Africa) 32–30	Second round, June 1968
Longest time for any Wimbledon match	5 hrs. 12 mins.	See any Wimbledon match above	
Wimbledon men's final	58	Jaroslav Drobny (then Egypt) bt. Kenneth R. Rosewall (Australia) 13–11, 4–6, 6–2, 9–7	Final, July 1954
Wimbledon men's doubles Final	70	John D. Newcombe–Anthony D. Roche (Australia) bt. Kenneth R. Rosewall–Frederick S. Stolle (Australia) 3–6, 8–6, 5–7, 14–12, 6–3	Final, July 1968
Wimbledon women's final	46	Margaret Smith Court (Australia) bt. Billie Jean Moffitt King (U.S.) 14–12, 11–9 (2 hrs. 25 mins.)	Final, July 1970
Wimbledon women's	38	Mme. Simone Mathieu (France)–Elizabeth Ryan (U.S.) bt. Freda James (now Hammersley)–Adeline Maud Yorke (both G.B.) 6–2, 9–11, 6–4	Final, July 1933
Doubles final		Rosemary Casals–Billie Jean King (both U.S.) bt. Maria E. Bueno (Brazil)–Nancy Richey (U.S.) 9–11, 6–4, 6–2	Final, July 1963

Wimbledon mixed Doubles final	48	Eric W. Sturgess-Mrs. Sheila Summers (S. Africa) bt. John E. Bromwich (Australia)-Alice Louise Brough (U.S.) 9-7, 9-11, 7-5	Final, July 1949
Any Davis Cup rubber	122	Stanley Smith-Erik Von Dillen (U.S.) bt. Jaime Filliol-Pat Cornejo (Chile) 7-9, 37-39, 8-6, 6-1, 6-3	American Zone Tie, 1973
Any Davis Cup singles	86	Arthur Ashe (U.S.) bt. Christian Kuhnke (Germany) 6-8, 10-12, 9-7, 13-11, 6-4	Challenge Round, Cleveland, O., 1970
Any Davis Cup tie i.e. 5 rubbers	281	Italy beat U.S. 3 rubbers to 2	Inter Zone Final, Perth, Western Australia, 1960

WOMAN GRAND SLAMMER: Margaret Smith Court (Australia) won all four major tournaments in 1970, but lost to 55-year-old Bobby Riggs (U.S.) in a famous female vs. male duel in 1973.

LONGEST WIMBLEDON MATCH: Pancho Gonzales (U.S.) played 112 games in 5 hours 12 minutes in 1969, and finally beat Charles Pasarell (U.S.).

Tennis ▪ 153

GRAND SLAM WINNERS: The only men to win all four major titles in the same year were Rod Laver (left) of Australia who performed the feat in 1962 and 1969, and Don Budge (right) of the U.S. who did it in 1937-38.

Pierre Etchbaster retired in 1955 at the age of 60 after 27 years as the world amateur tennis champion (see page 8).

Two women players also have won all these four titles in the same tennis year. The first was Maureen Catherine Connolly (U.S.). She won the United States title in 1951, Wimbledon in 1952, retained the U.S. title in 1952, won the Australian in 1953, the French in 1953 and Wimbledon again in 1953. She won her third U.S. title in 1953, her second French title in 1954, and her third Wimbledon title in 1954. Miss Connolly (later Mrs. Norman Brinker) was seriously injured in a riding accident shortly before the 1954 U.S. championships; she died in June, 1969, aged only 34.

The second woman to win the "grand slam" was Margaret Smith Court (Australia) in 1970. In the same year she earned $100,000 in prize money. (See photo, previous page.)

Greatest Crowd. The greatest crowd at a tennis match was the 30,492 who came to the Houston Astrodome in Houston, Texas, on September 20, 1973, to watch Billie Jean King beat Bobby Riggs in straight sets in the so-called "Tennis Match of the Century."

Fastest Service. The fastest service ever *measured* was one of 154 m.p.h. by Michael Sangster (U.K.) in June, 1963. Crossing the net the ball was traveling at 108 m.p.h. Some players consider the service of Robert Falkenberg (U.S.), the 1948 Wimbledon champion, as the fastest ever used.

Wimbledon Records

(The first Championship was in 1877. Professionals first played in 1968.) From 1971 the tie-break system was introduced, which effectually prevents sets proceeding beyond a 17th game, i.e. 9–8.

Most Appearances. Arthur W. Gore (1868–1928) of the U.K. made 36 appearances between 1888 and 1927, and was in 1909 at 41 years the oldest singles winner ever. In 1964, Jean Borotra (born August 13, 1898) of France made his 35th appearance since 1922. In 1972, he appeared in the Veterans' Doubles, aged 73.

Most Wins. Elizabeth (Bunny) Ryan (U.S.) (b. 1894) won her first title in 1914 and her nineteenth in 1934 (12 women's doubles with 5 different partners and 7 mixed doubles with 5 different partners). The post-war record is 17 championships by Billie Jean King (née Moffitt) (U.S.) with 5 singles, 9 women's doubles, and 3 mixed doubles, 1961–73.

The greatest number of wins by a man at Wimbledon has been 15 by Hugh Lawrence Doherty (1875–1919) who won 5 singles (1902–3–4–5–6), 8 men's doubles (1897–8–9–1900–1 and 1903–4–5), partnered by his brother Reginald F. Doherty (1872–1910), and two mixed doubles (then unofficial) in 1901–2, partnered by Mrs. Charlotte Sterry (née Cooper).

The greatest number of singles wins was eight by Mrs. F. S. Moody (née Helen Wills) (b. October 6, 1905) (U.S.), who won in 1927, 1928, 1929, 1930, 1932, 1933, 1935 and 1938.

The greatest number of singles wins by a man was seven by William C. Renshaw (G.B.) (1861–1904), in 1881–2–3–4–5–6–9. He also won 7 doubles titles (1880–1–4–5–6–8–9) partnered by his twin brother (James) Ernest.

WIMBLEDON CHAMPION: Billie Jean King (U.S.) has won 17 different titles since 1961, and has played in the longest women's singles and doubles finals. She also played before the largest crowd at a tennis match — 30,492 — in beating Bobby Riggs (U.S.) in a challenge match in the Astrodome, Houston, Texas, in 1973 and won $100,000 in prize money.

The greatest number of doubles wins by men was 8 by the brothers R. F. and H. L. Doherty (G.B.), as mentioned above.

The most wins in women's doubles were the 12 by Elizabeth Ryan (U.S.), mentioned above.

The greatest number of mixed doubles wins was 7 by Elizabeth Ryan (U.S.), as noted above. The men's record is four wins, shared by Elias Victor Seixas (b. August 30, 1923) (U.S.) in 1953–54–55–56, and Kenneth N. Fletcher (b. June 15, 1940) (Australia) in 1963–65–66–68.

Youngest Champions. The youngest champion ever at Wimbledon was Charlotte Dod (1871–1960), who was 15 years 8 months old when she won in 1887.

The youngest male singles champion was Wilfred Baddeley (born January 11, 1872), who won the Wimbledon title in 1891 at the age of 19.

Richard Dennis Ralston (born July 27, 1942), of Bakersfield, California, was 25 days short of his 18th birthday when he won the men's doubles with Rafael H. Osuna (1938–69), of Mexico, in 1960.

Professional Tennis

Highest Prize Money. The highest prize money won in a year is $292,717 by Rod Laver (Australia) in 1971. His career total in 9 professional seasons was thus brought to a record $1,006,947. In 1973, Mrs. Margaret Court (*née* Smith) (Australia) won more than $192,000 for a feminine record.

Tennis Marathons

The longest recorded non-stop tennis game is one of 73 hours 25 minutes by Mel Baleson, 21, and Glen Grisillo, 29, both of South Africa, who played 1,224 games at the University of Nevada, Reno, Nevada, May 6–9, 1971. The longest doubles is one of 41 hours 35 minutes by 4 players of Stobsmuir Lawn Tennis Club in Dundee, Scotland, ending July 1, 1973.

Davis Cup

Most Victories. The greatest number of wins in the Davis Cup (instituted 1900) has been (inclusive of 1973) the United States with 24 over Australia's 23 wins.

Individual Performance. Nicola Pietrangeli (Italy) played 164 rubbers, 1954 to 1972, winning 120. He played 110 singles (winning 78) and 54 doubles (winning 42). He took part in 66 ties.

In a singles match the greatest number of games played was 86 when at Cleveland, Ohio, in the 1970 Challenge Round, Arthur Ashe (U.S.) beat Christian Kuhnke (W. Germany) 6–8, 10–12, 9–7, 13–11, 6–4.

Tiddleywinks

Origin. This game was first espoused by adults in 1955 when Cambridge University issued a challenge to Oxford.

Speed. The record for potting 24 winks from 18 inches is 21.8

seconds by Stephen Williams of Altrincham Grammar School, England, in May, 1966.

Marathon. Allen R. Astles of the University of Wales potted 10,000 winks in 3 hours 51 minutes 46 seconds in February, 1966. The most protracted game on record is one of 170 hours by 6 players of Quinton Kynaston School, London, on January 1–8, 1973.

Track and Field

Earliest References. Track and field athletics date from the ancient Olympic Games. The earliest accurately known Olympiad dates from July 21 or 22, 776 B.C., at which celebration Coroebus won the foot race. The oldest surviving measurements are a long jump of 23 feet 1½ inches by Chionis of Sparta in *c.* 656 B.C. and a discus throw of 100 cubits by Protesilaus.

Fastest Runner. Robert Lee Hayes (born December 20, 1942), of Jacksonville, Florida, was timed at 26.9 m.p.h. at the 75-yard mark of a 100-yard race in May, 1964. It has been estimated that between the 60- and the 75-yard marks at St. Louis, Missouri, on June 21, 1963, Hayes was running at 27.89 m.p.h. in his world

FASTEST WOMAN: Wyomia Tyus (U.S.) (left) was clocked at 23.78 m.p.h. in Russia in 1965. FASTEST SPRINTER: Chi Cheng (Taiwan) (right) was the first and only woman to run 100 yards in 10 seconds flat. She also holds the record at 220 yards with turn at 22.6 seconds.

record 9.1 sec. 100 yards. Wyomia Tyus (U.S.) was timed at 23.78 m.p.h. in Kiev, U.S.S.R., on July 31, 1965.

Earliest Landmarks. The first time 10 seconds ("even time") was bettered for 100 yards under championship conditions was when John Owen recorded 9⅘ seconds in the A.A.U. Championships at Analostan Island, Washington, D.C., on October 11, 1890. The first recorded instance of 6 feet being cleared in the high jump was when Marshall Jones Brooks jumped 6 feet 0⅛ inch at Marston, near Oxford, England, on March 17, 1876. The breaking of the "4 minute barrier" in the one mile was first achieved by Dr. Roger Gilbert Bannister (born Harrow, England, March 23, 1929), when he recorded 3 minutes 59.4 seconds on the Iffley Road track, Oxford, at 6:10 p.m. on May 6, 1954.

World Record Breakers

Oldest. The greatest age at which anyone has broken a standard world record is 35 years 255 days in the case of Dana Zátopkova, (*née* Ingrova) (born September 19, 1922), of Czechoslovakia, who broke the women's javelin record with 182 feet 10 inches at Prague, Czechoslovakia, on June 1, 1958.

On June 20, 1948, Mikko Hietanen (Finland) (born September 22, 1911) bettered his own world 30,000-meter record with 1 hour 40 minutes 46.4 secs. at Jyväskylä, Finland, when aged 36 years 272 days.

Youngest. Doreen Lumley (born September, 1921) of New Zealand, equaled the world's 100-yard-dash record for women with 11.0 seconds at Auckland, N.Z., on March 11, 1939, when aged only 17 years 6 months.

Most Records in a Day. The only athlete to have his name entered in the world records 6 times in one day was J. C. "Jesse" Owens (U.S.) who at Ann Arbor, Michigan. on May 25, 1935, equaled the 100-yard running record with 9.4 secs. at 3:15 p.m.; long-jumped 26 feet 8¼ inches at 3:25 p.m.; ran 220 yards (straight away) in 20.3 secs. at 3:45 p.m., and 220 yards over low hurdles in 22.6 secs. at 4 p.m. The two 220-yard runs were also ratified as 200-meter world records.

Running Backwards. The fastest time recorded for running 100 yards backwards is 13.5 sec. by Bill Robinson (1878–1949) in the U.S. early in the century.

Standing High Jump. The best standing high jump is 5 feet 9¼ inches by Johan Christian Evandt (Norway) at Oslo, Norway, on March 4, 1962.

Standing Long Jump. Joe Darby (1861–1937), the famous Victorian professional jumper from Dudley, Worcestershire, England, jumped a measured 12 feet 1½ inches *without* weights at

Dudley Castle, on May 28, 1890. Evandt (see above) achieved 11 feet 11¾ inches as an amateur in Reykjavik, Iceland, on March 11, 1962.

Three-Legged Race. The fastest recorded time for a 100-yard three-legged race is 11.0 seconds by Harry L. Hillman and Lawson Robertson at Brooklyn, New York City, on April 24, 1909.

Highest Jumper. There are several reported instances of high jumpers exceeding the official world record height of 7 feet 6½ inches. The earliest of these came from unsubstantiated reports of Tutsi tribesmen in Central Africa clearing up to 8 feet 2½ inches, definitely however, from inclined take-offs. The greatest height cleared above an athlete's own head is 17⅝ inches, achieved by Ni Chih-chin of China (b. April 14, 1942) when clearing 7 feet 6⅛ inches in an exhibition at Changsha, Hunan, on November 8, 1970. He stands 6 feet 0½ inches tall.

The greatest height cleared by a woman above her own head is 7.48 inches by Yordanka Blagoyeva (Bulgaria) who stands 5 feet 8.9 inches and jumped 6 feet 4½ inches at Zagreb, Yugoslavia, on September 24, 1972.

Most Olympic Gold Medals. The most Olympic gold medals won is 10 (an absolute Olympic record) by Ray C. Ewry (U.S.) (b. October 14, 1873, d. September 29, 1937) with:

Standing High Jump	1900, 1904, 1906, 1908
Standing Long Jump	1900, 1904, 1906, 1908
Standing Triple Jump	1900, 1904

The most gold medals won by a woman is 4, a record shared by Francina E. Blankers-Koen (Netherlands) (b. April 26, 1918) with 100 m., 200 m., 80 m. hurdles and 4 × 100 m. relay (1948) and Betty Cuthbert (Australia) (b. April 20, 1938) with 100 m., 200 m., 4 × 100 m. relay (1956) and 400 m. (1964).

Most Olympic Medals. The most medals won is 12 (9 gold and 3 silver) by Paavo Johannes Nurmi (Finland) (1897–1973) with:

1920	Gold: 10,000 m.; Cross Country, Individual and Team; silver: 5,000 m.
1924	Gold: 1,500 m.; 5,000 m.; 3,000 m. Team; Cross Country, Individual and Team.
1928	Gold: 10,000 m.; silver: 5,000 m.; 3,000 m. steeplechase.

The most medals won by a woman athlete is 7 by Shirley de la Hunty (*née* Strickland) (Australia) (b. July 18, 1925) with 3 gold, 1 silver and 3 bronze in the 1948, 1952 and 1956 games.

Most Wins at One Games. The most gold medals at one celebration is 5 by Nurmi in 1924 (see above) and the most individual is 4 by Alvin C. Kraenzlein (U.S.) (1876–1928) in 1900 with 60 m., 110 m. hurdles, 200 m. hurdles and long jump.

WORLD RECORDS—MEN

The complete list of World Records for the 54 scheduled men's events (excluding the 6 walking records, see under Walking) passed by the International Amateur Athletic Federation as of February 2, 1974. Those marked with an asterisk * are awaiting ratification.

RUNNING

Event	mins. secs.	Name and Nationality	Place	Date
100 yards	9.1	Robert Lee Hayes (U.S.)	St. Louis, Missouri	June 21, 1963
	9.1	Harry Winston Jerome (Canada)	Edmonton, Alberta, Canada	July 15, 1966
	9.1	James Ray Hines (U.S.)	Houston, Texas	May 13, 1967
	9.1	Charles Edward Greene (U.S.)	Provo, Utah	June 15, 1967
	9.1	John Wesley Carlos (U.S.)	Fresno, California	May 10, 1969
	9.1	Steve Williams (U.S.)	Fresno, California	May 12, 1973
220 yards (straight)	19.5	Tommie C. Smith (U.S.)	San Jose, California	May 7, 1966
220 yards (turn)	20.0	Tommie C. Smith (U.S.)	Sacramento, California	June 11, 1966
440 yards	44.5	John Smith (U.S.)	Eugene, Oregon	June 26, 1971
880 yards	1:44.6	Richard Wohlhuter (U.S.)	Los Angeles, California	May 27, 1973
1 mile	3:51.1	James Ronald Ryun (U.S.)	Bakersfield, California	June 23, 1967
2 miles	8:13.8	Brendan Foster (U.K.)	London, England	Aug. 27, 1973
3 miles	12:47.8	Emiel Puttemans (Belgium)	Brussels, Belgium	Sept. 20, 1972
6 miles	26:47.0	Ronald William Clarke (Australia)	Oslo, Norway	July 14, 1965
10 miles	46:04.2	Willy Polleunis (Belgium)	Brussels, Belgium	Sept. 20, 1972
15 miles	1H 12:22.6*	Seppo Nikkari (Finland)	Jyväskylä, Finland	Oct. 14, 1973
100 meters	9.9	James Ray Hines (U.S.)	Sacramento, California	June 20, 1968
	9.9	Ronald Ray Smith (U.S.)	Sacramento, California	June 20, 1968
	9.9	Charles Edward Greene (U.S.)	Sacramento, California	June 20, 1968
	9.9	James Ray Hines (U.S.)	Mexico City, Mexico	Oct. 14, 1968
	9.9	Eddie Hart (U.S.)	Eugene, Oregon	July 1, 1972
	9.9	Reynaud Robinson (U.S.)	Eugene, Oregon	July 1, 1972
200 meters (straight)	19.5	Tommie C. Smith (U.S.)	San Jose, California	May 7, 1966
200 meters (turn)	19.8	Tommie C. Smith (U.S.)	Mexico City, Mexico	Oct. 16, 1968
400 meters	43.8	Lee Edward Evans (U.S.)	Mexico City, Mexico	Oct. 18, 1968
800 meters	1:43.7	Marcello Fiasconaro (Italy)	Milan, Italy	June 27, 1973
1,000 meters	2:16.0	Daniel Malan (South Africa)	Munich, West Germany	June 24, 1973

FASTEST HUMANS EVER: Tommie Smith (U.S.) (top left) holds world records at 200 yards and 200 meters, both straight and with turn. James Ray Hines (U.S.) (top right) has twice run 100 meters at 9.9 seconds to share that record, and also shares the 100-yard record at 9.1 seconds. Lee Evans (U.S.) (lower left) is the champion at 400 meters.

QUICKEST SIX MILES: Ron Clarke (Australia) holds the world record for 6 miles at 26 minutes 47 seconds.

RUNNING *(continued)*

Event	mins. secs.	Name and Nationality	Place	Date
1,500 meters	3:32.2	Filbert Bayi (Tanzania)	Christchurch, New Zealand	Feb. 2, 1974
2,000 meters	4:56.2	Michel Jazy (France)	Saint-Maur des Fossés, France	Oct. 12, 1966
3,000 meters	7:37.6	Emiel Puttemans (Belgium)	Aarhus, Denmark	Sept. 14, 1972
5,000 meters	13:13.0	Emiel Puttemans (Belgium)	Brussels, Belgium	Sept. 20, 1972
10,000 meters	27:30.8	David Colin Bedford (U.K.)	London, England	July 13, 1973
20,000 meters	57:44.4	Gaston Roelants (Belgium)	Brussels, Belgium	Sept. 20, 1972
25,000 meters	1H 14:55.6*	Seppo Nikkari (Finland)	Jyväskylä, Finland	Oct. 14, 1973
30,000 meters	1H 31:30.4	James Noel Carroll Alder (United Kingdom)	Crystal Palace, London	Sept. 5, 1970
1 hour	12 miles 1,609 yards	Gaston Roelants (Belgium)	Brussels, Belgium	Sept. 20, 1972

HURDLING

Event	mins. secs.	Name and Nationality	Place	Date
120 yards (3' 6" hurdles)	13.0	Rodney Milburn (U.S.)	Eugene, Oregon	June 25, 1971
	13.0	Rodney Milburn (U.S.)	Eugene, Oregon	June 20, 1973
220 yards (2' 6") (straight)	21.9	Donald Augustus Styron (U.S.)	Baton Rouge, Louisiana	Apr. 2, 1960
440 yards (3' 0")	48.8	Ralph Mann (U.S.)	Des Moines, Iowa	June 20, 1970
110 meters (3' 6")	13.1	Rodney Milburn (U.S.)	Zurich, Switzerland	July 6, 1973
	13.1	Rodney Milburn (U.S.)	Sienna, Italy	July 22, 1973
200 meters (2' 6") (straight)	21.9	Donald Augustus Styron (U.S.)	Baton Rouge, Louisiana	Apr. 2, 1960
200 meters (2' 6") (turn)	22.5	Karl Martin Lauer (West Germany)	Zurich, Switzerland	July 7, 1959
	22.5	Glenn Ashby Davis (U.S.)	Bern, Switzerland	Aug. 20, 1960
400 meters (3' 0")	47.8	John Akii-Bua (Uganda)	Munich, West Germany	Sept. 2, 1972
3,000 meters Steeplechase	8:14.0*	Ben Wabura Jipcho (Kenya)	Helsinki, Finland	June 27, 1973

HURDLING CHAMPION at 400 meters over 3-foot hurdles is John Akii-Bua (Uganda) (above, left) who set the world record in the 1972 Olympics. LONG DISTANCE CHAMPION: Gaston Roelants (Belgium) (right, #40) is the champion at 20,000 meters and ran a record 12 miles 1,609 yards in the one-hour race.

FASTEST 1,500 METERS: Filbert Bayi (Tanzania) (right) on his way to his record time of 3 minutes 32.2 seconds. John Walker of New Zealand (#483), who came in second, also bettered the previous record time.

WORLD RECORDS—MEN (Continued)

FIELD EVENTS

Event	ft.	ins.	Name and Nationality	Place	Date
High Jump	7	6¼	Dwight Stones (U.S.)	Munich, West Germany	July 11, 1973
Pole Vault	18	5¾	Robert Lloyd Seagren (U.S.)	Eugene, Oregon	July 2, 1972
Long Jump	29	2½	Robert Beamon (U.S.)	Mexico City, Mexico	Oct. 18, 1968
Triple Jump	57	2¾	Viktor Saneyev (U.S.S.R.)	Sukhumi, U.S.S.R.	Oct. 17, 1972
Shot Put	72	2½*	George Woods (U.S.)	Inglewood, California	Feb. 8, 1974
Discus Throw	224	5	L. Jay Silvester (U.S.)	Reno, Nevada	Sept. 18, 1968
	224	5	Rickard Bruch (Sweden)	Stockholm, Sweden	July 5, 1972
Hammer Throw	250	8	Walter Schmidt (West Germany)	Lahr, West Germany	Sept. 4, 1971
Javelin Throw	308	8	Klaus Wolfermann (West Germany)	Leverkusen, West Germany	May 5, 1973

RELAYS

Event	mins. secs.	Team	Place	Date
4 × 110 yards (two turns)	38.6	University of Southern California (U.S.) (Earl Ray McCullouch, Fred Kuller, Orenthal James Simpson, Lennox Miller (Jamaica))	Provo, Utah	June 17, 1967
4 × 220 yards	1:21.7	Texas Agricultural and Mechanical College (U.S.) (James Donald Rogers, Herbert Woods, Marvin Mills, Curtis Mills)	Des Moines, Iowa	Apr. 24, 1970
4 × 440 yards	3:02.8	Trinidad and Tobago (Lennox Yearwood, Kent Bernard, Edwin Roberts, Wendell A. Mottley)	Kingston, Jamaica	Aug. 13, 1966
4 × 880 yards	7:10.4*	University of Chicago Track Club (U.S.) (Tom Bach, Ken Sparks, Lowell Paul, Richard Wohlhuter)	Durham, N. Carolina	May 12, 1973
4 × 1 mile	16:02.8	New Zealand (Kevin Ross, Anthony Polhill, Richard Tayler, T. J. L. Quax)	Auckland, N.Z.	Feb. 3, 1972

The **POLE VAULT** record has been going up rapidly. Set by Bob Seagren at 18 feet 5¾ inches, it is more than 2 feet higher than in 1962.

GREATEST JUMP: Bob Beamon (U.S.) startled everyone when he exceeded the previous record long (broad) jump by 2 feet. No one has come close to his 29 feet 2½ inches, set in 1968.

WORLD RECORDS—MEN (Continued)

RELAYS (continued)

Event	mins. secs.	Team	Place	Date
4 × 100 meters	38.2	United States Olympic Team (Charles Edward Greene, Melvin Pender, Ronald Rey Smith, James Ray Hines)	Mexico City, Mexico	Oct. 20, 1968
	38.2	United States Olympic Team (Larry Black, Robert Tayler, Gerald Tinker, Eddie Hart)	Munich, West Germany	Sept. 10, 1972
4 × 200 meters	1:21.5	Italian Team (Franco Ossala, Pasqualino Abeti, Luigi Benedetti, Pietro Mennea)	Barletta, Italy	July 21, 1972
4 × 400 meters	2:56.1	United States Olympic Team (Vincent Matthews, Ronald Freeman, G. Lawrence James, Lee Edward Evans)	Mexico City, Mexico	Oct. 20, 1968
4 × 800 meters	7:08.6	West Germany "A" Team (Manfred Kinder, Walter Adams, Dieter Bogatzki, Franz-Josef Kemper)	Wiesbaden, West Germany	Aug. 13, 1966
4 × 1,500 meters	14:40.4•	New Zealand (Rodney Dixon, Anthony Polhill, John Walker, T. J. L. Quax)	Oslo, Norway	Aug. 22, 1973

DECATHLON

8.454 points		Nikolay Avilov (U.S.S.R.)	Munich, West Germany	Sept. 7–8, 1972

THE MARATHON

There is no official marathon record because of the varying severity of courses. The best time over 26 miles 385 yards (standardized in 1924) is 2 hours 08 minutes 33.6 seconds (av. 12.24 m.p.h.) by Derek Clayton (b. 1942 at Barrow-in-Furness, England) of Australia, at Antwerp, Belgium on May 30, 1969.

The fastest time by a female is 2 hours 46 minutes 30 seconds (av. 9.53 m.p.h.) by Adrienne Beames (Australia), at Werribee, Victoria, Australia on Aug. 31,1971 in a time trial. Cheryl Bridge (née Pedlow) (U.S.) ran 2 hours 49 minutes 40.0 seconds at Culver City, California on December 5, 1971.

WORLD RECORDS—WOMEN

RUNNING

Event	mins. secs.	Name and Nationality	Place	Date
100 yards	10.0	Chi Cheng (Taiwan)	Portland, Oregon	June 13, 1970
220 yards (turn)	22.6	Chi Cheng (Taiwan)	Los Angeles, California	July 3, 1970
440 yards	52.2	Kathleen Hammond (U.S.)	Urbana, Illinois	Aug. 12, 1972
880 yards	2:02.0	Dixie Isobel Willis (Australia)	Perth, Western Australia	Mar. 3, 1962
	2:02.0	Judith Florence Pollock (née Amoore) (Australia)	Stockholm, Sweden	July 5, 1967
1 mile	4:29.5	Paola Cacchi (née Pigni) (Italy)	Viareggio, Italy	Aug. 8, 1973
60 meters	7.2	Betty Cuthbert (Australia)	Sydney, N.S.W., Australia	Feb. 21, 1960
	7.2	Irina Robertovna Bochkaryova (née Turova) (U.S.S.R.)	Moscow, U.S.S.R.	Aug. 28, 1960
100 meters	10.8*	Renate Stecher (née Meissner) (East Germany)	Dresden, East Germany	July 20, 1973
200 meters (turn)	22.1*	Renate Stecher (née Meissner) (East Germany)	Dresden, East Germany	July 21, 1973
400 meters	51.0	Marilyn Neufville (Jamaica)	Edinburgh, Scotland	July 23, 1970
	51.0	Monika Zerht (East Germany)	Paris, France	July 4, 1972
800 meters	1:57.5	Svetla Zlateva (Bulgaria)	Athens, Greece	Aug. 24, 1973
1,500 meters	4:01.4	Ludmila Bragina (U.S.S.R.)	Munich, West Germany	Sept. 9, 1972

HURDLES

The I.A.A.F. scheduled world records for 100- and 200-meter hurdles were introduced on May 1, 1969. Inaugural ratifications have been made as follows:

100 meters	12.3*	Annelie Ehrhardt (East Germany)	Dresden, East Germany	July 22, 1973
200 meters (2' 6")	25.7	Pamela Ryan (née Kilborn) (Australia)	Melbourne, Australia	Nov. 25, 1971

FIELD EVENTS

Event	ft.	ins.	Name and Nationality	Place	Date
High Jump	6	4¼	Jordanka Blagoyeva (née Dimitrova) (Bulgaria)	Zagreb, Yugoslavia	Sept. 24, 1972
Long Jump	22	5¼	Heidemarie Rosendahl (West Germany)	Turin, Italy	Sept. 3, 1970
Shot Put	70	4¼*	Nadyezhda Chizhova (U.S.S.R.)	Varna, Bulgaria	Sept. 29, 1973
Discus Throw	227	11*	Faina Melnik (U.S.S.R.)	Edinburgh, Scotland	Sept. 7, 1973
Javelin Throw	216	10*	Ruth Fuchs (née Gamm) (East Germany)	Edinburgh, Scotland	Sept. 7, 1973

WORLD RECORDS—WOMEN (*Continued*)

PENTATHLON

4,932 points* .... Burglinde Polak (East Germany) .... Bonn, West Germany ... Sept. 22, 1973
(100 meter hurdles, 13.21 sec.; shot, 52 ft.; high jump 5 ft. 10¼ in.;
long jump, 21 ft. 2¼ in.; 200 meter dash, 23.35 sec.)

RELAYS

Event	mins. secs.	Team	Place	Date
4 × 110 yards	44.7	Tennessee State University (Diane Hughes, Debbie Wedgeworth, Mattline Render, Iris Davis)	Bakersfield, Calif.	July 9, 1971
4 × 220 yards	1:35.8	Australia (Marian Hoffman, Raelene Boyle, Pamela Kilborn, Jennifer Lamy)	Brisbane, Australia	Nov. 9, 1969
4 × 440 yards	3:33.9	United States Olympic Team (Kathleen Hammond, M. Ferguson, Madeline Jackson (*née* Manning), D. Edwards)	Urbana, Illinois	Aug. 12, 1972
4 × 100 meters	42.6*	East German Team (Petra Kandarr, Renate Stecher, Christina Heinisch, Doris Selmigkeit)	Potsdam, East Germany	Sept. 1, 1973
4 × 200 meters	1:33.8	United Kingdom National Team (Maureen Dorothy Tranter, Della P. James, Janet Mary Simpson, Valerie Peat (*née* Wild))	London, England	Aug. 24, 1968
4 × 400 meters	3:23.0	East German Olympic Team (Dagmar Käsling, Rita Kühne, Helga Seidler, Monika Zehrt)	Munich, West Germany	Sept. 10, 1972
4 × 800 meters	8:08.6	Bulgarian Olympic Team (Svetla Zlateva, Lilyana Tomova, Tonka Petrova, Stefka Yordanova)	Sophia, Bulgaria	Aug. 12, 1973

WOMEN'S WORLD RECORD HOLDERS: Heidemarie Rosendahl (left) (W. Germany) jumped 22 feet 5¼ inches in Turin, Italy, in 1970, a record that has held through many meets. Nadyezhda Chizhova (right) (U.S.S.R.) put the shot 70 feet 4½ inches in 1973.

Blind 100 Yards. The fastest time recorded for 100 yards by a blind man is 11.0 seconds by George Bull, aged 19, of Chippenham, Wiltshire, England, in a race at the Worcester College for the Blind, on October 26, 1954.

Pancake Race Record. The annual Housewives Pancake Race at Olney, Buckinghamshire, England, was first mentioned in 1445. The record for the winding 415-yard course is 63.0 seconds, set by Janet Bunker, aged 17, on February 7, 1967. The record for the counterpart race at Liberal, Kansas, is 59.1 seconds by Kathleen West, 19, on February 10, 1970.

Mass Relay Record. The record for 100 miles by 100 runners belonging to one club is 8 hours 9 minutes 42 seconds by Shore Athletic Club at Monmouth College, West Long Branch, New Jersey, on March 25, 1973.

Highest Race. The highest race regularly run is the Pike's Peak International Marathon (first held in 1955), covering 26.8 miles in Colorado. The runners begin at the railroad depot in Manitou Springs (6,563 feet above sea level), go to the summit of Pike's Peak

FASTEST SPRINTER: The new record holder at 100 meters (10.8 sec.) and 200 meters (22.1 sec.) is Renate Stecher of East Germany, shown here winning the 100-meter dash in the Olympics in Munich in 1972.

(14,110 feet) and return to Manitou Springs. The ascent of 7,547 feet covers 13 miles and the descent covers 13.8 miles. The best time for the race is 3 hours 53 minutes 57 seconds by John Ray Rose, aged 26, of Garden City, Kansas, on August 22, 1965. He completed the ascent in 2 hours 25 minutes.

Trampolining

Origin. The sport of trampolining (from the Spanish word *trampolin*, a springboard) dates from 1936, when the prototype "T" model trampoline was developed by George Nissen (U.S.). Trampolines were used in show business at least as early as "The Walloons" of the period, 1910–12.

Most Difficult Maneuvers. The most difficult maneuvers yet achieved are: the triple back somersault with a double twist, known as a Luxon after the first trampolinist able to achieve it—Paul Luxon (U.K.), the 1972 world amateur and 1973 world professional champion, achieved at the University of Southwest Louisiana in February, 1972; the women's Wills (5½ twisting back somersault) named after the five-time world champion, Judy Wills (U.S.)

(born 1948), of which no analyzable film exists, and the 8 consecutive triple somersaults performed by 15-year-old Ricky Virgin (Australia) (24 somersaults with 8 contacts with the bed) on August 26, 1972.

Marathon Record. The longest recorded trampoline bouncing marathon is one of 505 hours, set by a team of 8 from the Ottawa Street Community Y.W.C.A. at Pro's Golf Centre, Stoney Creek, Ontario, Canada, June 22–July 13, 1971. Each person jumped 63 hours 7½ minutes. The solo record is 63½ hours (with 5-minute breaks per hour permissible) by A. D. (Tony) Richardson of Dunedin Y.M.C.A., New Zealand, on October 20–22, 1972.

Most Titles. The only men to win a world title (instituted 1964) twice have been Dave Jacobs (U.S.) the 1967–68 champion and Wayne Miller (U.S.) the 1966 and 1970 champion. Judy Wills won 5 women's titles (1964–65–66–67–68).

FIVE-TIME WORLD CHAMPION ON TRAMPOLINE: Judy Wills (left) even has a difficult maneuver named after her.

Volleyball

Origin. The game was invented as Minnonette in 1895 by William G. Morgan at the Y.M.C.A. gymnasium at Holyoke, Massachusetts. The International Volleyball Association was formed in Paris in April, 1947. The ball travels at a speed of up to 70 m.p.h. when smashed over the net, which measures 7 feet 11.6 inches. In the women's game it is 7 feet 4.1 inches.

World Titles. World Championships were instituted in 1949. The U.S.S.R. has won six men's titles (1949, 1952, 1960, 1962, 1964 and 1968) in the eight meetings held. The U.S.S.R. won the women's championship in 1952, 1956, 1960, 1968 and 1970. The record crowd is 60,000 for the 1952 world title matches in Moscow, U.S.S.R.

Most Olympic Medals. The sport was introduced to the Olympic Games for both men and women in 1964. The only volleyball players of either sex to win three medals are Ludmila Bouldakova (U.S.S.R.) (b. May 25, 1938) and Inna Ryskal (U.S.S.R.) (b. June 15, 1944), who both won a silver medal in 1964 and golds in 1968 and 1972.

The record for gold medals for men is shared by four members of the U.S.S.R.'s 1968 team, who won a second gold medal in 1972: Eduard Sibiryakov, Yury Poyarkov, Yvan Bugayenkov, and Georgy Mondzolevsky.

Marathon. The longest recorded volleyball marathon is one of 168 hours played by 4 teams of 6 from Kirkby College of Further Education, Liverpool, England, on April 22–29, 1973.

One-Man Team. Bob L. Schaffer, 45, in Newark, New Jersey, specializes in taking on 6-man teams lone-handed. His last reported lifetime score was 876 wins to 1 loss—against the Fordham University team.

Walking

Road Walking. The record for walking across the U.S. from Los Angeles to New York is 53 days 12¼ hours by John Lees (England) between April 13 and June 6, 1972. The women's record for the 3,207-mile route is 86 days by Dr. Barbara Moore (*née* Varvara Belayeva, b. in Kaluga, Russia, December 22, 1903), ending on July 6, 1960.

1,000 Miles in 1,000 Hours. The first man to achieve 1,000 miles in 1,000 hours at one mile each hour was Capt. Robert Barclay-Allardice (b. 1780) at Newmarket, England, from June 1 to July 12, 1809. He lost 32 lbs. during the ordeal.

Most Olympic Medals. There have been 24 Olympic walking races covering every celebration since 1906 except for 1928. The only walker to win three gold medals has been Ugo Frigerio (Italy) (b. September 16, 1901) with the 3,000 m. and 10,000 m. in 1920 and the 10,000 m. in 1924. He also holds the record of most medals with four (having additionally won the bronze medal in the 50,000 m. in 1932) which total is shared with Vladimir Golubnitschyi (U.S.S.R.) (b. June 2, 1936), who won gold medals for the 20,000 m. in 1960 and 1968, the silver in 1972 and the bronze in 1964.

OFFICIAL WORLD RECORDS (Track Walking)

(As recognized by the International Amateur Athletic Federation)

Distance	hrs.	mins.	secs.	Name and Nationality	Date	Place
20,000 meters	1	25	19.4	Peter Frenkel and Hans-Georg Reimann (East Germany)	June 24, 1972	Erfurt
30,000 meters	2	14	45.6	Karl-Heinz Städmuller (East Germany)	April 16, 1972	East Berlin
20 miles	2	31	33.0	Anatoliy S. Vedyakov (U.S.S.R.)	Aug. 23, 1958	Moscow
30 miles	3	51	48.6	Gerhard Weidner (West Germany)	April 8, 1973	Hamburg
50,000 meters	4	00	27.2	Gerhard Weidner (West Germany)	April 8, 1973	Hamburg
2 hours 16 miles 1,270 yards				Karl-Heinz Städmuller (East Germany)	April 16, 1972	Berlin

UNOFFICIAL WORLD BEST PERFORMANCES (Track Walking)

(Best valid performances over distances or times for which records are no longer recognized by the I.A.A.F.)

	hrs.	mins.	secs.	Name and Nationality	Date	Place
5 miles		34	21.2	Kenneth Joseph Matthews (U.K.)	Sept. 28, 1960	London
10 miles	1	09	40.6	Kenneth Joseph Matthews (U.K.)	June 6, 1964	Walton-on-Thames
50,000 meters (road)	3	52	44.6	Bernd Kannenberg (West Germany)	1972	West Germany
1 hour 8 miles 1,294 yards				Grigoriy Panichkin (U.S.S.R.)	Nov. 1, 1959	Stalinabad
24 hours 133 miles 21 yards				Huw D. M. N. Neilson (U.K.)	Oct. 14–15, 1960	Walton-on-Thames

Walking on Crutches. David Ryder, 21, a polio victim from Essex, England, left Los Angeles on March 30 and arrived at New York City on August 14, 1970, after covering 2,960 miles on his crutches.

Water Polo

Origins. Water polo was developed in England as "Water Soccer" in 1869 and was first included in the Olympic Games in Paris in 1900.

Olympic Victories. Hungary has won the Olympic tournament most often with five wins, in 1932, 1936, 1952, 1956 and 1964. Five players share the record of three gold medals: George Wilkinson (b. 1880) in 1900–08–12; Paulo (Paul) Radmilovic (1886–1968), and Charles Sidney Smith (b. 1879) all G.B. in 1908–12–20; and the Hungarians Deszö Gyarmati (b. October 23, 1927) and György Kárpáti (b. June 23, 1935) in 1952–56–64.

Radmilovic also won a gold medal for the 4×200 m. relay in 1908.

MOST GOLD MEDALS:
György Kárpáti of Hungary is one of the five men who have won three gold medals in Olympic competition.

Most Caps. The greatest number of internationals is 168 by Aurel Zahan (Rumania) to 1970.

Water Skiing

Origins. The origins of water skiing lie in plank gliding or aquaplaning. A photograph exists of a "plank-riding" contest in a regatta won by a Mr. S. Storry at Scarborough, Yorkshire, England, on July 15, 1914. Competitors were towed on a *single* plank by a motor launch. The present-day sport of water skiing was pioneered by Ralph W. Samuelson on Lake Pepin, Minnesota, on two curved pine boards in the summer of 1922, though claims have been made for the birth of the sport on Lake Annecy (Haute Savoie), France, in 1920. The first World Water Ski Organization was formed in Geneva, Switzerland, on July 27, 1946.

Jumps. The first recorded jump on water skis was by Ralph W. Samuelson, off a greased ramp at Miami Beach, Florida, in 1928. The longest jump recorded is one of 169 feet by Wayne Grimditch, 17 (U.S.), at Callaway Gardens, Pine Mountain, Georgia, July 15, 1972. A minimum margin of 8 inches is required for sole possession of the world record.

The women's record is 119 feet by Linda Giddens (U.S.) at Picture Lake, Petersburg, Va., on August 10, 1973.

Buoys and Figures. The world record for slalom is 38 buoys (6 passes through the course plus 2 buoys with a 75-foot rope shortened by 36 feet) by Mike Suyderhoud (U.S.) at Ruislip, England, on June 6, 1970, and by Robi Zucchi (Italy) at Canzo, Italy, on September 6, 1970. The highest recorded point score for tricks is 5,970 points by Ricky McCormick (U.S.) at Bedfont, near London, England, in August, 1970.

Longest Run. The greatest distance traveled non-stop is 818.2 miles by Marvin G. Shackleford round McKellar Lake, Memphis, Tennessee, in 34 hours 15 minutes in September, 1960.

Highest Speed. The water skiing speed record is 125.69 m.p.h. recorded by Danny Churchill (U.S.) at the Oakland Marine Stadium, California, in 1971. Sally Younger, 17, set a feminine record of 105.14 m.p.h. at Perris, California, in June, 1970.

Most Titles. World championships (instituted 1949) have been twice won by Alfredo Mendoza (U.S.) in 1953–55 and Mike Suyderhoud (U.S.) in 1967–69 and three times by Mrs. Willa McGuire (*née* Worthington) of the U.S., in 1949–50 and 1955.

Water Ski Kite Flying. The altitude record is 4,750 feet by Bill Moyes (Australia) on March 14, 1972. He was towed by a 435-h.p. Hamilton Jet Boat over Lake Ellesmere, New Zealand. The duration record is 15 hours 3 minutes by Bill Flewellyn (N.Z.) over Lake Bonney, South Australia, in 1971.

TWICE WORLD CHAMPION, Mike Suyderhoud (U.S.), holds the world record for the slalom and was the first man ever to jump over 160 feet.

FASTEST WOMAN WATER SKIER: Sally Younger, at the age of 17, sped 105.14 m.p.h. in June, 1970.

Barefoot. The barefoot duration record is 67 minutes over about 36 miles by Stephen Z. Northrup (U.S.) in 1969. The backwards barefoot record is 33 minutes 19 seconds by Paul McManus (Australia) in 1969. A barefoot jump of 43 feet has been reported from Australia. The barefoot speed records are 87.46 m.p.h. by John Taylor (U.S.) on Lake Ming, California, on March 27, 1972, and for women 52.44 m.p.h. by Lynn Cowles (U.S.) over 440 yards at Long Beach, California, on August 18, 1973.

Weightlifting

Origins. Amateur weightlifting is of comparatively modern origin, and the first world championship was staged at the Café Monico, Piccadilly, London, on March 28, 1891. Prior to that time, weightlifting consisted of professional exhibitions in which some of the advertised poundages were open to doubt. The first 400-lb. clean and jerk is, however, attributed to Charles Rigoulet (1903–62), a French professional, with 402½ lbs. on February 1, 1929.

Greatest Lift. The greatest weight ever raised by a human being is 6,270 lbs. in a back lift (weight raised off trestles) by the 364-lb. Paul Anderson (U.S.) (b. 1933), the 1956 Olympic heavyweight champion, at Toccoa, Georgia, on June 12, 1957. (The heaviest Rolls-Royce, the Phantom VI, weighs 5,600 lbs.) The greatest by a woman is 3,564 lbs. with a hip and harness lift by Mrs. Josephine Blatt (*née* Schauer) (U.S.) (1869–1923) at the Bijou Theatre, Hoboken, New Jersey, on April 15, 1895.

The greatest overhead lifts made from the ground are the clean and jerks achieved by super-heavyweights which now exceed 500 lbs. (see table).

The greatest overhead lift ever made by a woman, also professional, is 286 lbs. in a Continental jerk by Katie Sandwina, *neé* Brummbach (Germany) (born January 21, 1884, died as Mrs. Max Heymann in New York City, in 1952) in *c.* 1911. This is equivalent to seven 40-pound office typewriters. She stood 6 feet 1 inch tall, weighed 210 lbs., and is reputed to have unofficially lifted 312½ lbs. and to have once shouldered a 1,200-lb. cannon taken from the tailboard of a Barnum & Bailey circus wagon.

Power Lifts. Paul Anderson as a professional has bench-pressed 627 lbs., achieved 1,200 lbs. in a squat, and dead-lifted 820 lbs. making a career aggregate of 2,647 lbs. The record (A.A.U.) for a single contest is an aggregate of 2,370 lbs. by Jon Cole (U.S.) set in October, 1972.

The highest official two-handed dead lift is 882 lbs. by Jon Cole (U.S.). Hermann Görner performed a one-handed dead lift of 734½ lbs. in Dresden on July 20, 1920. He once raised 24 men weighing 4,123 lbs. on a plank with the soles of his feet and also carried on his back a 1,444-lb. piano for a distance of 52½ feet on June 3, 1921.

STRONGEST WOMAN WEIGHTLIFTER: Lifting her 182-lb. brother was child's play to Katie Sandwina (1884-1952), who once unofficially lifted 312½ lbs. over her head. She herself weighed 220 lbs.

LIFTS MORE THAN
THREE TONS: Paul
Anderson of Toccoa, Georgia,
who weighs 364 lbs., raised
the greatest weight ever
lifted by a human—6,270 lbs.
——in a back lift.

Peter B. Cortese (U.S.) achieved a one-arm dead lift of 22 lbs. over triple his body weight with 370 lbs. at York, Pennsylvania, on September 4, 1954.

The highest competitive two-handed dead lift by a woman is 392 lbs. by Mlle. Jane de Vesley (France) in Paris on October 14, 1926.

It was reported that a hysterical 123-lb. woman, Mrs. Maxwell Rogers, lifted one end of a 3,600-lb. car which, after the collapse of a jack, had fallen on top of her son at Tampa, Florida, on April 24, 1960. She cracked some vertebrae.

OFFICIAL WORLD WEIGHTLIFTING RECORDS

(As of January 1, 1974)

Flyweight				
(114½ lb.–52 kg.)				
Snatch	232½	Takeshi Horikoshi (Japan)	Cuba	Sept. 15, 1973
Jerk	308½	Mohamed Nassiri (Iran)	Cuba	Sept. 15, 1973
Total	528¾	Mohamed Nassiri (Iran)	Cuba	Sept. 15, 1973
Bantamweight				
(123¼ lb.–56 kg.)				
Snatch	259¾	Koji Miki (Japan)	Cuba	Sept. 16, 1973
Jerk	332	Mohamed Nassiri (Iran)	Turkey	Aug. 2, 1973
Total	567½	Atanas Kirov (Bulgaria)	Cuba	Sept. 16, 1973
Featherweight				
(132¼ lb.–60 kg.)				
Snatch	276½	Yoshinobu Miyake (Japan)	Japan	Oct. 28, 1969
Jerk	349¼	Yuri Golubtsov (U.S.S.R.)	U.S.S.R.	Mar. 17, 1973
Total	611½	Yoshinobu Miyake (Japan)	Japan	Oct. 28, 1969
Lightweight				
(148¾ lb.–67.5 kg.)				
Snatch	303	Waldemar Baszanowski (Poland)	Poland	Apr. 23, 1971
Jerk	391¼	Murkharbi Kirzhinov (U.S.S.R.)	West Ger.	Aug. 30, 1972
Total	688¾	Murkharbi Kirzhinov (U.S.S.R.)	West Ger.	Aug. 30, 1972
Middleweight				
(165¼ lb.–75 kg.)				
Snatch	331¾	Leif Jensen (Norway)	Denmark	Apr. 28, 1973
Jerk	418¾	Nedelcho Kolev (Bulgaria)	Cuba	Sept. 19, 1973
Total	743¾	Nedelcho Kolev (Bulgaria)	Cuba	Sept. 19, 1973
Light-heavyweight				
(181¾ lb.–82.5 kg.)				
Snatch	356	Vladimir Rizhenkov (U.S.S.R.)	U.S.S.R.	Dec. 16, 1973
Jerk	444	Vladimir Rizhenkov (U.S.S.R.)	Spain	June 15, 1973
Total	788	Vladimir Rizhenkov (U.S.S.R.)	U.S.S.R.	Dec. 16, 1973
Middle-heavyweight				
(198¼ lb.–90 kg.)				
Snatch	374¾	David Rigert (U.S.S.R.)	Spain	June 16, 1973
Jerk	470½	David Rigert (U.S.S.R.)	Spain	June 16, 1973
Total	837¾	David Rigert (U.S.S.R.)	U.S.S.R.	Apr. 5, 1973
Heavyweight				
(242½ lb.–110 kg.)				
Snatch	391¼	Pavel Pervushin (U.S.S.R.)	Spain	June 17, 1973
Jerk	493¾	Valeri Vstyuzhin (U.S.S.R.)	U.S.S.R.	Oct. 14, 1973
Total	881¾	Pavel Pervushin (U.S.S.R.)	Spain	June 17, 1973
Super-heavyweight				
(Over 242½ lb.–110 kg.)				
Snatch	408	Leonid Zhabotinski (U.S.S.R.)	U.S.S.R.	Feb. 21, 1974
Jerk	529	Vasili Alexeev (U.S.S.R.)	Spain	June 18, 1973
Total	920¼	Vasili Alexeev (U.S.S.R.)	Spain	June 18, 1973

HIGHEST TOTAL LIFT:
Vasili Alexeev (U.S.S.R.) set
world records for Super-
heavyweight lifters in the Jerk
and Total Weight categories.

Most Olympic Gold Medals. Of the 81 Olympic titles at stake,
the U.S.S.R. has won 21, the U.S. 15 and France 9. Eight lifters
have succeeded in winning an Olympic gold medal in successive
Games. Of these, three have also won a silver medal:—

Louis Hostin (France)	Gold, light-heavyweight 1932 and 1936; Silver, 1928.
John Davis (U.S.)	Gold, heavyweight 1948 and 1952.
Tommy Kono (Hawaii/U.S.)	Gold, lightweight 1952; Gold, light-heavyweight 1956; Silver, middleweight 1960.
Charles Vinci (U.S.)	Gold, bantamweight 1956 and 1960.
Arkady Vorobyov (U.S.S.R.)	Gold, middle heavyweight 1956 and 1960.
Yoshinobu Miyake (Japan)	Gold, featherweight 1964 and 1968; Silver, bantamweight 1960.
Waldemar Baszanowski (Poland)	Gold, lightweight 1964 and 1968.
Leonid Schabotinsky (U.S.S.R.)	Gold, heavyweight 1964 and 1968.

Most Olympic Medals. Winner of most Olympic medals is
Norbert Schemansky (U.S.) with four; gold, middle-heavyweight
1952; silver, heavyweight 1948; bronze, heavyweight 1960 and 1964.

Wrestling

Earliest References. The earliest depiction of wrestling holds and falls are from the walls of the tomb of Ptahhotap (Egypt) so proving that wrestling dates from *c.* 2350 B.C. or earlier. It was introduced into the ancient Olympic Games in the 18th Olympiad in *c.* 704 B.C. The Graeco-Roman style is of French origin and arose about 1860. The International Amateur Wrestling Federation (F.I.L.A.) was founded in 1912.

Sumo Wrestling. The sport's origins in Japan certainly date from *c.* 200 A.D. The heaviest performer was probably Dewagatake, a wrestler of the 1920's who was 6 feet 5 inches tall and weighed up to 420 lbs. Weight is amassed by over-eating a high protein sea food stew called *chanko-rigori.* The tallest was probably Ozora, an early 19th century performer, who stood 7 feet 3 inches tall. The most successful wrestler has been Koki Naya (born 1940), *alias* Taiho ("Great Bird"), who won his 26th Emperor's Cup on September 10–24, 1967. He was the *Yokozuna* (Grand Champion) in 1967. The highest *dan* is Makuuchi. (See photos.)

Most Olympic Titles. Three wrestlers have won three Olympic titles. They are:

Carl Westergren (Sweden)
(b. Oct. 13, 1895)

Graeco-Roman Middleweight A	1920
Graeco-Roman Middleweight B	1924
Graeco-Roman Heavyweight	1932

Ivar Johansson (Sweden)
(b. Jan. 31, 1903)

Free-style Middleweight	1932
Graeco-Roman Welterweight	1932
Graeco-Roman Middleweight	1936

Aleksandr Medved (U.S.S.R.)
(b. Sept. 16, 1937)

Free-style Light-heavyweight	1964
Free-style Heavyweight	1968
Free-style Super-heavyweight	1972

The only wrestler with more medals is Imre Polyák (Hungary) who won the silver medal for the Graeco-Roman featherweight class in 1952, 56–60 and the gold in 1964.

SUMO WRESTLERS: Dewagatake (left) who weighed 420 lbs., and Taiho (right photo, with both feet planted), the current champion in Japan.

Best Record. Osamu Watanabe (Japan) won the free-style featherweight event in the 1964 Olympic Games. This was his 186th successive win and he has never been defeated.

Most World Championships. The greatest number of world championships won by a wrestler is seven by the freestyler Aleksandr Medved (U.S.S.R.), with the light-heavyweight titles in 1964 (Olympic) and 1966, the heavyweight 1967 and 1968 (Olympic), and the super-heavyweight title 1969, 1970 and 1971. The only other wrestler to win world titles in 6 successive years has been Abdullah Movahad (Iran) in the lightweight division in 1965–70. The record for Graeco-Roman titles is five shared by Roman Rurua (U.S.S.R.) with the featherweight 1966, 1967, 1968 (Olympic), 1969 and 1970 and Victor Igumenov (U.S.S.R.) with the welterweight 1966, 1967, 1969, 1970 and 1971.

Longest Bout. The longest recorded bout was one of 11 hours 40 minutes between Martin Klein (Estonia, representing Russia) and Armas Asikainen (Finland) in the Graeco-Roman middleweight "A" event in the 1912 Olympic Games in Stockholm, Sweden.

Professional Wrestling. Modern professional wrestling dates from *c*. 1875 in the United States. Georges Karl Julius Hackenschmidt (1877–1968) made no submissions in the period 1898–1908.

The highest paid professional wrestler ever is Antonino ("Tony") Rocca with $180,000 in 1958. The heaviest wrestler was William J. Cobb of Macon, Georgia, who was billed in 1962 as the 802-lb. "Happy" Humphrey. What he lacked in mobility he possessed in suffocating powers. By July, 1965, he had reduced to a modest 232 lbs.

Most Successful. Ed "Strangler" Lewis (1890–1966), *né* Robert H. Friedrich, fought 6,200 bouts in 44 years losing only 33 matches. He won world titles in 1920, 1922 and 1928.

Yachting

Origin. Yachting dates from the £100 (now $250) stake race between King Charles II of England and his brother James, Duke of York, on the Thames River, on September 1, 1661, over 23 miles, from Greenwich to Gravesend. The earliest club is the Royal Cork Yacht Club (formerly the Cork Harbour Water Club), established in Ireland in 1720. The word "yacht" is from the Dutch, meaning to hunt or chase.

Most Successful. The most successful racing yacht in history was the British Royal Yacht *Britannia* (1893–1935), owned by King Edward VII while Prince of Wales, and subsequently by King George V, which won 231 races in 625 starts.

Highest Speed. The highest speed achieved in trials run by a national yachting governing body has been 29.2 knots or 33.62 m.p.h. by the 60-foot *Crossbow* (sail area 932 sq. ft.) designed by Rod McAlpine-Downie, with T. Coleman as helmsman, off Portland, Dorset, England, on September 29, 1973. The U.S. Navy experimental hydrofoil craft *Monitor* is reported to have attained speeds close to 40 knots (46 m.p.h.).

Longest Race. The longest regularly contested yacht race is the biennial Los Angeles-Tahiti Trans Pacific event which is over 3,571 miles. The fastest time has been 8 days 13 hours 9 minutes by Eric Taberley's *Pen Duick IV* (France) in 1969.

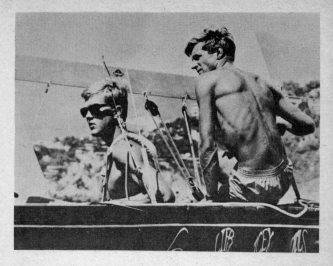

OLYMPIC REGATTA WINNER with lowest number of penalty points was the "Superdocius" of the Flying Dutchman Class, 1968.

Olympic Victories. The first sportsman ever to win individual gold medals in four successive Olympic Games has been Paul B. Elvström (b. February 25, 1928) (Denmark) in the Firefly class in 1948 and the Finn class in 1952, 1956 and 1960. He has also won 8 other world titles in a total of 6 classes.

The lowest number of penalty points by the winner of any class in an Olympic regatta is 3 points [6 wins (1 disqualified) and 1 second in 7 starts] by *Superdocius* of the Flying Dutchman class sailed by Lt. Rodney Stuart Pattison (b. August 5, 1943), British Royal Navy and Ian Somerled Macdonald-Smith (b. July 3, 1945), in Acapulco Bay, Mexico, in October, 1968.

America's Cup. The América's Cup was originally won as an outright prize by the schooner *America* on August 22, 1851, at Cowes, England, but was later offered by the New York Yacht Club as a challenge trophy. On August 8, 1870, J. Ashbury's *Cambria* (G.B.) failed to capture the trophy from the *Magic*, owned by F. Osgood (U.S.). Since then the Cup has been challenged by Great Britain in 15 contests, by Canada in two contests, and by Australia thrice, but the United States holders have never been defeated. The closest race ever was the fourth race of the 1962 series, when the 12-meter sloop *Weatherly* beat her Australian challenger *Gretel* by about $3\frac{1}{2}$ lengths (75 yards), a margin of only 26 seconds, on September 22, 1962. The fastest time ever recorded by a 12-meter boat for the triangular course of 24 miles is 2 hours 46 minutes 58 seconds by *Gretel* in 1962.

Little America's Cup. The catamaran counterpart to the America's Cup was instituted in 1961 for International C-class catamarans. The British club entry has won on each annual occasion to 1968 vs. the U.S. (1961–66 and 1968) and vs. Australia (1967). In 1969, Denmark beat G.B. and in 1970 Australia beat Denmark and has held the cup since.

Admiral's Cup. The ocean racing series to have attracted the largest number of participating nations (three boats allowed to each nation) is the Admiral's Cup held by the Royal Ocean Racing Club in the English Channel in alternate years. Up to 1971 when 17 nations took part, Britain had won 5 times, U.S. twice and Australia once.

Largest Yacht. The largest private yacht ever built was Mrs. Emily Roebling Cadwalader's *Savarona* of 4,600 gross tons, completed in Hamburg, Germany, in October, 1931, at a cost of $4,000,000. She (the yacht), with a 53-foot beam and measuring 407 feet 10 inches overall, was sold to the Turkish government in March, 1938. Operating expenses for a full crew of 107 men approached $500,000 per year.

LARGEST SAIL ever made was the parachute spinnaker on the "Ranger," Harold S. Vanderbilt's yacht, in 1937.

The largest private sailing yacht ever built was the full-rigged 350-foot auxiliary barque *Sea Cloud* (formerly *Hussar*), owned by the oft-married Mrs. Marjorie Merriweather Post-Close-Hutton-Davies-May (1888–1973), one-time wife of the U.S. Ambassador to the U.S.S.R. Her four masts carried 30 sails with the total canvas area of 36,000 square feet.

Largest Sail. The largest sail ever made was a parachute spinnaker with an area of 18,000 square feet (more than two-fifths of an acre) for Harold S. Vanderbilt's *Ranger* in 1937.

Highest Altitude. The greatest altitude at which sailing has been conducted is 14,212 feet on Lake Pomacocha, Peru, by *Nusta*, a 19-foot Lightning dinghy owned by Jan Jacobi, reported in 1959.

PICTURE CREDITS

American Bowling Congress; Associated Newspapers Ltd.; Associated Press; Associated Press Ltd., London; Atlanta Braves; Australian News and Information Bureau, New York; Boston Bruins; Boston Garden; Buffalo Bills; California State Library; Camera Press Ltd.; Central Press Photos Ltd., London; Daily Express, London; John Eagle; Bill Halkett; Harmsworth Photo Library; Marion Kaplan; Keystone Press Agency Ltd.; E. D. Lacey; Ladies' Professional Golf Association; London Art Tech.; National Baseball Hall of Fame and Museum, Inc.; National Baseball League; National Basketball Association; National Football League Properties, Inc.; N.B.C. Sports, New York; New Hungary; New York Rangers; New York Times; Novosti Press Agency, Moscow; Photo-Reportage Ltd.; Planet News; Press Association Photos, London; Professional Football, Office of the Commissioner; Pro Football Hall of Fame; Radio Times Hulton Picture Library; Reaction Dynamics, Inc.; Remington Arms Co.; Bernard Rouget; Al Ruelle; Robert L. Smith; A. G. Spalding and Bros.; Sport and General Press Agency Ltd., London; The Thomson Organisation Ltd., London; United Press International (U.K.); United Press International (U.S.); United States Lawn Tennis Association; Universal Pictorial Press; Fiona Vigors; Wide World Photos; Wilson Sporting Goods Company.

INDEX

Archery, earliest sport 7, earliest references, flight shooting, highest scores, most titles, marathon 11

Auto Racing, longest sport 7, earliest races 11–12, fastest circuits, fastest races 12, toughest circuits 12–13, Le Mans, most wins 15, Indianapolis 500 15–16, fastest pit stop, duration record 16, most successful drivers 17, oldest and youngest Grand Prix winners and drivers 18, land speed records 18–19, drag racing, piston-engined, rocket or jet-engined, stock car racing 19, earliest and longest rallies, smallest car 20, go-kart circumnavigation, Pike's Peak race 21

Badminton, origins 21, international championships 21–22, most titles won, longest hit 22

Baseball, origins, earliest games, home runs, fastest pitcher 22, youngest player, highest catch 23, major league all-time records, individual batting 23–27, base running 27, pitching 28–30, club batting, club fielding 30, general club records 30–31, World Series records, pitchers' records, World Series winners 31

Basketball, origins, Olympic champions, world champions, greatest attendances 32, tallest players, highest scoring, marathon 34, most accurate shooting 35, National Basketball Association regular season records, service 35, scoring 35–37, rebounds, assists, personal fouls 37, disqualifications 38, team records 38–40

Bicycling, longest sport 7, largest crowd 9–10, earliest race, slow cycling, highest speed, most Olympic titles, Tour de France, world titles, one-hour and 24-hour records 41, coast to coast 42

Billiards, earliest mention 42, highest breaks, fastest century, most world titles, most amateur titles 43

Boat Racing, see Powerboat Racing and Yachting

Bobsledding, origins, Olympic and world titles 43, tobogganing, lugeing, most world titles, highest speed 44

Bowling, origins 44–45, lanes, organizations, world championships, highest game, league scores, highest men's, highest women's, consecutive strikes, most perfect scores 45, ABC tournament scores, highest individual, highest doubles, perfect scores 46, best finishes in one tournament 46–47, attendance, prize winnings,

youngest and oldest winners, strikes and spares in a row, marathon 47

Boxing, earliest references 47, longest fight 48, shortest fight 48–49, tallest and heaviest, world heavyweight champions, longest and shortest reigns, heaviest and lightest, tallest and shortest 49, oldest and youngest, undefeated, earliest title fight, world champions (any weight), longest and shortest reign 50, youngest and oldest, longest fight, most recaptures 51, most titles simultaneously, greatest "tonnage," smallest champions, most knockdowns in title fights, all fights, largest purse, highest attendances 53, highest receipts 53, highest earnings in career, most knockouts, most fights, most fights without loss 54, greatest weight difference, longest career, most Olympic gold medals 55

Bridge (Contract), earliest references, highest possible scores 55, perfect deals, world titles, longest session, most master points 56

Bull Fighting, largest stadiums and gate, most successful matadors, most kills in a day, highest paid matadors 57

Canoeing, origins, most Olympic gold medals, longest journey, eskimo rolls, transatlantic, downstream canoeing 58

Cave Exploration, world's deepest caves 59, progressive caving depth records, duration 60

Champions, youngest, oldest 8

Checkers, origins, longest game, most opponents 60

Chess, origins, world champions, longest games, marathon 61, shortest game, most opponents 62

Crowd, largest 9–10

Curling, origins, largest rink, most titles, marathon, most durable player 62

Cycling, see Bicycling and Motorcycling

Disasters, worst 8

Diving, see Swimming

Drag Racing, see Auto Racing

Equestrian Sports, origin, most Olympic medals 63, jumping records, marathon 64

Fencing, origins, most Olympic titles 65, most world titles 65–66

Index by Daniel Burt